Reading Derrida and Ricoeur

SUNY series: Insinuations: Philosophy, Psychoanalysis, Literature

Charles Shepherdson, editor

Reading Derrida and Ricoeur

Improbable Encounters between
Deconstruction and Hermeneutics

Eftichis Pirovolakis

"The Word: Giving, Naming, Calling" by Jacques Derrida was originally published in French as: "La parole: Donner, nommer, appeler," in *Paul Ricoeur*, ed. Myriam Revault d'Allones and François Azouvi, L'Herne, no. 81 (Paris: Éditions de L'Herne, 2004) 19–25, Copyright © 2004 Éditions de L'Herne. It is reproduced here with permission by Éditions de L'Herne and Marguerite Derrida. English translation © 2010 Eftichis Pirovolakis.

Published by State University of New York Press, Albany

For information, contact State University of New York Press, Albany, NY
www.sunypress.edu

Production by Eileen Meehan
Marketing by Anne M. Valentine

Library of Congress Cataloging-in-Publication Data

Pirovolakis, Eftichis, 1970–
    Reading Derrida and Ricoeur : improbable encounters between deconstruction and hermeneutics / Eftichis Pirovolakis.
        p. cm. — (SUNY series, insinuations: philosophy, psychoanalysis, literature)
    Includes bibliographical references and index.
    ISBN 978-1-4384-2949-6 (hc : alk. paper) ISBN 978-1-4384-2950-2 (pb : alk. paper)
    1. Deconstruction.   2. Derrida, Jacques—Criticism and interpretation.   3. Ricœur, Paul—Criticism and interpretation.   4. Phenomenology and literature.
5. Hermeneutics.   6. Literature—Philosophy.   7. Criticism—History—20th century.
I. Title.

    PN98.D43P57 2010
    801'.95—dc22   2009014349

10 9 8 7 6 5 4 3 2 1

For Antony and Cleopatra

Contents

Acknowledgments

In the course of writing this book, I have been indebted to the support and friendship of many people. I would like to thank Laura Marcus and Vicky Margree for their help and vital advice; Sean Gaston for his friendship and numerous thought-provoking conversations on Derrida and Ricoeur; the anonymous readers for State University of New York Press for their encouraging and constructive comments; and the series editor Charles Shepherdson and James Peltz for helping the finished manuscript through its last stages.

I would also like to express my gratitude to Joanna Hodge and Nick Royle for examining my Sussex doctoral thesis on which this book is based, for kindly making available to me some of their unpublished papers and for their very positive contributions towards the completion of this project. I am especially grateful to Céline Surprenant for her vital supervisory role during the later stages of the research, and for her generosity in reading very closely and offering incisive criticism and invaluable advice on the original manuscript. I am also greatly indebted to Geoff Bennington for the range of knowledge he has brought to my work, for helping me clarify my arguments at certain important points during the early stages of this project and, most of all, for continuous inspiration and encouragement since 1993. Very special and singular thanks are due to Vassiliki Dimitropoulou for her patience, understanding, and overall support.

Finally, I would like to record my gratitude to the Alexander S. Onassis Public Benefit Foundation for its financial assistance between 2001 and 2004, and to Marguerite Derrida and Éditions de L'Herne for kindly authorizing the translation into English of Jacques Derrida's "La parole: Donner, nommer, apeller," which appears here as an appendix. Some of the arguments on Ricoeur's narrative theory in the second section of chapter 3 have been anticipated in my " 'Donner À Lire': Unreadable Narratives," *Literature Interpretation Theory* 19, no. 2 (2008): 100–122.

List of Abbreviations

The following abbreviations will be used in the main body of the text and the notes. They will be followed by volume number, where appropriate, and page number to the English translation. Details of the edition referred to appear under the author's name and title in the bibliography.

Works by Jacques Derrida

AF   *Archive Fever: A Freudian Impression*

AP   *Aporias: Dying—Awaiting (One Another at) the "Limits of Truth"*

FSW   "Freud and the Scene of Writing"

GD   *The Gift of Death*

LI   "Limited Inc a b c . . ."

MPM   *Mémoires: For Paul de Man*

PG   *The Problem of Genesis in Husserl's Philosophy*

PM   "Perhaps or Maybe"

SEC   "Signature Event Context"

SP   *Speech and Phenomena: And Other Essays on Husserl's Theory of Signs*

SF   "To Speculate—On 'Freud' "

VM   "Violence and Metaphysics: An Essay on the Thought of Emmanuel Lévinas"

W   "The Word: Giving, Naming, Calling"

Works by Paul Ricoeur

FM   *Fallible Man*

FP   *Freud and Philosophy: An Essay on Interpretation*

H   *Husserl: An Analysis of His Phenomenology*

IT   *Interpretation Theory: Discourse and the Surplus of Meaning*

MHF   *Memory, History, Forgetting*

OA   *Oneself as Another*

QS   "The Question of the Subject: The Challenge of Semiology"

RM   *The Rule of Metaphor: The Creation of Meaning in Language*

SWE   "Structure, Word, Event"

TA   *From Text to Action: Essays in Hermeneutics II*

TN   *Time and Narrative*

Works by Sigmund Freud

SE   *The Standard Edition of the Complete Psychological Works of Sigmund Freud*

Works by Edmund Husserl

CM   *Cartesian Meditations: An Introduction to Phenomenology*

Ideas I *Ideas: General Introduction to Pure Phenomenology*

PITC   *The Phenomenology of Internal Time-Consciousness*

Introduction

An encounter simultaneously tangential, tendentious, and intangible begins to emerge but also slips away.

— Jacques Derrida, "The Word: Giving, Naming, Calling"

Any account of the contentious relation between Paul Ricoeur and Jacques Derrida cannot fail to be marked, initially at least, by a feeling of melancholy and a certain mournfulness. Not only because the two thinkers, having recently passed away within only a few months of each other, will not have the opportunity to contribute to or revisit the various debates in which they jointly participated for approximately fifty years. But also because, even when they were alive, most of their public encounters could be described, at best, as missed opportunities of a fruitful dialogue. Hence a sense of sorrowfulness with respect to the distance separating deconstruction and hermeneutics, those two most influential streams of contemporary European thought.

The first public instance of a miscarried dialogue was a roundtable discussion following a conference on "Communication" in Montreal in 1971, organized by The Association of the Society for Philosophy in the French Language.[1] Both Ricoeur and Derrida contributed formal presentations to the conference and actively participated in the roundtable discussion, which was dominated, to say the least, by an animated confrontation between them.[2] A debate between the two thinkers apparently did take place at the time. Considering, however, that the word *debate* implies the willingness of each partner in a conversation to resolve any initial disagreement by being open to what the other has to say, or, according to its Latin *etymon*, the reversal of an incipient discordance,[3] it is clear that this exchange constituted, rather, a spirited altercation. And even though Derrida, on three or four occasions, begins responding by declaring that he agrees with Ricoeur, he hastens to temper and complicate this scene of agreement by adding another twist to his argument. Whether the dichotomy between semiology and semantics, the event of signature, or *différance* is at

1

issue, Ricoeur and Derrida seem to be talking at cross-purposes throughout this discussion. At certain points, the confrontation becomes so lively that the two interlocutors cannot help interrupting each other, thereby rendering the possibility of a patient dialogue very difficult indeed.

Nor is a series of publications that appeared in the seventies on metaphor a debate, as in none of the three texts of this exchange do they fully engage with each other's arguments. The first one, Derrida's "White Mythology: Metaphor in the Text of Philosophy" (1971), is a "deconstructive" interpretation of the vicissitudes of metaphor in philosophical discourse and does not contain any reference to Ricoeur.[4] It is the latter who instigates the polemic by providing, in the eighth study of *The Rule of Metaphor: The Creation of Meaning in Language* (1975), a critical reading of Derrida's essay.[5] In no way does that reading amount to a detailed response to Derrida. Ricoeur chooses to focus on two very specific aspects of "White Mythology," whose argument, moreover, he hastily assimilates to Heidegger's conviction that the metaphorical exists only within the limits of metaphysics, and to which he devotes just a few pages. Finally, "The *Retrait* of Metaphor" (1978) was supposed to be Derrida's rejoinder to Ricoeur's polemical comments.[6] Yet, the explicit references to Ricoeur are limited to a few observations to the effect that he mistakenly attributed to Derrida assertions that "White Mythology" was specifically intended to put into question. Derrida goes on to devote the largest part of his essay to a meticulous examination of certain Heideggerian motifs. As a result, their debate on metaphor could also be portrayed as a failed attempt to engage in constructive dialogue.[7]

More recently, in his *Memory, History, Forgetting* (2000), Ricoeur affirmatively draws attention to Derrida's paradoxical formulation that forgiveness is impossible to the extent that one, in order genuinely to forgive, should forgive the unforgivable. Despite, however, his acknowledgment of an asymmetry between the act of forgiving and the demand to forgive the unforgivable, Ricoeur defines forgiveness, on the first page of his "Epilogue," entitled "Difficult Forgiveness," in terms of an infinite horizon or a task that may be *difficult* but not *impossible*.[8] Derrida refers to this third instance of disagreement in his brief essay paying tribute to Ricoeur.[9] He wonders about the difference between an impossible and a difficult forgiveness, and points out that at stake, in the final analysis, is the concept of the "self" and Ricoeur's insistence on determining selfhood on the basis of the "I can."[10] *A contrario*, for Derrida, it is always the other, be that other myself, who decides, forgives, or acts, a structure that, introducing an absolutely irreducible alterity into the heart of the experience of forgiveness, renders problematic its construal as activity or possibility, even a difficult one.

Finally, the controversial issue of selfhood resurfaces in a discussion on the promise, in which both thinkers participated. On the one hand, Ricoeur's "La promesse d'avant la promesse" (2004) contains no reference to Derrida and explicitly opposes the promise to betrayal and perjury. Invoking J. L Austin's and John R. Searle's speech acts theory, Ricoeur associates the promise with the self-constancy of a self that ought to keep the word given to the other within a horizon regulated by the Kantian Idea of a universal civil society.[11] On the other hand, Derrida distances himself from Ricoeur's reliance on the notion of the "self" and establishes an inextricable link between the promise and an originary pervertibility. The latter points to a certain otherness that cannot be subordinated to the authority of the self, to an ineluctable multiplicity that will always minimally contaminate the self-constancy and ethical responsibility that Ricoeur's "selfhood" prioritizes. Derrida underscores that both speech acts theory and hermeneutics cannot help acknowledging the inherence of this structural pervertibility in every act of promising, even if they strive to minimize its effects and significance.[12]

The sense of failure emanating from these four occasions is aggravated by their reluctance to confront directly or discuss in detail each other's philosophy. With the exception of Derrida's essay on Ricoeur, it is only rarely and merely in passing that one can identify in their writings brief references to each other's work.[13] They have both been disinclined to embark on a productive and genuine *Auseinandersetzung*, to discuss the other's positions publicly in a way that would have made it easier for their readers clearly to determine the individual standpoints of the two philosophers, and, therefore, the elusive relationship between them. It is in view of such discrepancy and such reticence about explicitly taking on each other that the debate between them can be qualified as an unavailing one.[14] Now that both thinkers have passed away, this abortive dialogue takes on an absolute dimension. The situation today seems irreversible and the opportunity of a fruitful encounter, of which they did not take advantage in the past, appears to have been irremediably missed, something which gives rise to a certain poignancy.

In response to this situation, some commentators tend to affirm an incongruity between the thought of Ricoeur and Derrida, no matter how much they may disagree over the philosophical merit of each thinker. If one briefly focuses on two of the most polarizing approaches, one finds, at one end of the spectrum, J. Hillis Miller's acerbic 1987 review of Ricoeur's *Time and Narrative* (1983–85). Miller attributes to Ricoeur "a conspicuously reactionary role within current critical theory and practice," and bluntly claims that *all* of his basic presuppositions are mistaken, while opposing such conservatism to Derrida's infinitely more rigorous and radical formulations.[15] At the other end, Stephen H. Clark criticizes Derrida for his dependency "on a series of restrictive and unstated premises derived from structuralism," his profound orthodoxy and tendency "to merge back into the pack, distinguished only by his absence of generosity towards a past history of error." At the same time, Clark praises Ricoeur for his exploratory, radical interventions and "cross-disciplinary thought," which he designates as post-structuralist.[16] However differently they may perceive the intellectual value of Ricoeur and Derrida, Miller and Clark concur in opposing the two thinkers to one another, in portraying their relation in terms of difference and divergence.

Leonard Lawlor's *Imagination and Chance* offers a much more balanced account. This book-length study does not fall prey to the simplifying temptation to oppose Ricoeur to Derrida by hastily endorsing a watertight division between them. On the contrary, Lawlor cautiously admits that things are much more complicated and synopsizes, in his introduction entitled "A Barely Visible Difference," the similarities between the two philosophers as follows: they both agree that thought cannot achieve self-knowledge by means of intuitive self-reflection, that thought has to externalize and mediate itself in repeatable signs, and that linguistic mediation disallows the possibility of a "complete mediation" whereby the origin would be recovered in all of its determinations.[17] In light of such overwhelming and blurring affinities, the work of Derrida is said to be "almost indistinguishable" from Ricoeur's.[18]

And yet, Lawlor identifies "a barely visible difference" as far as the role of mediation is concerned. On the one hand, mediation, for Derrida, is qualified as originary non-presence, discontinuity, and difference, and incorporates an element of chance that forestalls any safe transition from thought back to thought. Derridean *différance*, argues Lawlor, accounts for the unforeseeable accident that is considered to be inherent in the sign's structure; as a result, it cannot be conceived of as circularity or linearity but, rather, as a zigzag movement. On the other hand, Ricoeur's mediation constitutes a dialectical concept articulating origin and end, *archē* and *telos*. Functioning as a safe passage from present back to present, mediation is always placed into the service of presence, identity, immediacy, and continuity. While Ricoeur accepts that mediation is intimately bound up with a distance or absence that prevents it from reaching an absolute degree, still, complete mediation is maintained as a task and distanciation is said to be regulated by the always receding horizon of complete identity.[19]

Accordingly, Lawlor purports to have pinned down an almost imperceptible difference, the illumination of which constitutes the thematic axis of *Imagination and Chance*. His conclusion, suggestively entitled "The Difference Illuminated," consolidates the idea of differentiation in terms of four specific motifs: the origin of mediation, the transitional point or mediation itself, the end or destiny of mediation, and, finally, the Idea in the Kantian sense.[20] I will return below to Lawlor's fine study, but what needs to be stressed here is his insistence on a difference that, albeit "barely visible," is nonetheless thought to belong to the order of a metaphorical visibility or phenomenality.[21]

As one of my objectives is clearly and accurately to bring into focus the difference between these two most prominent continental philosophers, this study constitutes a continuation and expansion of Lawlor's project.[22] I will juxta-pose and reflect on texts in which Derrida and Ricoeur address similar issues or scrutinize the work of thinkers such as Edmund Husserl, Sigmund Freud, and Emmanuel Lévinas. The thematic organization of my project involves interpreta-tive decisions, and, in this respect, a margin of contingency appears inevitable. Without wishing to reduce this margin, I would like to point up some of the reasons that have led to these decisions.

The confrontation staged in the first two chapters, whose thematic focus is the relation between continuity and discontinuity, takes place on the basis of a certain commonality, namely, their shared interest in phenomenology and psy-choanalysis. Ricoeur's translation of and commentary on Husserl's *Ideas: General Introduction to Pure Phenomenology* (1913) appears as early as 1950 and is the work that establishes his reputation as a leading expert on phenomenology.[23] The appeal of Husserl's thought remains undiminished throughout Ricoeur's career and he keeps returning to it even in his later writings. It is not by chance that his own philosophy has been portrayed as a ramification of "hermeneutic phenomenology."[24] Similarly, the early phases of Derrida's career are marked by an intense preoccupation with phenomenology thanks, to a great extent, to Ricoeur's rigorous reflection on the *Ideas I*.[25] Derrida's first published work in 1962 is a translation and extended commentary entitled *Edmund Husserl's "Origin of Geometry": An Introduction*, but, already before that, his higher studies dissertation, written in 1953–54 and published belatedly in 1990, was devoted to the problem of genesis in Husserl's philosophy.[26] Both Ricoeur and Derrida turn to Freud in the mid '60s in order to address, in their own idiosyncratic ways, problems left unresolved by Husserl.[27]

My concentration specifically on the two thinkers' readings, on the one hand, of Husserl's exegesis of temporalization, and, on the other, of psycho-analysis as a radicalization of phenomenology, has been motivated by two inter-dependent factors. Firstly, I believe that this juxtaposition allows one to gain a vantage point from which to examine the gulf separating Ricoeur's dialectical construal of the present from Derrida's affirmation of discontinuity and inter-ruption. Secondly, by virtue of the fact that Lawlor devotes only a few pages to Husserl's analysis of time-consciousness and makes almost no reference to Freud, my discussion brings to light some aspects of the encounter between Ricoeur and Derrida that perhaps lie beyond the scope of *Imagination and Chance*.[28] This exigency of investigating the link between Husserl and Freud is underlined by Derrida's coupling of phenomenology to hermeneutics, both of which he distinguishes from psychoanalysis, a gesture already anticipated in one of his questions to Gadamer in 1981 that concerned the challenge of psychoanalysis to hermeneutics.[29]

The thematic framework of the third and fourth chapters is provided by the two philosophers' preoccupation with singularity and generality, which will be initially studied on the basis of their sustained attention to signification and language. I mentioned, above, Lawlor's remark that both thinkers reject the idea of transparent self-reflection and admit that thought is possible only if it is mediated by signs and externalized. Several of Ricoeur's works published between the late '60s and the mid '80s are characterized by their focus on spoken or written discourse, hence the use of the phrase "linguistic" or "hermeneutic turn" to describe that phase of his career.[30] Similarly, Derrida is interested, right from the beginning, in the functioning of the linguistic sign. In "The Time of a Thesis: Punctuations" (1983), he recalls that the title he had submitted around 1957 for his first thesis topic was "The Ideality of the Literary Object," a study of the problematics of communication and literary meaning.[31] Subsequently, the overwhelming majority of his published work in the '60s and '70s is concerned with the structure of signification as attested to by *Writing and Difference*, *Of Grammatology* (1967), *Speech and Phenomena* (1967), *Dissemination* (1972), *Positions* (1972), and *Margins of Philosophy*.[32]

As Lawlor has extensively studied the two philosophers' debate on metaphor, I will focus here on their analyses of deixis and the first-person perspective, which, with the help of Ricoeur's "hermeneutics of the self" and dialectics of narration and prescription, will function as points of transition leading to the ethical relation between self and other. I will investigate their disparate accounts of Husserl's interpretation of intersubjectivity, but also their response to some of Lévinas's writings on alterity and responsibility.[33] On the basis of this confrontation on singularity and generality, I will explicate Ricoeur's self-characterization as a "post-Hegelian Kantian,"[34] as well as Derrida's tendency to resist, without straightforwardly opposing, the dialectical structure germane to Ricoeur's thought.

To avoid, however, subscribing to too teleological a construal of the difference between the two thinkers—a construal indissociable from the terms *debate* and *dialogue*—another strand of this book will reflect, following Derrida, on the nature of this difference. A radical thinking of difference will be announced, a thinking that, while allowing for the ordinary teleological conceptuality, takes difference seriously into account and cautiously refuses to determine it in a negative and provisional way. This alternative interpretation turns out to have serious implications for the debate between Ricoeur and Derrida, as this has been portrayed thus far.

In a sense, if a debate is not to be reduced to a banal situation where two partners harmoniously communicate to each other beliefs they already share, it has to presuppose a moment of absolute distance. Without this moment of interruption or discord, there is no dialogue but simply a complacent confirmation of ideas the interlocutors know they anyway share. If such a radical difference constitutes the a priori requirement of any event of dialogue, if there is no genuine encounter without or before that moment of violent interruption, then this moment can be relegated neither to an empirical accident nor to a negative and provisional necessity. Rather, alterity and non-dialogue have to be construed as *positive* structural possibilities without which dialogue *stricto sensu* would not stand a chance.

Although Ricoeur's and Derrida's shared thematic concerns, their common intellectual context and their philosophical discrepancies may constitute interesting empirico-historical information, they cannot function as necessary conditions able to give rise to a genuine encounter between them. Such a condition can be supplied by an ineluctable and positively determined distance alone. It is in this light that the non-dialogue or non-event apparently lamented at the beginning of this introduction, far from regretfully instantiating a contingent failure, functions as the positive condition of a promised debate. The missed opportunity of a fruitful exchange in the past will have succeeded in making possible an encounter respectful of the two thinkers' irreplaceability. What is at stake here is a non-dialogue whose "non" does not indicate a negative actuality but a radical heterogeneity that promises the event of an encounter worthy of its name.[35] Owing, however, to the essential character of such heterogeneity, a dialogue or a debate, in the ordinary sense of these terms, is rendered at the same time impossible. To the extent that the chance of an encounter depends on an a priori required distance, this chance will always be marked by alterity, so it will never become a dialogue, given that the latter is intended, by definition, to overcome and suppress difference.

If the chance of a genuine debate cannot indeed be disengaged from the exigency of absolute alterity and non-dialogue, is the term *debate* worthy of this structure? If the possibility of dialogue is grounded in an originary non-dialogue, is this not to say that the words *debate* or *dialogue*, which imply some common ground or a shared objective, cannot appropriately bear witness to this complex configuration? This is why it is tempting to describe the "relation" between Ricoeur and Derrida in terms of "improbable encounters."[36] This expression, to the extent that it affirms both a radical difference and the chance of a meeting of texts bearing their signature, respects the two thinkers' irreducible singularity. The improbable or uncanny encounter between them, which the second strand of this study calls for, will never be a debate in the sense of a juxtaposition simply or dialectically opposing their work in view of a synthesis or reconciliation. At best, one can speak of an apposition, a placement next to each other of discussions of texts, which perhaps, like two parallel lines, may meet at infinity.[37]

The belief in such improbable encounters, indebted to Derrida's thought, constitutes a fundamental methodological presupposition reflected in the structuring principle of my study. On the one hand, the first and the third chapters focus on Ricoeur's work, whereas chapters 2 and 4 are devoted to Derrida. It is possible prima facie to delimit and identify the position the two thinkers occupy vis-à-vis the texts they read. On the other hand, the two chapters on Derrida will reveal a reading strategy that will give rise to another thinking of difference, identity, and position. According to a familiar Derridean gesture that differentiates between the author's declared intentions and his or her descriptions,[38] I will briefly revisit Ricoeur's texts to see if one can discover therein any moments interrupting his expressly hermeneutic assertions. Ricoeur's discourse will be shown to include possibilities that can be hardly maintained simultaneously, and, as a consequence, the relation between the two philosophers will turn out to be more complicated than initially thought. I will argue that such a complication alone, which is not without a parallel as far as Derrida's relation to reflective philosophy and hermeneutics is concerned, allows for an uncompromising singularity without seeking to negate, exclude, or subordinate difference to a desired commonality. Moreover, this reading does justice to the complexity and richness of Ricoeur's and Derrida's texts by resisting the temptation of associating them, once and for all, with either deconstruction or hermeneutics.

Before delineating in greater detail the thematics of this study, it has to be underlined that there is significant overlapping between all four chapters in more than one way. The themes specific to any one chapter are imbricated across the whole book. As a result, the link between singularity and generality is broached much earlier than the third chapter, and the movement of temporalization constitutes a motif overflowing the limits of the first two chapters. In addition, there are thematic concerns of equal salience diffused throughout the book, such as the finitude-infinity binary, the exigency of distance and interruption, the relation between repetition and difference, or that between possibility and impossibility.

The first chapter focuses on the coupling of consciousness and presence in Ricoeur's construal of Husserl and Freud. The third volume of *Time and Narrative* considers Husserl's theory of temporalization to provide a coherent approach to the *human* experience of time to be opposed to the *cosmological* time of nature. Ricoeur examines the phenomenological "thick present," and underscores that Husserl's major contribution was the intercalation of the concept of "retention" into the realm of perception. What is crucial, however, is the relation between primary intuition and retention, and the extent to which Ricoeur endorses the phenomenological emphasis on continuity. According to Husserl's manifest declarations, this continuity is interrupted as soon as one crosses the borderline separating perception from memory, whose corollary is the coupling of intuition and immediate presence. Dissatisfied with such a coupling, Ricoeur draws upon Kant's conception of temporality and Freudian psychoanalysis in order to question the self-sufficiency and immediacy of the Husserlian ego.

By virtue of his early quantitative hypothesis and the later topographical and economic models, Freud introduces distance into the very heart of perception, thereby casting into doubt the transparency of conscious presence. In the first instance, Ricoeur embraces Freud's critique of immediate consciousness and commends the anti-phenomenological reduction by means of which psychoanalysis suspends the properties of the transcendental subject. At the same time, he does not wish to give up all hope with respect to the possibility that the subject may attain, with the help of the analyst and the analytical technique, a certain self-reflexivity. Consequently, although Ricoeur admits to the necessary alterity of Freudian categories such as the primary process, the pleasure principle, the unconscious, the death drive, etc., still, these are determined as negative phases dialectically linked to a positive and meaningful reappropriation.

Ricoeur's nuanced discourse both allows for the idea that unconscious activity *as such* remains inaccessible and highlights that the dialectical character of most psychoanalytical divisions makes possible the appropriation of an initial non-presence. He articulates the *actual impossibility* of attaining an absolute mediation with the *conceptual possibility* of such a mediation posited as a *telos* or a task never to be actually achieved. The infinite idea of a reflective consciousness gives rise to a mediated self purged from the hubristic belief in self-constitution. In spite of incorporating some Freudian insights in order to expose the illusion of a transparent consciousness, Ricoeur's philosophy remains indebted to a continuist and dialectical conception of presence.

Chapter 2 begins by exploring Derrida's response to Husserl's lectures on time-consciousness in *Speech and Phenomena* with a view to revealing the extent to which Ricoeur underplays the implications of the introduction of retention qua alterity into the perceptual present. According to a reading gesture outlined above, Derrida distinguishes Husserl's declared intentions from his actual descriptions. As a result of this tension, a certain distance between original intuition and retention turns out to be absolutely irreducible, which entails that one is not justified in stressing the primacy of continuity. If difference is neither an empirical eventuality that may befall the temporal present here and there, nor a negative necessity anticipating a plenitude of presence, in what terms is one supposed to think of its irreducibility? The philosophical configuration of "necessary possibility" and the quasi-concept of *différance* will reveal a paradoxical commingling of presence and absence, continuity and discontinuity. Although this aporetic structure and its syncopated temporality are far removed from Husserl's manifest declarations, his analyses contain traces that invite one to conceive of non-presence in a nonnegative, non-teleological fashion.

Next, following Derrida's early work on Freud, I will evaluate Ricoeur's conviction about the dialectical nature of psychoanalysis. If such a dialectics rests on the oppositional determination of perception and memory, life and death, pleasure and reality, etc., are these oppositions safely sustained by Freud's accounts of the psychical apparatus? Or does Freudian discourse bear witness, on the contrary, to a permeable-impermeable borderline that gives rise to all those values while excluding a watertight dichotomy between them? Derrida affirms a peculiar diastem that is the only chance of a present intuition, the memory trace, and psychical life in general. Paradoxically, this diastem has to be thought of in terms of a *différance* that complicates opposition and, by extension, dialectics. Freud's *Nachträglichkeit* goes some way toward capturing the discontinuous temporality involved in such a structure. To what extent does psychoanalysis differ from phenomenology in light of the fact that Husserl too allows, by virtue of retention, for a certain difference as constitutive of the living present?

Another set of issues I will address here is the significance of Freud's portrayal of psychical processes in terms of increasingly intricate scriptural metaphors. What does this metaphorics imply not only for perception and memory but also for the act of writing itself? Does psychical writing function according to a topography, or does it disturb any ordinary understanding of spatiality? Can the psychical text be understood on the basis of conventional temporal categories, or does it originate in an aporetic temporalization resistant to permanence and identity? I will explore the disjuncture between Freud's commitment to interpretation and certain descriptive moments that call upon one to think the *impossibility* of acceding to an original psychical inscription or mnemic trace. Finally, I will revisit Ricoeur's discourse in order to identify therein instances that, by allowing for a more interruptive thinking of non-presence, undercut his dialectics of archaeology and teleology. This latter gesture complicates any attempt definitely and securely to differentiate Ricoeur's thought from Derrida's.

The last two chapters will focus on singularity and the relation between self and other. Chapter 3 will present Ricoeur's hermeneutics of the self, which admittedly has taken on board the criticism leveled by psychoanalysis and structuralist linguistics at various "philosophies of the subject," thereby resisting any straightforwardly Cartesian, Kantian, or Husserlian conception of subjectivity.[39] In both early and more recent writings, Ricoeur is keen to establish a link between the subject or the self and singularity. As far as language is concerned, the use of the personal pronoun is claimed to designate transparently and singularly the speaker of discourse. By underlining the self-referential and singularizing function of the speech act, he seeks to achieve a mediation between Husserl's belief in the subject as the self-constituting principle of language and the structuralist rejoinder that language is an autonomous entity that cannot be reduced to a medium at the disposal of a sovereign self.

Besides, I will examine the two types of identity, *idem* and *ipse*, introduced in *Time and Narrative* but more fully developed in *Oneself as Another*. Their dialecticization will lead to "narrative identity," a motif that takes into consideration both the possibility of change and the self-constancy that ethics requires. Insofar as such self-constancy cannot be guaranteed on the level of literature, it has to be linked to the prescriptive realm of ethics where a truly responsible agent ought to take the initiative and publicly declare "Here I stand!" The hermeneutic functions of "refiguration" and "appropriation" serve as the points of transition from the literary to the ethical. This passage from plurality to a singular responsibility is ensured by the regulative Idea of the "good life," on whose basis the notion of the "ethical self" is developed. The ethical self is yoked together with action, decision, and benevolence, categories mediated by a certain passivity and finitude originating in the call of the suffering other. Ricoeur defines the ethical relation in terms of friendship and reciprocity, whose corollary is the dialectical pairing of selfhood and alterity, activity and passivity. His reflection is dominated by this dialectic, through which he negotiates a median position between Husserl's assimilative interpretation of the alter ego and Lévinas's hyperbolic discourse on absolute exteriority.

Does Ricoeur succeed in reinscribing the philosophies of the cogito after assimilating the challenges of psychoanalysis and structuralism? What are the implications of the concepts of benevolence, mutuality, and friendship with respect to the other's alterity? Is the idea of a singular self compatible with the generality that inheres in a prescriptive ethical domain regulated by the Idea of the "good life"? Does the public declaration "Here I stand!" sufficiently guarantee one's ethical behavior and singularly assumed responsibility?

Chapter 4 complicates the link between selfhood and singularity. I will initially concentrate on Derrida's discussion of the personal pronoun, which casts doubt upon the supposedly singularizing role of language. Insofar as the phenomenon of deixis in general can be shown to be subject to the law of iterability, the latter introduces a minimal exemplarity or generalizability into the heart of a singular referent. Although this gesture might be regarded as assimilating deictics to other words, thus subordinating referential singularity to the transcendental conditions of language, the argument is far more subtle than this. Derrida infiltrates the realm of signification with a "referentiality" that cannot be dialectically opposed to an interior sense or conceptuality.

If iterability cannot be disengaged from the necessary possibility of non-presence, the self-identity of the referent is rendered problematic, and along with it the belief in language as a means of expression and singular responsibility. In some of his recent writings, Derrida reveals an originary co-implication of language and secrecy that gives rise to language while excluding the possibility of pure truthfulness or transparency. This secrecy does not refer to something that can be provisionally dissimulated but remains nonetheless subject to representation. Rather, at issue here is a secret that, heterogeneous to visibility and phenomenality, is responsible for the promissory and aleatory nature of language. Such a construal anchors the possibility of truthful speech and singular responsibility in an anterior pervertibility. Paradoxically, Ricoeur's theory of discourse will be found to contain traces that call upon one to think a similar commingling of speech and secrecy, something that corroborates my contention about the "improbable encounters" between the two philosophers.

Subsequently, beginning with Derrida's reflection on the phrase "to be in memory of the other," I will unpack the aporetic structure whereby singularity and alterity are deconstituted by what makes their emergence possible.[40] A rigorous concept of singularity requires a priori the other's radical alterity, hence Derrida's concurrence with Lévinas's views on absolute exteriority. At the same time, in order for one to be able to refer to such alterity, the other has to be somewhat phenomenalizable. This exigency of a minimal contact, on whose basis Derrida reveals resources of Husserl's account of intersubjectivity that remain unexplored by both Lévinas and Ricoeur, entails yoking together necessity and chance, and leads to a differentiation between "absolute alterity" and "irreducible alterity." Derrida's approach can be seen as radicalizing, in a sense, Lévinas's thought. By virtue of his insistence on an ineluctable discontinuity between self and other, the possibility of singularity and the impossibility of a purely singular self cannot be teleologically organized. Strangely enough, it is this non-teleological structure and the corollary interruption that ensure the infinity of the Idea in the Kantian sense.

This study makes no pretence of constituting an exhaustive investigation into all the contexts and authors one could legitimately claim to have played a significant role in shaping Derrida's and Ricoeur's thought. Any such contention would be clearly out of the question considering the vast array of issues that have preoccupied the two thinkers over a period of seventy years, the complexity of the philosophical problems they have addressed, but also the sheer magnitude of their published output. Rather, these readings illuminate, on the basis of some major themes in their work, the *barely visible* difference that Lawlor identifies, and simultaneously put forward the idea of an *absolutely invisible* difference giving rise to a " 'singular' dialogue,"[41] promised interchanges, and improbable encounters between hermeneutics and deconstruction. Those two strands will remain inextricably interrelated throughout this book, and the second one will keep impinging, in principle and in fact, upon the first one.

Chapter 1

Ricoeur on Husserl and Freud

From a Perceptual to a Reflective Present

In his well-informed and instructive *Imagination and Chance* and, more specifically, in a brief chapter on Husserlian temporalization, Lawlor maintains that "Ricoeur's reading of Husserl discovers that immediacy and continuity precede spatial separation and discontinuity. Mediation or distanciation, traces or absence, derive for Ricoeur from immediacy and should return to it. Immediacy, as we shall see, supports all of Ricoeur's theories."[1] This chapter will evaluate Lawlor's claim with respect to Ricoeur's approach to consciousness and temporality.

The first section will focus on the constitution of the perceptual present and on Ricoeur's interpretation of Husserl's account of time-consciousness in *Time and Narrative.* One of the issues at stake here is Husserl's introduction of "retention" into the heart of the living present. How does Ricoeur interpret the relation between primary impression and retention? To what extent does he privilege identity and immediacy at the expense of difference? Does he unreservedly subscribe to the self-evidence of an original intuition, or does he, on the contrary, problematize the idea of immediate presence? How does he deal with the tension between, on the one hand, the phenomenological yoking together of intuition and the punctual *stigmē*, and, on the other, the description of time as continuous and flowing, something that compromises the rigorous identity of the now? Although Ricoeur admits that Husserl cannot be reproached for ousting difference altogether from the realm of perception, he maintains nonetheless that phenomenology construes mediation and exteriority as secondary to an originarily self-present consciousness. Ricoeur's reservation is grounded in his belief that Husserl regards perception primarily through the prism of the ego's self-identity and immediacy.

The last two sections will establish that, for Ricoeur, Freud's thought, by allowing for an irreducible distance in the conscious present, instantiates a radical break with phenomenology. Freud's neurological reflections and later metapsychological texts on the unconscious and repression directly challenge the phenomenological claims about a self-sufficient and self-constituting subject. In this light, Freud is said to be a better archaeologist than Husserl, to be capable of reaching deeper into the psyche in order to discover an origin more ancient and more secret than the transcendental ego. However, Ricoeur will eventually assert that the primordial non-presence unearthed by the psychoanalytical "archaeology of the subject" is dialectically articulated with a *telos* where the meaningful presence of a reflective consciousness is not so much a given as a task to be pursued jointly by the analyst and the patient.[2] Both Ricoeur's endorsement of a continuous, albeit mediated, temporality in Husserl, and his insistence on the teleological organization of Freud's thought will reveal the extent to which he is committed to a dialectical reading of difference and identity.

Ricoeur Reading Husserl: The Thick Present and Continuity

The first section of the third volume of *Time and Narrative*, entitled "The Aporetics of Temporality," is a comparative investigation into various philosophical readings of time: Aristotle versus Augustine, Kant versus Husserl, and finally Heidegger.[3] The Aristotelian and Kantian accounts are classified as cosmological, in view of the fact that they regard time as either an objective category or an a priori intuition that remains inscrutable and invisible. Augustine and Husserl are thought to have interpreted time in terms of its constitution within subjectivity; as a result, they are subsumed under the phenomenological approach. Heidegger reached the highest point of critical reflection and perplexity by resolving many of the aporias of Husserlian and Augustinian thought. However, he is seen as still working within the limits of a hermeneutic phenomenology that verges on hermeticism.[4]

The discussion of Husserl's theory of temporalization, anchored directly in perception in *The Phenomenology of Internal Time-Consciousness* (1928),[5] is strategically situated immediately after Ricoeur's reflection on Aristotle, and is said to address many of the issues left unresolved by the Greek philosopher. The objective of this volume of *Time and Narrative* is to establish the "mutual occultation" of the phenomenological time of human experience and the cosmological time of physics with a view to affirming narrated time as a "third time" mediating between the two opposing perspectives (TN, 3:245). The discussion of Husserl functions as a rejoinder to Aristotle's conception of time on the basis of measurable movement, and to the prioritization of the undifferentiated instant at the expense of a dialectically unified present. As a consequence, Ricoeur's reading of Husserl makes a point, against Aristotle, in favor of the continuity and unitariness of the human experience of time.[6]

Ricoeur initially draws attention to Husserl's ambition to make time itself appear by means of an appropriate method, to submit the appearance of time as such to a direct description. In order to gain access to the internal time-consciousness freed from every aporia, Husserl had to exclude objective time and all "transcendent presuppositions concerning existents" (PITC, §1, 22). His work, therefore, begins by performing the famous "phenomenological reduction" or *epochē*, by bracketing out objective time; the latter coincides with the first level of temporal constitution where things are experienced in world time.

The second level of temporal constitution is that of immanent unities, the order of temporal objects (*Zeitobjekte*). Husserl seeks to provide an explanation of the duration in consciousness of such objects as the same from moment to moment. How is it possible for our perception of these objects to endure, and how does this lived experience come about? It is in response to these questions that his two great discoveries, according to Ricoeur, occur: the description of the phenomenon of retention (*Retention*), and the distinction between retention (primary remembrance) and recollection (secondary remembrance) (TN, 3:25–26). Husserl is interested in sensed objects and their mode of continuance rather than perceived or transcendent objects. In this respect, the central example in his discussion of retention is that of a sound, a minimal temporal object that can be constituted, thanks to its simplicity, in the sphere of pure immanence. A melody would be something far too complex to deal with on this level.

One of the first things Husserl affirms is that the immanent object that the sound is has a beginning and an end. Its beginning coincides with a now-point that corresponds to a primal impression (*Urimpression*) or impressional consciousness involved in continuous alteration. When the sound stops, one is conscious of this now-point as the end-point when the duration expires. The whole duration of the sound is made up of individual nows, each of which corresponds to a primal impression that gradually sinks back into the past as the duration proceeds toward its end. While the impression of a tonal now sinks back into the past, says Husserl, "I still 'hold' it fast, have it in a 'retention,' and as long as the retention persists the sound has its own temporality. It is the same and its duration is the same" (PITC, §8, 44). Before the sound began, one was not conscious of it. After it has stopped, one is still conscious of it in retention for a while. For as long as the sound lasts, one is conscious of one and the same sound as enduring now.

The retention of a just passed now in each actual now guarantees that the *same* sound continues to resonate throughout a succession of individual nows. Defined as a "modification" of the primal impression (PITC, §11, 50–51), retention makes possible the expansion of an immediate intuition taking place in an actual now into a duration. Husserl designates each intuitive now as a "source-point" (*Quellpunkt*), remarks Ricoeur, "precisely because what runs off from it 'still' belongs to it. Beginning is beginning to continue. . . . Each point of the duration is the source-point of a continuity of modes of running-off and the accumulation of all these enduring points forms the continuity of the whole process" (TN, 3:30). "Modification" implies that each actually present now is modified into the recent past, and that the original impression passes over into retention, thereby thickening the now of perception into a broadened present including both a new impression and the retention of a just passed impression. The determination of retention as a "modification" bears witness to Husserl's wish "to extend the benefit of the original character belonging to the present impression to the recent past" and its retentional consciousness (TN, 3:30).

Thanks to the expansion of the punctual now-point, not only is the recent past connected with the present now but also it retains its intuitive aspect even if it is no longer present *stricto sensu*. As soon as a now-point has expired, the primal intuition corresponding to it continues to exist in the form of retentional rather than impressional consciousness. The two kinds of consciousness are intimately bound up with each other and with protention, hence the transformation of a point-like *stigmē* into a thick present. One of Husserl's major contributions to philosophical reflection on time was the idea that

> the "now" is not contracted into a point-like instant but includes a
> transverse or longitudinal intentionality (in order to contrast it with
> the transcendent intentionality that, in perception, places the accent
> on the unity of the object), by reason of which it is at once itself
> and the retention of the tonal phase that has "just" [*soeben*] passed,
> as well as the protention of the imminent phase. (TN, 3:26)

Each tonal now of consciousness retains the now that has just passed and anticipates the next one. As a consequence, it encompasses a continuity of retentional modifications while at the same time being itself a point of actuality that shades off and becomes a recent past in order to give rise to the next now which will be itself a continuous modification of the previous one, and so on and so forth.

Commenting upon Husserl's phrase "the sound still resonates," Ricoeur notes that the adverb "still" entails both sameness and otherness. There is otherness not only because of the diminishing clarity of the impression of expired now-points but also because of the incessant piling up of retained contents. Far from saying that Husserl dogmatically excludes discontinuity, Ricoeur admits that he allows for a certain difference between impression and retention, and that this difference is indispensable: "[If it] were not included in the continuity, there would be no temporal constitution, properly speaking. The continuous passage from perception to nonperception (in the strict sense of these terms) is temporal constitution" (TN, 3:33).

Nevertheless, he underlines that "what Husserl wants at all cost to preserve is the continuity in the phenomenon of passing away, of being drawn together, and of becoming obscure. The otherness characteristic of the change that affects the object in its mode of passing away is not a difference that excludes identity" (TN, 3:28). In spite of the fact that, by putting forward the lingering on of the just passed now, Husserl has introduced some otherness into the perceptual present, such otherness does not pose a threat to the continuity of the duration. Ricoeur observes that Husserl, in order to account for the provenance of continuity, splits intentionality into two interdependent aspects: one of them, designated as "longitudinal intentionality," is directed toward the continuity between the retained and the actual now, whereas the other is an "objectifying intentionality" directed toward the transcendent correlate that is always other through the succession of nows. Retention and the longitudinal intentionality ensure the continuation of the now-point in the extended present of the unitary duration and preserve "the same in the other" (TN, 3:28).

Temporal constitution entails first and foremost continuity, even though the prefix *re-* of "retention" indicates a chasm between itself and impression. The motif of broadened perception is claimed to privilege sameness, immediacy, and continuity at the expense of a radical discontinuity. Difference is regarded as a smooth passage from intuition to retention, and is relegated to a secondary position with respect to the primacy of continuity:

> The notions of difference, otherness and negativity expressed by the "no longer" [of the retained now] are not primary, but instead derive from the act of abstraction performed on temporal continuity by the gaze that stops at the instant and converts it from a source-point into a limit-point. . . . Primary remembrance is a positive modification of the impression, not something different from it.[7] (TN, 3:30–31)

Subsequently, Ricoeur turns to Husserl's second major discovery, and argues that his claim about the prioritization of continuity is corroborated by the apparently unbridgeable chasm between retention and recollection. On the one hand, primary remembrance retains the just passed now-point within a thick present that has some duration; it is the "comet's tail" of a just passed source-point while being a new source-point itself (PITC, §11, 52). On the other hand, secondary remembrance or memory refers to a distant past that has no foothold in the present. Husserl deploys the example of a melody recently heard at a concert: whereas retention takes place for as long as the melody lasts and when it has just stopped, memory begins a while after the melody has ended.

After the event recalled has finished, one's memory aims to do no more than reproduce it. When one tries to remember it, the melody is "no longer 'produced' but 'reproduced,' no longer presented (in the sense of the extended present) but 're-presented' (*Repräsentation* or *Vergegenwärtigung*)" (TN, 3:32). Husserl stresses the "*wieder*" of "*Wiedererinnerung*" (recollection), which marks a discontinuity between perception and reproduction, presentation and representation. Prima facie, Ricoeur rightly diagnoses that this account downplays the role of difference and consolidates the continuity between impression and retention:

> This primacy of retention finds further confirmation in the unbridgeable aspect of the break that separates re-presentation from presentation. Only the latter is an original self-giving act. . . . The "once again" has nothing in common with the "still." What might mask this phenomenological difference is that major feature of retentional modification that, in fact, transforms the original or reproduced "now" into a past. But the continuous fading-away characteristic of retention must not be confused with the passage from perception to imagination that constitutes a discontinuous difference. (TN, 3:33)

What is at issue, then, is the difference between two types of difference: a continuous one between the just passed now and the actual now yoked together under the aegis of a broadened perception, and a discontinuous one between perception and recollection or imagination. The before-instant of impression and the after-instant of retention are different point-like nows. Yet the gap between them is considered to be a continuous one; it is this temporal continuity that gives rise to internal time-consciousness. Any *proper* difference is subsequent to this primordial continuity. Ricoeur underlines the radical discontinuity between perception and memory, whose corollary is that the *represented* past is relegated to the realm of the "as if," which has nothing in common with *presentative* intuition.

Ricoeur's discussion of the second level of temporal constitution concludes with two critical remarks. The first one concerns Husserl's privileging of the past and memory to the detriment of expectation. One reason for this is that his major preoccupation was to resolve the issue of temporal continuity, so the distinction between retention and recollection was sufficient to that end. Moreover, to the extent that the future takes its place in the temporal surroundings of the present and that expectation is integrated in those surroundings as an empty intention, Husserl did not think he could deal directly with such futural categories. Expectation is portrayed as merely an anticipation of perception: either it is characterized by the emptiness of the not-yet, or, if the anticipated perception has already become present, it has sunk down into the past. Expectation is not regarded as the counterpart of memory, which remains, says Ricoeur, "the major guideline" of Husserl's analysis (TN, 3:37). This remark signals Ricoeur's belief that Husserl conceives of intuition and recollection in terms of a *fulfilled* intention alone, which somehow contravenes his declaration, in "Kant and Husserl" (1954), that the distinction between intuition and an unfulfilled intention is totally unknown in Husserl.[8]

The paradoxical effect of such emphasis on memory is its insertion into the same series of internal time where retention belongs, something that mitigates the previously established opposition between recollection and retention. If memory is directed toward a perception that has already occurred in the past, it can be aligned with retention under the aegis of the past. Ricoeur draws attention to Husserl's contradiction whereby he first affirms a rigorous dichotomy between memory and retention, between the "*wieder*" and the "*re*," only in order to bring them back together by inserting them into a single temporal flow: "Reproduction is itself also called a modification, in the same way as retention. In this sense, the opposition between 'quasi' and 'originary' is far from being the last word concerning the relation between secondary and primary remembrance" (TN, 3:37).

Ricoeur's second remark concerns the extent to which Husserl's discussion of temporal objects remains inseparable from a previous understanding of objective time, despite having initially set time out of play. The temporal series in which both memory and retention are inserted is a serial order made up of identifiable temporal positions (*Zeitstelle*). This is not to suggest that Husserl collapsed the material of lived experience to the formal objectivity of those temporal positions, for he cautiously distinguished between the two phases of temporal constitution: one focusing upon the immanent object and its appearance to consciousness, the other upon the identity of the temporal position. Ricoeur, however, points toward what appears to be an essential law in Husserl:

> The sinking back of one and the same sound into the past implies a reference to a fixed temporal position. "It is part of the essence of the modifying flux that this temporal position stands forth as identical and necessarily identical" (p. 90). Of course, unlike what has to do with an a priori of intuition in Kant, the form of time is not superimposed on pure diversity, since the interplay of retentions and representations constitutes a highly structured temporal fabric. It remains nonetheless that this very interplay requires a formal moment that it does not seem capable of generating. (TN, 3:39)

By highlighting Husserl's unsuccessful attempt to derive a homogeneous objective time from the lived continuum of a transcendental ego's retentions, Ricoeur questions the constituting ability of intrasubjective temporality. The closest

Husserl gets to such a derivation is when he defines recollection as the power to transpose every instant into a zero-point or a quasi-present. This gesture marks a possible transition from the time of monadic remembrance to a world time that goes beyond the memory of each individual.[9] But even then, this transition turns out to take for granted what it is supposed to lead to, that is, objective time. In the final analysis, Husserl cannot avoid having recourse to some a priori temporal laws and, in Ricoeur's words, "whenever we attempt to derive objective time from internal time-consciousness, the relation of priority is inverted" (TN, 3:40).

Husserl's presupposition of objective time recurs on the third level of temporal constitution, that of the absolute flux of consciousness. Ricoeur contends that it is only here that the true sense of the Husserlian enterprise comes into view, and continues: "The originality of the third level thus lies in bracketing the tempo-objects and formalizing the relations among point-source, retention, and protention, without regard for the identities, even the immanent ones, constituted here; in short, in formalizing the relation between the originary 'now' and its modifications" (TN, 3:41). On this level, which precedes all constitution, there is no identity and nothing that endures. What one finds here is just a flux of alteration, even though, absurdly enough, there is no identifiable object to be altered. Husserl sought to go beyond immanent objects and *constituted* unities toward the *constituting* level of consciousness, which he defined as absolute subjectivity. He encountered serious difficulties in providing a philosophical description of that level, hence his well-known phrases "For all this, names are lacking" and "Here, one can say nothing further than: 'See'" (PITC, §36, 100 and §38, 103). The difficulty with any description of the constituting flux is that one can either name it after whatever is constituted, or resort to analogy and metaphors such as flux, source-point, etc. One cannot help wondering here whether it is by chance that Kant had to resort to analogy in order to represent the formal conditions of experience, and that Freud also used scriptural and mechanical metaphors to account for the perceptual process.[10]

Ricoeur critically points out that Husserl regarded simply as intuitions the formal conditions of experience, which can be subsumed under three headings: the unity of the flux of consciousness, the common form of the now (the origin of simultaneity), and the continuity of the modes of running-off (the origin of succession) (TN, 3:41).[11] A question arising here is the following: How can one have knowledge of the unity of the flux if there is no constituted objectivity at this level? Here one can speak neither of identity, nor of difference, nor of distinction. Even the temporal objects of the second level are excluded and the relations between source-point, retention, and protention are formalized. Aware of this problem, Husserl tried to resolve it by differentiating a transverse intentionality turned toward the immanent object and its temporal unity from a longitudinal one directed toward the unity of the absolute flux itself.[12] The two intentionalities are indissociable aspects of one and the same thing; they are homogeneous and intertwined with each other. As Ricoeur notes, in order to have something that endures (an immanent object), there must be a flux that constitutes itself, and the necessity of such self-constitution results from the fact that Husserl had to avoid infinite regress. The flux does not need a backdrop against which to appear, but is, as a phenomenon, self-constituting. Here is Ricoeur on this act of self-evident self-constitution:

> The enterprise of a pure phenomenology is completed with this self-constitution. Husserl claims the same self-evidence in its regard as his phenomenology grants to internal perception. There is even a "self-evident consciousness of duration" (p. 112), just as indubitable as that of immanent contents. The question remains, however, whether the self-evident consciousness of duration can be sufficient to itself without relying in any way on that of a perceptual consciousness. (TN, 3:42)

Ricoeur's objection to the idea of a self-evident and self-constituting consciousness of duration is that such a formalization and any knowledge of the unity of the flux depend on a perceptual consciousness and some constituted objectivity. Husserl's appeal to "unity," "succession," and "simultaneity" presupposes objective time, for it is only on this basis that these concepts make sense. The belief in a continuous flux takes for granted the objective time that Husserl had initially set out of play. One can enter the phenomenological problematic only by bracketing out the time of nature; simultaneously, the phenomenology of time can be articulated only by borrowing from world time. The unity of the flux of consciousness entails a time divided up into now-points, so Ricoeur contends that Husserl inadvertently has recourse to objective temporal categories despite his determination to achieve a pure phenomenology.

This objection results neither from Ricoeur's distrust of the ordinary concept of time, as is the case in Heidegger, nor from his wish to question the metaphysical implications of Husserl's appeal to objective time. On the contrary, it is grounded, as is clear from the first lines of the discussion of Kant's approach, in Husserl's failure to *acknowledge* the irreducibility of certain temporal a priori:

> I want to find in Kant the reason for the repeated borrowings made by the phenomenology of internal time-consciousness with respect to the structure of objective time, which this phenomenology claims not only to bracket but actually to constitute. In this regard, what the Kantian method refutes are not Husserl's phenomenological analyses themselves but their claim to be free of any reference to an

objective time and to attain, through direct reflection, a temporality
purified of any transcendent intention. (TN, 3:44)

For Ricoeur, who follows to a great extent Kant's critical philosophy where
objective time always remains a presupposition,[13] Husserl was wrong not to
have realized that time as such cannot appear before consciousness, for time
constitutes the very condition of appearing. Husserl is rebuked for refusing
to acquiesce in the irreducibility of the intersubjective time of nature, and
for seeking in vain phenomenologically to reflect on its constitution by the
transcendental ego. Ricoeur's argument gestures toward an invincible time, a
gesture reminiscent of Augustine's professed inability to provide a philosophical
explanation of time when asked what it is.[14]

In the "Conclusion," while discussing the third aporia of temporality,
Ricoeur maintains that "time, escaping any attempt to constitute it, reveals itself
as belonging to a constituted order always already presupposed by the work
of constitution" (TN, 3:261). He attributes the Kantian epithet "inscrutable"
to a time that thwarts the attempts of human thinking to posit itself as the
master of meaning. Finally, with a view to indicating the antinomy between a
finite and an infinite temporality, he turns to lyric poetry whose elegiac tone
appropriately expresses the "nonmastery and the grief that is ceaselessly reborn
from the contrast between the fragility of life and the power of time that
destroys" (TN, 3:273).

Ricoeur concludes his reading of Husserl by stressing that "the phenomenology of internal time-consciousness ultimately concerns immanent intentionality interwoven with objectifying intentionality. And the former, in fact,
rests on the recognition of something that endures, which the latter alone can
provide for it" (TN, 3:44). Husserl's analyses cannot free themselves from any
reference to objective time, and fail to attain a temporality extricated from
transcendent presuppositions.

Admittedly, Ricoeur is uneasy about Husserl's reduction to consciousness and the tendency to regard the perceptual present as self-constituting,
self-sufficient, and immediate. One may object here that the present does not
amount to a category altogether exclusive of difference, for retention is strictly
speaking a non-perception. Moreover, toward the end of his discussion, Ricoeur
perceptively refers to the "weightier implication" of Husserl's surprising and
even "contradictory" assertion that even representation or presentification is in
the final analysis a present impression (TN, 3:43): "Every act of presentification, however, is itself actually present through an impressional consciousness.
In a certain sense, then, all lived experiences are known through impressions
or are impressed" (PITC, §42, 116). It is by virtue of the potential disruption
inherent in such admission of the nonoriginary into the identity of the present

that Ricoeur accepts, in *Freud and Philosophy*, that Husserl allows for a certain problematic of a wounded, dispossessed, and mediated consciousness.[15]

Nevertheless, he falls short of pursuing that insight and its weighty implications any farther and, rather, chooses to adhere to a more conventional construal of Husserl's declarations. Accordingly, he focuses on the continuous transition from impression to retention, and on the concomitant thickening of the present. Broadened perception is inseparable from an *essentially* smooth continuity where difference and discontinuity are regarded as secondary modalities to be subordinated to the continuous movement that defines the transcendental ego. If Aristotle is reproached for his failure, due to his excessive emphasis upon the individual instant, to account for the continuity of lived experience, phenomenology, for Ricoeur, succeeds in producing a more human or subjective conception of time without exposing it to the threat of an interrupting difference.

This success amounts at the same time to a failure, for the prioritization of a continuous and immediate living present signals toward a consciousness cut off from the world and unable to constitute itself and time single-handedly. Ricoeur clearly wants to keep his distance, in *Time and Narrative* and elsewhere, from a theory that, positing the transcendental subject as the first fact, considers difference to be secondary and inessential. In *Freud and Philosophy*, he regrets that phenomenology begins with an act of suspension, an *epoché* "at the free disposition of the subject" (FP, 391). Similarly, in "The Question of the Subject," he argues that Husserl's thought, in *Cartesian Meditations: An Introduction to Phenomenology* (1931), goes much farther in the direction of an autonomous consciousness, and culminates in "a radical subjectivism which no longer allows any outcome other than conquering solipsism by its own excesses and deriving the other from the originary constitution of the *ego cogito*" (QS, 257).[16]

Isn't Ricoeur's accusation of subjectivism at variance with Husserl's confession, attendant upon his phrase "for all this, names are lacking," about the indeterminacy of the flux of consciousness? Such indeterminacy, however, turns out to be applicable, as Derrida usefully specifies, to the properties of the flux rather than consciousness itself.[17] The latter, affirms Husserl, "is absolute subjectivity and has the absolute properties of something to be denoted metaphorically as 'flux,' as a point of actuality, primal source-point, that from which springs the 'now,' and so on. . . . For all this, names are lacking" (PITC, §36, 100). Despite maintaining that its *properties* have to be indicated metaphorically, Husserl does not hesitate to designate consciousness as "absolute subjectivity."

By deploying this expression in order to refer to an essence distinct from its attributes, is it not clear that Husserl conceived of consciousness, as Derrida notes, on the basis of presence as substance, *ousia, hypokeimenon,* that is, a self-identical being in self-presence which forms the substance of a subject? Is not the construal of the flux and the living present in terms of consciousness and subjectivity the result of the phenomenological requirement that the presence of sense to a full and primordial intuition be the guarantee of all value? I will discuss this point in detail in chapter 2, but it has to be said here that the ultimate court of appeal for Husserl is the noematic presence of an object to consciousness. Therefore, conscious intuition taking place in the living present constitutes the source of self-giving evidence. Husserl was strongly opposed to any talk of a non-present, unconscious sensation or content:

> It is certainly an absurdity to speak of a content of which we are "unconscious," one of which we are conscious only later. Consciousness is necessarily *consciousness* in each of its phases. Just as the retentional phase was conscious of the preceding one without making it an object, so also are we conscious of the primal datum—namely, in the specific form of the "now"—without its being objective. . . . Were this consciousness not present, no retention would be thinkable, since retention of a content of which we are not conscious is impossible.[18]

Husserl establishes in one fell swoop the complicity between intuition, consciousness, certitude, and the present. None of these terms can be eliminated without causing his project to collapse. It appears then that Derrida would concur with Ricoeur apropos of Husserl's endorsement of an immediate and self-sufficient perceptual consciousness.

By drawing attention to the transcendental self's inability to generate objective time, Ricoeur contests the phenomenological authority of consciousness, and points out the necessity of articulating it with non-presence and exteriority. Husserl's recourse to a priori temporal laws bears witness to his failure to set out of play not only the time of reality and history but also intersubjectivity, in which objective time is ineluctably anchored. Far from being self-evident and immediate, the unity of consciousness that Husserl strives to account for remains dependent on the exteriority of objective time, which is itself reliant upon the communalization of individual experiences. Even though Ricoeur acknowledges that the phenomenological theory of temporalization allows, perhaps at the price of a certain contradiction,[19] for some discontinuity, he suggests that Husserl could have admitted more expressly to the necessity of difference and exteriority at the very core of a supposedly unified consciousness.[20]

In this light, one is not only tempted to remain vigilant about Lawlor's remark that immediacy supports the entire Ricoeurean edifice, but also surprised by the fact that Lawlor himself observes that Ricoeur's criticism is aimed at "Husserl's failure to reconcile his subjective descriptions with irreversible temporal succession."[21] To the extent that Ricoeur holds that the modalities of difference and exteriority, attendant upon the objective time that phenomenology presupposes, introduce an element of alterity into the thick perceptual present, he cannot be reproached for embracing a fully present, self-sufficient and immediate consciousness. This claim is corroborated by the concerns that Ricoeur voices in *Freud and Philosophy*, written approximately twenty years before *Time and Narrative*, regarding the phenomenological prioritization of conscious perception and Husserl's mistrust of the unconscious. Ricoeur turns to Freud in response to a double demand: firstly, to acknowledge, against Husserl, a certain non-presence as absolutely necessary and original, and, secondly, to establish that nonetheless this non-presence is dialectically bound up with a positive meaningfulness. The latter is not grasped in the immediate experience of a perceptual consciousness but is to be sought by a reflective consciousness mediated by the interaction between the patient and the psychoanalyst.

Freud's Quantitative Hypothesis and Unconscious Autonomy

In "The Question of the Subject," Ricoeur expresses a double uneasiness about what he calls "reflective philosophy" or, more hesitantly, "philosophy of the sub- ject," one instance of which is Husserlian phenomenology (QS, 236–37). Firstly, his hesitation originates in the acknowledgment that no such philosophy puts forward an immutable proposition affirming unreflectively and unreservedly the subject's sovereignty. With respect to phenomenology, I have shown that Ricoeur accepts that Husserl does not oust *all* difference from the perceptual present. Secondly, Ricoeur's uneasiness arises from the contemporary challenge, first and foremost by psychoanalysis and structuralism, to the pretensions of immediate consciousness and to the primordial and founding act of absolute subjectivity.

In his detailed investigation in *Freud and Philosophy*, psychoanalysis is said to suspend the properties of consciousness by means of an anti-phenomenological reduction. The Freudian text situates the possibility of a certain non-presence of meaning within the very heart of conscious perception, thereby undermin- ing the primacy accorded by Husserl to a continuous and self-sufficient living present. Ricoeur, however, wishes to reappropriate such absence by inscribing it within a teleology claimed to be inherent in the Freudian discourse itself. Accordingly, I will explore here what many commentators have affirmatively described as Ricoeur's "double reading" of Freud,[22] and will also raise specific questions that this double gesture fails to address.

The part of Freud's oeuvre that remains the most resistant to phenomeno- logical concepts such as "conscious experience," "subjective intention," "mean- ing," "certainty," etc., is the one designated as "energetics," which refers to Freud's neurological work and, more specifically, to his "Project for a Scientific Psychology" (1950 [1895]).[23] Freud's early thought is dominated by the notion of the "psychical apparatus" conceived of on the basis of principles borrowed from physics and compliant with a quantitative treatment of energy. Ricoeur's presentation begins by quoting the opening statement of the "Project" where Freud sets out the fundamental tenets of his theory:

> The intention is to furnish a psychology that shall be a natural science: that is, to represent psychical processes as quantitatively determinate states of specifiable material particles, thus making those processes perspicuous and free from contradiction. Two principal ideas are involved: [1] What distinguishes activity from rest is to be regarded as Q, subject to the general laws of motion. (2) The neurones are to be taken as the material particles. (SE, 1:295)

Freud goes on to affirm that pathological clinical observation suggested to him the conception of neuronal excitation as quantity in a state of flow, and stipulates that the basic principles of neuronal activity in relation to quantity are those of constancy and inertia. According to the latter, the nervous system tends to discharge its quantities trying to reduce its tensions to zero; this is its primary function. Considering that any excitation that produces energy can be subsumed under the concept of "quantity," Freud distinguishes between quantity originating in the external world (Q) and intercellular quantity arising within the somatic element ($Q\dot{\eta}$). Whereas the organism can withdraw from external stimuli, it cannot do so with respect to endogenous ones; these have their origin in the needs of hunger, respiration and sexuality, and cease only under specific conditions. In order to bring about these conditions, the organism is required to make an effort independent of and greater than the intercellular $Q\dot{\eta}$. Therefore, it needs to abandon its original trend to inertia and to put up with a certain store of $Q\dot{\eta}$ in order to be able to accomplish such an action. The system is unable to bring the level of $Q\dot{\eta}$ down to zero, but seeks nonetheless to maintain the level of tension as low as possible and to guard against any increase of it; this is the principle of constancy associated with the secondary function. As Freud notes, "[A]ll the functions of the nervous system can be comprised either under the aspect of the primary function or of the secondary one imposed by the exigencies of life" (SE, 1:297).

Subsequently, Freud identifies two classes of neurones: the permeable ones (φ), which offer no resistance and retain no trace of quantity, and the impermeable ones (ψ), which are loaded with resistance and constitute the vehicles of memory and other psychical processes (SE, 1:299–300). This distinction is necessitated by the fact that any serious psychology should provide an explanation of memory to the extent that this is one of the main characteristics of nervous tissue. If memory is defined as the capacity of protoplasm to be permanently differentiated by excitation, an equally important function of the system is perception. Capable of remaining infinitely fresh to new excitations, the receiving substance must be essentially unalterable too. The nervous system must be both permanently altered and unaltered, hence the differentiation between φ and ψ.

Oddly, Ricoeur does not mention almost anything at all about the complex functioning of the two classes of neurones to which Freud devotes substantial space in the "Project." Rather, he is content to refer, in very general terms, to the mechanical description of quantity on the model of physical energy, and to insist that excitation is conceptualized as a "current which flows, which 'stores,' 'fills' or 'empties,' and 'charges' neurons [sic]; the all-important notion of 'cathexis' was first elaborated within this neuronic framework as a synonym of storing up and filling (Origins, pp. 358–62). Thus the 'Project' talks about cathected or empty neurons [sic]" (FP, 73–74).[24] Then he goes on to focus on the third system related to consciousness, perception and quality (ω), while drawing attention to Freud's alignment, on the one hand, of the increase in neuronal tension with unpleasure, and, on the other, of the discharge of tension with pleasure. Experiences of pleasure or unpleasure leave in the ψ system traces that are considered to be the intermediaries responsible for translating quantity into quality.[25]

In what sense exactly is Freud's quantitative conception said, initially at least, to defy interpretation and meaning? Why does Ricoeur consider the quantitative treatment of psychical energy and the work of hermeneutics to be mutually exclusive? Precisely because Freud's explanation, by conceiving of the nervous system in terms of a purely mechanistic principle, regards it as an apparatus essentially purposeless and, therefore, resistant to the intentionality with which psychical life is usually coupled. If the provenance of the psyche is an unconscious level dominated by automatic forces and incompatible with "quality," "reality," and "time," then every process is a mechanical reaction to the threat of an increase in quantity and unpleasure. Quality is thought to originate in quantity, and even conscious desire and wishes, says Ricoeur, are assumed to depend primarily on a mechanistic or "hedonistic" principle (FP, 80). What counts on this primordial level is measurable forces in relation to which the conscious processes of discrimination, inhibition, judgment, interaction with the external world and other persons, etc., are regarded as secondary and supervenient. By approaching the psyche in terms of quantities of excitation, currents of energy, and cathected neurones, Freud has provided an anatomy of the brain, thereby construing psychical processes as more or less static phenomena laid bare by a mechanical explanation.

For Ricoeur, the corollary of Freud's anatomical psychology is a certain determinism that is in conflict with a teleological interpretation. Quoting Ernest Jones, he points out that such a "deterministic hypothesis" prevailed over against a theory of desire incorporating the values of purpose, aim, and intention (FP, 86). The neurology of the "Project" was intended as a scientific explanation of how the psychical apparatus functions without, however, placing this mechanical functioning under the service of a higher objective or *telos*. If there is something essentially inventive about such a quantitative hypothesis, it has to do with the conception of the psyche on the model of a machine defined in terms of its pure functioning rather than a final purpose. To the extent that Freud could envisage a machine without finality, intention, or meaning, he introduces an irreducible non-presence into the heart of consciousness and, thereby, undercuts the phenomenological belief in a living perceptual present.

The dispossession of immediate consciousness is sustained in *The Interpretation of Dreams* (1900), whose difficult seventh chapter is, according to Ricoeur, the unquestionable heir to the "Project."[26] However, inasmuch as the *Traumdeutung* subordinates the systematic explanation to interpretation, it is to Ricoeur's discussion of Freud's papers on metapsychology that I will now turn in order to examine the extent to which this more mature expression of psychoanalysis corroborates the idea of an initial non-presence, independent of and resistant to meaningfulness. Ricoeur draws attention once again to the anti-phenomenological character of Freud's topographical-economic explanation. Freud adopts a systematic perspective as opposed to a descriptive one, and performs the reverse of Husserl's *epochē*: whereas the latter consists in an act of suspension at the disposal of the subject, Freud's *epochē* amounts to a reduction of consciousness, where the very control and certitude of a conscious self is put into question.[27]

In order for such a reduction to be possible, Freud postulates, in the essay on "The Unconscious" (1915), the organization of psychical experience in three independent localities in compliance with the first topography: the unconscious (*Ucs.*), the preconscious (*Pcs.*) and consciousness (*Cs.*).[28] Every psychical act, considered to belong at first to the system *Ucs.*, in order to be allowed into *Cs.*, should pass a certain type of testing or censorship understood by Ricoeur on the model of the barrier (*la barre*). If it passes the testing without difficulty, it enters the *Pcs.*, and the possibility of it becoming conscious is not a remote one. If, however, the act is rejected by censorship, it is cut off from the *Cs.* and repressed into the *Ucs.* According to the topography, the process of becoming conscious

> is a possibility which may or may not eventuate. Consciousness does not occur unconditionally and as a matter of course. The barrier of resistance leads us to represent the process of becoming conscious as a transgression, a crossing of a barrier; to become conscious is to penetrate *into*, to be unconscious is to keep apart *from* consciousness. (FP, 118)

"Repression," in conjunction with "topography," gives rise to relations of exclusion, which, in turn, result in the metaphorics of the barrier. If the latter is invoked whenever Ricoeur wishes to underline the difference between Husserl and Freud, it is by virtue of the fact that the separation between the unconscious and consciousness is a rigorous one, and the entailed non-presence is much more radical than that allowed for by Husserl. In the third part of *Freud and Philosophy*, Ricoeur remarks that the main barrier dividing psychical localities is that between the unconscious and the preconscious rather than that between the preconscious and the conscious: "To replace the formula *Cs./Pcs., Ucs.* by the formula *Cs., Pcs./Ucs.* is to move from the phenomenological point of view to the topographic [*sic*] point of view" (FP, 392). Repression is responsible for dissociating the *Ucs.* from the *Pcs.* and *Cs.*, and, in this light, the unconscious is no longer determined as an implicit consciousness or latency *continuously* yoked to the perceptual present; rather, it is autonomous and wholly different from the *Cs.* The specificity of the unconscious is indicated by the fact that it is governed by its own systemic laws such as the primary process, the absence of negation, timelessness, etc., outlined in the fifth section of "The Unconscious."[29]

Similarly, in "The Question of the Subject," Ricoeur reaffirms that these psychical localities are "in no way defined by descriptive, phenomenological properties but as *systems*, that is, as sets of representations and affects governed by specific laws which enter into mutual relationships which, in turn, are irreducible to any quality of consciousness, to any determination of the 'lived' " (QS, 237). Insofar as consciousness is denied direct access to the unconscious, where meaning is constituted, it is not the principle or measure of all things; it is, therefore, suspended or reduced. The key idea of the topography is that the unconscious is beyond the reach of consciousness, hence the demand for an interpretative technique adapted to distortions and displacements. By exposing the illusion of immediate consciousness, not only does psychoanalysis undermine the philosophies of the subject but it also establishes the anteriority and primordiality of unconscious activity, which is now placed at the center of existence.

That Freud wished to affirm a distance between the *Ucs.* and *Cs.*, thereby introducing an ineluctable alterity into the heart of the conscious present, is evident in the following comparison he makes: when an unconscious thought gains access into consciousness, the ensuing conscious perception is similar to that of the external world by means of our sense-organs. By assigning psychical activity to the unconscious, psychoanalysis differentiates the conscious perception of an unconscious process from this process itself, in the same way that Kant cautiously avoided identifying a subjectively conditioned perception of a thing with the thing itself. Freud points out that, "like the physical, the psychical is not necessarily in reality what it appears to us to be" (SE, 14:171). Commenting on this comparison, Ricoeur underlines that Freud, by endorsing the idea of *essentially* and *originarily* remote unconscious operations, questions the phenomenological preeminence of the living present and complicates the coupling of perception, certainty, and consciousness. Given that the conscious text is subject to distant impulses that originate in a system outside its own control, it is regarded not as immediately meaningful and transparent but as a "lacunary, truncated text" (FP, 119–20).

Freud's systematic perspective comes more forcefully to the fore when his topography becomes an economy, when he posits drive (*Trieb*) as one of the fundamental concepts of his psychology. Such a stipulation brings us back to the "Project," for the notion of "drive" cannot be divorced from the hypothesis of the constancy principle.[30] An instinctual stimulus does not arise in the external world but from within the organism itself. In this respect, it can also be called a "need." It is the function of the nervous system to reduce to the lowest possible level the stimuli that reach it. The activity of the psychical mechanism, affirms Freud in "Instincts and Their Vicissitudes" (1915), is "subject to the pleasure principle, i.e. is automatically regulated by feelings belonging to the pleasure-unpleasure series."[31] This implies not only that every psychical operation is ultimately understood as a vicissitude of drives, but also that the source *itself* of these drives cannot become the object of knowledge.

Nevertheless, if one can talk of drives, it is thanks to the fact that their energetic component is represented by something psychical: "An 'instinct' appears to us as a concept on the frontier between the mental and the somatic, as the psychical representative [*Repräsentant*] of the stimuli originating from within the organism and reaching the mind" (SE, 14:121–22).[32] Repression consists in cutting off drives from consciousness and not in cutting them off from their psychical representatives. This is what Freud specifically labels "primal repression," according to which the psychical representative of the drive is denied access into consciousness.[33]

In his detailed exposition of the complex role of psychical representatives, which are themselves subdivided into ideas or groups of ideas (*Vorstellungen*) and quotas of affect (*Affektbetrag*),[34] Ricoeur does not fail to draw attention to Freud's terms *remoteness* (*Entfernung*) and *distortion* (*Entstellung*), which indicate the necessary distance separating the two realms in question: on the one hand, drives, unconscious activity, and the quantitative factor of instinctual energy; on the other, the ideational or psychical representatives of these drives and the possibility of gaining access into consciousness. By virtue of this irreducible remoteness, drives *as such* are averred to be energy and tension. Their biological reality or source (*Quelle*) is inaccessible: "We do not in fact know what instincts are in their own dynamism. We do not talk of instincts in themselves" (FP, 136).

The move from the topography in the direction of a pure economics and the concomitant affirmation of the anteriority and independence of drives recur in the fourth and fifth sections of "The Unconscious." Freud's analysis here, concerned solely with the placement and displacement of cathexis, the withdrawal of cathexis and anticathexis, veers toward the economic viewpoint, which "endeavours to follow out the vicissitudes of amounts of excitation and to arrive at least at some *relative* estimate of their magnitude" (SE, 14:181).

In addition, the nucleus of the unconscious is said to consist of "instinctual representatives which seek to discharge their cathexis; that is to say, it consists of wishful impulses" (SE, 14:186). Freud, once again, claims Ricoeur, defines "the unconscious system much more in terms of the discharge of affects than in terms of ideas" (FP, 148), thereby banishing any relations of meaning.

The reading of the papers on metapsychology concludes with a double gesture epitomizing Ricoeur's approach to psychoanalysis in general. On the one hand, Freud is shown to favor the autonomy of instinctual and unconscious activity, hence the economic and automatic regulation of pleasure and unpleasure as the intractable provenance of the psychical system. The latter functions according to mechanistic principles devoid of any sense of purposefulness or intentionality. Such an anti-phenomenological account posits a *necessary* and *originary* non-presence, which is precisely why Ricoeur turns to Freud in order to question Husserl's emphasis on self-evidence, immediacy, continuity, and self-sufficiency. Insofar as psychoanalysis regards difference as necessary and anterior to a self-identical consciousness, it introduces absence into the perceptual present much more decisively than Husserl did. Ricoeur stresses that unconscious desire, rather than the cogito, is the first fact of existence: "Before the subject consciously and willingly posits himself, he has already been posited in being at the instinctual level. That instinct [or drive] is anterior to awareness and volition signifies the anteriority of the ontic level to the reflective level, *the priority of the* I am *to the* I think" (QS, 265). As a result of Freud's anti-phenomenology, "consciousness is now the least known; it has ceased to be self-evident and has become a problem" (FP, 133).

On the other hand, Ricoeur is keen to place the Freudian emphasis on a detached unconscious under the service of the *demand* for interpretation and meaningfulness. Following this second strand of his reading, I will now focus on the dialectical articulation between the quantitative-economic hypotheses and the possibility of attributing a meaning to otherwise purely biological processes, a possibility designated as Freud's "semantics of desire" (QS, 263). Commenting on such a double reading, Thomas R. Koenig remarks that Freud's naturalistic approach is considered by Ricoeur to be "only a provisional reference point which eventually is to be integrated into the existential."[35] Although the necessity and chronological priority of unconscious activity is affirmed, it is teleologically and, in the final analysis, *negatively* determined as always looking forward to a meaningful *positivity*.

From a Perceptual to a Reflective Present

Ricoeur's negative interpretation of non-presence is predicated upon his complaint that Freud's abstract science, albeit necessary, is inadequate and cannot single-handedly provide a satisfactory account of the psychical system. Insofar

as the "Project" construes the psyche on the model of the principles of physics, biology, and anatomy, it deprives it of the properly psychical qualities that
distinguish its meaningfulness from the automatism of an apparatus. What
cuts Freud's scientific explanation off "from any work of deciphering, from
any reading of symptoms and signs, is the pretension of making a quantitative
psychology of desire . . . correspond to a mechanical system of neurons [*sic*]"
(FP, 82). On the contrary, argues Ricoeur, the "pleasure-unpleasure combination sets into play much more than the isolated functioning of the psychical
apparatus" (FP, 77). He insists that Freud, dissatisfied with his natural scientific
representation of the primary function, was forced to move gradually away
from his quantitative conception and the metaphorics of the apparatus toward
a certain semantics.

This transition to a more dialectical approach is evident in his reluctance,
even in the "Project," to endorse the unpredictable and discontinuous functioning of the psychical machine. Freud is said to have affirmed the *meaningful* and
productive transformation of quantity into quality, and the smooth passage from
the primary to the secondary function. Accordingly, having hardly explained
how the ψ neurones and their unconscious traces work, brief references to which
are largely confined to his footnotes, Ricoeur moves to the third neuronal class
related to consciousness.

One of the axioms of Freudian theory is that conscious perception and
memory are mutually exclusive. Consciousness knows nothing of the quantities
of excitation that constitute the origin of memory cathecting the ψ system:
"Consciousness gives us what are called *qualities*—sensations which are *different*
in a great multiplicity of ways and whose *difference* is distinguished according
to its relations with the external world. Within this difference there are series,
similarities and so on, but there are in fact no quantities in it" (SE, 1:308).
Consciousness makes us aware of certain sensations by qualitatively differentiating them from other ones that belong to the order of quantity and that
are registered by means of unconscious traces. How and where do qualities
originate? Freud reaches the conclusion that "there is a third system of neurones—ω perhaps [we might call it]—which is excited along with perception,
but not along with reproduction, and whose states of excitation give rise to
the various qualities—are, that is to say, *conscious sensations*" (SE, 1:309).[36] The
ω neurones, which will later be inserted between φ and ψ, are responsible for
receiving qualities, or, rather, for converting external incoming excitation into
quality. The ω system is moved by very small quantities, and conscious sensations (quality) come about only where quantities are so far as possible excluded.
Largely permeable and retaining no memory of the sensations they receive, the
ω neurones seem to be the antipodes of the ψ system at this stage.[37]

Ricoeur defines this difference between the perceptual neurones and their
mnemic counterparts in terms of an "opposition" between receiving and retain-

ing, perceiving and remembering (FP, 76 n. 15). Such an opposition, however, does not amount to a radical heterogeneity, and Ricoeur recalls Freud's metaphorical description of ψ and ω as intercommunicating pipes. Moreover, the perceptual neurones are linked to the mnemic ones by means of a temporal property, a certain periodicity of neuronal motion that is transmitted without inhibition in every direction. This periodicity changes into time as soon as it enters consciousness, hence the correlation of the latter with time and reality, to be opposed to the timelessness of the unconscious.[38] By portraying the ω and ψ neurones as two entities at variance with each other, and by affirming the smooth transformation not only of quantity into quality but also of periodicity into time, Ricoeur puts forward the idea of their dialectical articulation, thereby denying the quantitative system a radical alterity. As a result, the mechanical component of the apparatus is not regarded as *entirely* autonomous but as a necessary and provisional negativity to be eclipsed by quality and consciousness.

One indication, for Ricoeur, that Freud's mechanistic model is not self-sufficient is that it starts to break down when one realizes that the principle of inertia cannot adequately explain experiences such as pleasure, unpleasure, satisfaction, etc., all of which involve much more than mere mechanics. The pleasure-unpleasure combination sets into play one's interaction with the external world and other persons, a process that cannot be accounted for by invoking currents of physical energy alone. The avoidance of unpleasure implies several operations that are scarcely quantifiable and that are germane to the secondary function and the ego organization. Some such processes are discrimination, inhibition, satisfaction, judgment, observant thought, etc., which, as Freud concedes, do not function in compliance with a purely naturalistic law.[39]

In addition, the fact that the amounts of excitation cannot be measured also signifies the inadequacy of the quantitative hypothesis. Freud's quantities, far from being proper quantities comparable to those studied by physics, have been derived from pathological clinical observation, so, strictly speaking, there is nothing measurable about them; what matters is their intensive aspect. Ricoeur underlines that all the "mechanisms" Freud describes in this early period will soon be raised to the level of "work" (dream-work, work of mourning, etc.), where agency and purposefulness are introduced into the previously neurological account (FP, 84–85).

Although Ricoeur is aware that the quantitative hypothesis will never be completely abandoned and that consciousness will always remain a quasi-cortex, he stresses the tendency of psychoanalysis to move gradually away from an organic explanation, and quotes many passages where Freud proclaims the inadequacy of his neurological model and the need for more psychical, non-anatomical categories. Such a tendency is already evident in the "Project," which "is not merely a mechanical system cut off from interpretation by its anatomical hypothesis; it is already a topography, linked by underground connections to the work of deciphering symptoms. Hermeneutics is already present in this text" (FP, 84).[40] Freud is said to have been more and more willing to describe his concepts from both an anatomical and a psychological perspective, and it is the dialectical continuity between the two that allows for the possibilities of analysis and interpretation.

The claim about Freud's intention to distance himself from the mechanical model appears problematic, for it fails to take into consideration that his descriptions of the psyche drew increasingly upon a metaphorics of the machine, culminating in the "Note upon the 'Mystic Writing-Pad' " (1925), where the nervous system is likened to the famous *Wunderblock*.[41] Moreover, this transition from neurology to hermeneutics is authorized by the dialectical interpretation of various oppositional pairs such as memory and perception, quantity and quality, the primary and secondary processes, the mechanical and the psychical, etc. This gesture is indissociable from a teleological construal whereby one of the terms of these binaries is thought to exist for the sake of the other one, to be always in sight of the other higher term whose function is to absorb without negating the first one. Such conceptuality entails the determination of the two poles of the dialectic on the basis of a positive-negative relation. On the one hand, Freud is credited with introducing an original and necessary non-presence into perceptual consciousness; on the other, Ricoeur determines this non-presence as a provisional negativity to be subsumed by a positive and meaningful *telos*. His reading of Freud's topographical-economic model sheds more light on this dialectic.

Initially, Ricoeur laments Freud's drifting toward a pure economics in his metapsychology. The pleasure principle and the terminology of biological needs or discharge of affects are inseparable from the idea of an apparatus functioning according to a mechanistic, nonintentional principle. As long as the primary process prevails and forces of quantitative energy are dominant, "impulses coexist without any relations of meaning" (FP, 148). Although Freud's economics is instrumental in reducing phenomenological illusions and unmasking a false consciousness, it has to be supplemented by a semantics intended to restore meaning. Ricoeur claims that such a semantics of desire, whose implication is the dialectical coupling of suspicion and faith, is evident in the Freudian discourse itself.

The barrier, for instance, separating psychical localities, far from imposing an absolute limit on interpretation, is precisely what calls for the collaborative work of the analyst and the patient. In the final analysis, "The Unconscious" ends not with the *intra*systemic laws governing each system but with the *inter*-systemic relations that make the communication between the three localities possible: " 'The Unconscious' ends with a significant circular movement that takes us back to the starting point, that is, to the deciphering of the unconscious in its 'derivatives' " (FP, 150). These derivatives, which are the psychical representatives referred to earlier, function as intermediaries between the systems, as the points of transition capable of providing access, on condition that one is willing to undertake the laborious work of analysis, to the repressed contents of the unconscious. In this sense, economics forms the background of a properly hermeneutic phase: "[Psychoanalysis] never confronts one with bare forces, but always with forces in search of meaning; this link between force and meaning makes instinct a psychical reality, or, more exactly, the limit concept at the frontier between the organic and the psychical" (FP, 151).

What is one supposed to conclude from this attribution to Freud of an unequivocally hermeneutic agenda? Perhaps that one should not take Ricoeur's words à la lettre when he speaks of a "barrier" separating the Ucs. from Cs. Of course, Ricoeur never said that this barrier entails a relation of radical exteriority between the two systems. On the contrary, he insists that the barrier unites as much as it separates: "In spite of the barrier that separates the systems, they must be assumed to have a common structure whereby the conscious and the unconscious are equally psychical. . . . [This structure] assures a close 'contact' [Berührung] between conscious and unconscious psychical processes' (FP, 135). And closer to the end of the book, he affirms that "the barrier functions both as a relation between signifying and signified factors and as a force of exclusion between dynamic systems" (FP, 403–404).[42] The double functionality of the word barrier, not only indicating exclusion but also constituting a point of transition between distinct psychical domains, excellently serves the dialectical agenda of Freud and Philosophy.

Firstly, the term barrier is instrumental in distancing Freud and Ricoeur from Husserl's emphasis on the transparency of a sovereign consciousness. Doesn't "barrier," by opposing the unconscious to consciousness and by allowing for a necessary and anterior non-presence, make Ricoeur impervious to any criticism of solipsism, subjectivism, or subscription to the immediacy of a perceptual present? "Barrier" indicates the separation of two realms determined reciprocally and in opposition to each other. The corollary of such separation is the attribution of a more or less rigorous identity to each system, which remains in principle self-identical, unaltered, and distinguishable from what lies on the other side. Hence Ricoeur's allusions, in Freud and Philosophy but also in more recent work, to the indestructibility and permanence of unconscious traces.[43]

Secondly, insofar as the barrier allows for communication and translation, what is at issue is a dialectical opposition, which is precisely why the barrier does not constitute a radical limit. The acknowledged difference between the unconscious and consciousness does not amount to an irreducible heterogeneity. The two realms are conceptually opposed to one another, which means that they share a minimal common ground, that of the common barrier. The unconscious is not conceived of on the basis of an ineluctable alterity but on that of a necessary remoteness which nonetheless communicates with consciousness. In the third section of *Freud and Philosophy*, entitled "Dialectic: A Philosophical Interpretation of Freud," Ricoeur asserts that "the unconscious is homogeneous with consciousness; it is its relative other, and not the absolute other" (FP, 430). In this respect, he interprets the link between the two spheres as a dialectical one, and regards the transcription of content from one to the other as a teleological process.

An essential feature of such dialectics is the directionality from the unconscious to consciousness, from non-meaning to meaningfulness, from quantity to quality, from secrecy to expression. This directionality is evident in Ricoeur's delineation of the unconscious as a "drive toward language" (FP, 453–54). Notwithstanding its unnameable and disjunctive character, the unconscious is a potentiality, a provisional state of affairs looking forward to the possibility of a meaningful present: "If desire is the unnameable, it is turned from the very outset toward language; it wishes to be expressed; it is in potency to speech. What makes desire the limit concept at the frontier between the organic and the psychical is the fact that desire is both the nonspoken and the wish-to-speak" (FP, 457). Mute at a given moment, the unconscious is congruous with phenomenality and expression, toward which it is claimed unfailingly to tend. According to Hegelian phenomenology, to which Ricoeur's reading of Freud is indebted, every dialectic consists in a progressive synthetic movement whereby each form or figure receives its meaning from the subsequent one. The truth of the unconscious lies in the subsequent moment of consciousness, which, having incorporated its other, assumes the form of the mediated self of reflection rather than the allegedly transparent self of perception. Ricoeur alludes to Jean Hyppolite's designation of this complex conceptuality as a "dialectical teleology."[44]

Most of Freud's operative concepts are arranged in oppositional pairs, which is what makes possible a dialectical correlation giving the whole system the directionality characteristic of a teleological process. Anyone "familiar with the philosophical mentality of Hegelianism," says Ricoeur, "cannot help noticing the constant use of opposition in the structure of Freud's concepts" (FP, 475). Some of the binaries identified are the primary and the secondary process, the unconscious and consciousness of the first topography, life and death instincts, the id and the superego of the second topography, the libido and a nonlibidinal culture, and the intersubjective dialectical nature not only of the analytical situation but also of unconscious impulses. The terms of these pairs "are all presented, as in the Hegelian dialectic, as master-slave relationships that must be overcome" (FP, 477).

Unconscious activity, then, is not regarded as imposing a radical limit on interpretation but as the negative condition of a positively reflective process aiming at self-understanding by means of recovering, with the analyst's help, an archaic, hidden meaning. This original dialectic between the unconscious and consciousness is instrumental both in giving rise to the archaeological urge of psychoanalysis to return to the most originary and principial psychical state, and in authorizing that other interpretative dialectic between archaeology and teleology. Firstly, the concept of "archaeology" is introduced to complement the economic point of view:

> We must now see the underlying compatibility between the eco-
> nomic model and what I henceforth shall call the archeological
> [sic] moment of reflection. Here the economic point of view is no
> longer simply a model, nor even a point of view: it is a total view
> of things and of man in the world of things. . . . For my part, I
> regard Freudianism as a revelation of the archaic, a manifestation
> of the ever prior. (FP, 440)

Ricoeur explains that the expression "archaeology of the subject," borrowed from Merleau-Ponty, was motivated by a "sense of depth" pertaining to the hidden timelessness of the unconscious as opposed to the temporality of a more easily available consciousness (FP, 442). Furthermore, this very timelessness cannot be disengaged from the Freudian belief in the indestructibility of unconscious traces that is the task of the analytical work to excavate. Ricoeur refers to Freud's portrayal of instinctual activity in terms of a dark, inaccessible locality or even a chaos, and, arguably, the affinity between such metaphorics and Hegel's description of subjectivizing interiorization (*Erinnerung*) as a dark abyss is hardly coincidental.[45]

Secondly, if such archaeology and what Ricoeur calls Freud's "realism of the unconscious" lead to the dispossession of immediate consciousness, this is only a provisional phase inextricably bound up with the demand for a higher reflective consciousness: "What I wish to demonstrate, then, is that if Freudianism is an explicit and thematized archeology [sic], it relates of itself, by the dialectical nature of its concepts, to an implicit and unthematized teleology" (FP, 461). The necessary stage of dispossession refers to the patient's supposedly transparent consciousness whereas the final return to consciousness at the end of the analysis pertains to a "scientific consciousness" that belongs not to a private but to a "transcendental subjectivity" (FP, 431). The reappropriation of such consciousness constitutes the *telos* of the psychoanalytical enterprise, and it is on this basis that the reality of the id has to be dialectically yoked to the ideality of meaning. The transparency of meaning must be suspended for the work of analysis to be jointly undertaken by the analyst and the patient, and for the return journey toward an ideal intersubjective meaning to begin: "I understand," maintains Ricoeur, "the Freudian metapsychology as an adventure of reflection; the dispossession of consciousness is its path, because the act of becoming conscious is its task" (FP, 439).

The dialectic between dispossession and reappropriation, between archaeology and teleology, brings together under the same roof the psychoanalytical
critique of a phenomenologically living present and the possibility of attaining
a reflective present on a higher level of consciousness. Insofar as the unconscious trace that constitutes the object of archaeology functions according to
mechanistic principles, it is something unnameable and unpresentable that cannot appear as such before a *perceiving* subject; hence the acknowledgment of
distance, absence, and secrecy. Nevertheless, although the unconscious itself
does not appear and does not speak, it is conceived of, thanks to the linking
capacity of the barrier, as a tendency toward phenomenality, language, and
meaning. This tendency can be made use of by the onerous and reflective work
of analysis undertaken jointly by the analyst and the analysand. Consciousness
has to lose itself, to distance itself from the myth of immediate perception, in
order for the *reflective* subject to achieve a genuine self-awareness through the
detour of the psychoanalytical technique, another consciousness and its own
working-through (*Durcharbeitung*).[46]

Ricoeur's discussion leaves little doubt as to his approach to those two
interpretative phases in terms of a dialectic between a positivity and a negativity.
Although the diagnosis of the inadequacies and illusions of consciousness is a
necessary and original stage, it is a negative gesture that has to be complemented
by the postulation of a positive *telos*: "We must now take a further step and
speak no longer merely in negative terms of the inadequacy of consciousness,
but in positive terms of the emergence or positing of desire through which
I am posited, and find myself already posited" (FP, 439). Similarly, in "The
Question of the Subject," he reiterates that "the task of a reflective philosophy
following Freud will be to dialectically relate a teleology to this archaeology,"
and underlines that "rooting subjective existence in [unconscious] desire permits
a *positive* implication of psychoanalysis to appear, one which goes beyond the
negative task of deconstructing the false *cogito*" (QS, 244 and 243). As Ricoeur
explains in "What is Dialectical?" (1975), every dialectical process has to welcome negative instances, to incorporate foreign elements in order to be able
to attain a higher order of truth and objectivity.[47] Thus, the appropriation of
meaning through psychoanalysis and interpretation entails the negative realization that the conscious subject is an enigma or a problem for reflection rather
than the measure of all things.

The Freudian insights find completion in a philosophy of reflection,
where the archaeology of the subject aims at a purposeful meaning. It is on
account of such a dialectics that Ricoeur's reading of Freud claims to retain the
critique of immediate consciousness without, however, giving up all belief in
the possibility of achieving a mediated self-consciousness. The latter is inscribed
within the course of a progressive synthetic movement of what Ricoeur calls,
after Hegel, "spirit" or "mind":

The subject must also discover that the process of "becoming conscious," through which it *appropriates* the meaning of its existence as desire and effort, does not belong to it, but belongs to the *meaning* that is formed in it. The subject must mediate self-consciousness through spirit or mind, that is, through the figures that give a telos to this "becoming conscious." (FP, 459)

The journey of self-consciousness, its mediation by an abysmal unconscious and the eventual *Aufhebung* of the perceptual present, comes to be represented by an imagery of darkness and light arrived at through a reinterpretation of *Oedipus Rex*. In response to Freud's insistence on the Oedipal drama of childhood, Ricoeur proposes that the pivotal theme of the play is "the tragedy of self-consciousness" and Oedipus's relation to revelation or insight, where the sphinx represents the unconscious and Tiresias the force of truth (FP, 516–17).[48] Paradoxically, Oedipus, who can see the light of day, remains in darkness with regard to his initial hubris and pretension to mastery. He can achieve spiritual insight only after his pretension has been shattered by suffering. The possibility of light and self-consciousness depends on the realization of his arrogance and false mastery: "As in the Hegelian dialectic, Oedipus is not the center from which the truth proceeds; a first mastery . . . must be broken; the figure from which truth proceeds is that of the seer" (FP, 517). It is in light of such a tendency to endorse dialectics that Jean-François Lyotard draws attention, in *Discours, figure* (1971), to Ricoeur's Hegelian reading of Freud.[49]

To what extent is Ricoeur's dialecticization of psychoanalysis compatible with his deployment, throughout *Freud and Philosophy*, of a metaphorics of language, discourse, and text in order to describe the functioning of the unconscious? If he claims that the unconscious is analogous to a linguistic process, the latter is not the transparent one of ordinary language. By virtue of repression, distortion, displacement, condensation, and pictorial representation, unconscious activity does not coincide with language, nor does it obey any linguistic laws: "It is impossible to make the absence of logic in dreams, their ignorance of 'No,' accord with a state of real language" (FP, 397). The instinctual representatives, which are the signifying elements in that secret realm, belong to the order of images and have little to do with ordinary language. The only case where ordinary language may be involved in the unconscious is when words are treated as images in schizophrenia or the more schizophrenic aspect of dreams. Ricoeur admits that "if we take the concept of linguistics in the strict sense of the science of language phenomena embodied in a given and therefore organized language, the symbolism of the unconscious is not *stricto sensu* a linguistic phenomenon" (FP, 399). The unconscious is operative prior to language and does not function in agreement with orderly relations between signifiers and signifieds. Ricoeur, therefore, purports to have resisted the Lacanian belief that "the unconscious is structured like a language" (FP, 395).

And yet, this is far from saying that the linguistic analogy is altogether abandoned. Rather, Ricoeur complicates things by putting forward, following Émile Benveniste, the analogy between the unconscious and rhetoric, which is an equivocal language of tropes where the link between signifier and signified is not given but something to be arrived at by means of a toilsome process.[50] This analogy presupposes that in ordinary language there is a more or less direct relation between the sensible and the intelligible, that the access to the signified via the signifier is unproblematic and unequivocal. Such a straightforward transition is absent from metaphorical language, insofar as involved therein is the substitution of one signifier for another and the displacement of literal meaning. A necessary distance is acknowledged between signifier and signified, and the latter, not readily available to the conscious subject, is posited as a *telos* to be partially reappropriated. Repression resembles the mechanism of metaphor because it leads, in the case of dreams, to condensation and displacement of unconscious contents.[51]

Ricoeur cautiously refrains from affirming an absolute coincidence between metaphor and repression, for repression entails an economy of forces incompatible with the linguistic point of view. The impossibility of *totally* recovering or appropriating an unconscious meaning originates in the inscrutable nature of somatic needs and impulses. This is precisely why psychoanalytical truth always remains, for Ricoeur, a "task" or an "infinite Idea" (FP, 458), never to be actually and fully realized but regulating nonetheless the horizon within which the collaborative work of the patient and the analyst takes place.

The analogy, however, is upheld with the qualification that "the interpretation of repression as metaphor shows that the unconscious is related to the conscious as a particular kind of discourse to ordinary discourse" (FP, 403). Ricoeur refers to unconscious processes as "paralinguistic distortions of ordinary language" or a "quasi language" (FP, 404–405). No matter how much he seeks to displace and complicate the relation between the sensible and the intelligible in his metaphorical portrayal of the unconscious, the psychical representatives are regarded as signifying elements mediating between an anterior non-presence and a positive meaningfulness. If non-presence and presence are dialectically linked thanks to a middle term ensuring the smooth transition from the former to the latter, their difference is internal rather than external. I will come back to this in chapters 3 and 4, so it suffices here to stress, in an elliptical fashion, that the sensible and intelligible components of language have always been understood in terms of a dialectical relation whereby one can reach a signified content on the basis of a signifying form. The dialectical teleology Ricoeur diagnoses in the consciousness-unconscious relation is consolidated by his recourse to a linguistic or, rather, rhetorical metaphorics.

In light of Ricoeur's endorsement of a dialectical logic in Freud, but also of his attempt to introduce an intersubjective mediation into the living present of phenomenology, one has to agree with Richard Kearney's affirmation of

> Ricoeur's resolute refusal of the idealist temptation—extend-
> ing from Hegel to Husserl and Sartre—to reduce being to
> being-for-consciousness. . . . Consciousness must pass through
> the unconscious; intuition through critical interpretation; reason
> through language; and reflection through imagination. . . . The way
> of appropriation must always go through the way of disappropria-
> tion. There is no belonging except through distantiation.[52]

With the reservation that my insistence on Ricoeur's dialectics is not my last word on his reading of Freud, one can pose here several questions, anticipat-ing the investigation of Derrida's approach to psychoanalysis. To what extent does Ricoeur's dialectics do justice to Freud's supposedly major contributions to thought, namely, the concept of the unconscious and the process of repression? Does the construal of the unconscious as a potentiality on its way to meaning-fulness not detract from Freud's radical thinking? What would the implications for a hermeneutics of the psyche be if Freud's bipolar distinctions were shown to be essentially nonoppositional? If it could be shown that the psychical system functions according to a differential law that infinitely problematizes the dialec-tical opposition of all those terms, would this not signify that any progressive movement is interrupted in a way unaccounted for by Ricoeur's reading? I will now turn to Derrida with a view not only to seeing whether his interpretation of Freud is compatible with Ricoeur's idea of a "psychical discourse" compliant with the continuist understanding of "language," "signification," "communica-tion," "medium," "form," and "content," but also to exploring the extent to which he upholds Ricoeur's association of Husserlian phenomenology with a continuous and flowing temporality.

Chapter 2

Derrida and
Rhythmic Discontinuity

In order to counterbalance Husserl's conception of the living present in terms of immediacy and transparency, Ricoeur turned to Freudian psychoanalysis, which complicates, he claims, the idea of a self-constituting consciousness. It is worth now going back to Husserl's text, regarding it this time through the prism of Derrida's analysis in his highly controversial *Speech and Phenomena.* The first two sections of this chapter will reexamine Husserl's theory of temporalization from a Derridean perspective. I will argue that Derrida's construal is more appreciative than Ricoeur's of the incongruities of Husserl's *Phenomenology of Internal Time-Consciousness,* and that these incongruities reflect, in turn, an originary aporia that constitutes the sine qua non of the living present and temporality in general.

The remaining three sections will focus on Derrida's reading of Freud's archaeological quest and findings with respect to an absolutely original psychical trace. Although Derrida admits to the dialectical structure of Freudian conceptuality, he also insists on the tendency of psychoanalysis to resist interpretation and teleology. In order to throw some light on such a paradoxical gesture of self-resistance, I will discuss Derrida's interpretation of certain moments in Freud's neurological and metapsychological accounts where psychical inscription is at issue. This process will be revealed to constitute a differential movement taking place on the frontier between the inside and the outside, and giving rise to mysterious unconscious traces that remain essentially heterogeneous to presence and permanence. I will also explore the peculiar temporality of this psychical writing, as well as the implications of Freud's scriptural metaphorics not only for the functioning of the psyche but also for what one could designate as "mundane writing." Finally, in a quasi-circular and apparently contradictory fashion, I will investigate the possibility of discovering in Ricoeur's text indications that, despite appearances, he goes some way toward thinking the Freudian tension brought out by Derrida's reading.

Husserl's Aporia: Discontinuity and Repetition

In *The Problem of Genesis in Husserl's Philosophy*, in order to portray the problematic relationship between objective time and immanent time-consciousness in Husserl, Derrida has abundant recourse to the terms *dialectic* and *contradiction*.[1] One, therefore, might justifiably believe that this early work concurs with Ricoeur's interpretation. This vocabulary, however, is largely abandoned in *Edmund Husserl's "Origin of Geometry"* and, subsequently, a certain adjustment in Derrida's vocabulary apropos of Husserl's account of temporalization is evident in *Speech and Phenomena*, where he thematizes what he calls Husserl's "irreconcilable possibilities" (SP, 67).[2] For Derrida, Husserl's analyses are perplexing insofar as they are tormented by two simultaneous demands: on the one hand, there is the necessity of a faithful description of lived experiences of time, which are nonpunctual and enduring, whereas, on the other, there is the requirement that the living now be the absolute *principium* and ultimate source of authority for all knowledge.

The first necessity, whose phenomenological provenance I will now attempt to flesh out, concerns the modalities of continuity and repetition accentuated by Ricoeur. Husserl's theory was intended to make time itself appear before a pure and transcendental consciousness, hence his avowal to set world time out of play. In the form that his transcendental project took in his mature years from 1905 onward, it was defined by the attempt to reach a primordial sphere of originary lived experience (*Erlebnis*).[3] With a view to opposing both empiricism and historicism, he sought to get beyond mere facts of experience and the worldly present to the eidetic structures of consciousness prior to facticity. In order for the objects and contents of such experience to come properly into view in their essence, all constituted knowledge and presuppositions originating in metaphysics, psychology, and the natural sciences had to be bracketed, hence the reduction. The latter reveals the naïveté of the natural attitude, which is now suspended together with the totality of the natural world and any judgment concerning spatiotemporal existence. By thus excluding metaphysical naïveté and everything belonging to the order of the already constituted, the reduction amounts to a removal of being leading to a primordial region of consciousness called a "phenomenological residuum" (*Ideas I*, §33, 112–14 and §§49–50, 150–55).[4]

This residuum refers to a living present in its "essential purity" and "*unconditioned necessity*" (*Ideas I*, §36, 120), to a transcendental consciousness directed toward an intentional and ideal object not to be confused with the apprehended thing. The distinction between immanence and transcendence is crucial here to the extent that it points to a fundamental difference between two modes of being given. On the one hand, a transcendent thing is perceived through the perspectival manifestations of its determinate qualities. On the other hand, unlike spatial objects, the immanent correlates of transcendental experience have no hidden profiles or perspectives. Their presence before consciousness is not affected by any form of exteriority, contingency, difference, or absence; in this respect, they are given as absolute.[5]

Therefore, the phenomenological slogan "to the things themselves" must be understood as referring not to perceived objects or empirical facts but to transcendental experiences analyzable in the pure generality of their essence. Insofar as the contents of experience are treated, after the *epochē*, as self-given and immanent phenomena, transcendental phenomenology provides access to a domain of apodeictic evidence and certitude. If all reality and exteriority is excluded, if everything is ideal, if nothing gets lost by going forth in the world, space, or nature, then experience is diaphanously present to the transcendental subject.[6]

As far as *The Phenomenology of Internal Time-Consciousness* is concerned, the reduction of objective time would provide access to a purely phenomenological present, to a primordial temporal essence constituted within the immanence of consciousness. Paola Marrati explains that Husserl, aiming to reflect on temporality in a way that would define the specificity of phenomenology in relation to psychologism and Kant's theory of knowledge, had to exclude not only the time of nature and the psyche but also time as the empty form of the Kantian subject.[7] This exclusion alone could lead to a domain of consciousness that, unencumbered by naturalistic distortions, could think of an immanent time endowed with absolute evidence. The appearance of the noematic sense of time in all its purity and freedom from exteriority is facilitated by the repetitious structure of retention. The *eidos* of time hinges on the possibility of repetition within the intimacy of the transcendental consciousness, where the ideal sense of temporality can be reproduced in the absence of all contingency. An account faithful to the phenomena Husserl is interested in requires the continuity between impression and retention.

This is why Husserl insists that the punctual instant in which the present is anchored constitutes only an ideal limit that cannot be isolated as such. Section 19 affirms that "what we term originary consciousness, impression, or perception is an act which is continuously gradated. Every concrete perception implies a whole continuum of such gradations. . . . It belongs to the essence of lived experiences that they must be extended in this fashion, that a punctual phase can never be for itself" (PITC, §19, 70). The temporality described here is not punctual, and Derrida, already in *The Problem of Genesis*, drew attention to the unity or "*a priori* synthesis" of impression, retention, and protention:

> I cannot reduce an originary impression to the purity of a real point, and that is a matter of essence. The absolute point is still less perceptible in time than in space. . . . It is an *a priori* necessity of the perception of time and of the time of perception that

an originary impression have some temporal density. As a result, absolute originarity is *already a synthesis* since it implies *a priori* a "retentional modification." (PG, 62)

Husserl places both intuition and retention under the aegis of a broadened perception in section 16 too, which reiterates the indispensability of continuity: "[The] ideal now is not something *toto caelo* different from the not-now but continually accommodates itself thereto. The continual transition from perception to primary remembrance conforms to this accommodation" (PITC, §16, 63). Derrida, who cites this passage in *Speech and Phenomena*, admits that intuition is continuously compounded with retention, thereby agreeing with Ricoeur.

Moreover, he accepts that Husserl, well aware of the disturbing implications of his introduction of retention into the present, put forward the idea of a radical discontinuity between primary and secondary remembrance so as to safeguard the primordiality of perception against representative memory and imagination. Section 17 refers to the *discontinuous* difference between perception and reproduction, which functions as a foil highlighting the *continuous* difference between impression and retention:

> If we call perception *the act in which all "origination"* lies, which *constitutes originarily*, then *primary remembrance is perception*. For only in *primary remembrance do we see what is past*; only in it is the past constituted, i.e., *not in a representative but in a presentative way*. The just-having-been, the before in contrast to the now, can be seen directly only in primary remembrance. It is the essence of primary remembrance to bring this new and unique moment to primary, direct intuition, just as it is the essence of the perception of the now to bring the now directly to intuition. On the other hand, recollection, like phantasy, offers us mere presentification. (PITC, §17, 64)

This passage confirms the preeminence of continuity between impression and retention as well as the latter's presentative character. Husserl's gesture originates in the phenomenological necessity of describing the concrete lived experience of temporality, the presence of the present from the standpoint of ideal interiority.[8] The sphere of primordiality is extended to include the retentional now, whose repetitious nature alone can prepare the ground for the ideality of the living present. As Derrida remarks, "the living now is constituted as the absolute perceptual source only in a state of continuity with retention taken as nonperception. Fidelity to experience and to 'the things themselves' forbids that it be otherwise" (SP, 67).

At the same time, and according to a second necessity whose implications are underlined by Derrida but downplayed by Ricoeur, the idea of a smooth continuity is complicated by the fact that the lived experience of temporality must be referable to a source-point qua *absolute* beginning. In order for the perceptual present to constitute a zone of primordial experience and to function as the source of self-giving evidence, it has to exclude all absence or difference, even temporal difference; it has to be narrowed down to the punctuality of the now. Intuition has to be instantaneous, it has to take place in the present moment without any need of exteriorization, indication, or representation. Derrida makes much of this precept, and contends that, for Husserl, "despite all the complexity of its structures, temporality has a nondisplaceable center, an eye or living core, the punctuality of the real now" (SP, 62).

He supports his claim by citing the following passage, where Husserl affirms the derivation of the living present from a punctual source-point: "We emphasize that modes of running-off of an immanent temporal Object have a beginning, that is to say, a source-point. This is the mode of running-off with which the immanent Object begins to be. It is characterized as now" (PITC, §10, 48–49). The original sensation, which constitutes a self-giving presentation (*Gegenwärtigung* or *Vorstellung*), has to be distinct from retention, let alone from memory and imagination, both of which are demoted to the order of representation (*Vergegenwärtigung* or *Repräsentation*).[9] Notwithstanding his portrayal of retention as a modification, Husserl also maintains that each sensation corresponding to a stigmatic now-point remains "absolutely unaltered" (PITC, §31, 90), thereby provoking Derrida's legitimate complaint that "one no longer understands then how retentional and protentional modifications are still possible out of an originarity that is not modified" (PG, 67).

Despite referring in a footnote to Derrida's emphasis on the Husserlian demand for a punctual beginning, Ricoeur is keen to draw a rigorous demarcation line between the account of a largely continuous time-consciousness and the prioritization of the point-like now in Husserl's theory of intuition (TN, 3:283 n. 12).[10] However, such a division is not justified in light of the allusions, throughout *The Phenomenology of Internal Time-Consciousness*, to the absolutely unaltered now of the primal impression. The latter, in section 8, is defined as a generative and "productive point" (PITC, §8, 45), which implies a radical break from all anterior instants but also from the passivity of retention. This view is corroborated in Appendix I, where Husserl introduces the notion of "*genesis spontanea*": "The primal impression is the absolute beginning of this generation—the primal source, that from which all others are continuously generated. In itself, however, it is not generated; it does not come into existence as that which is generated but through spontaneous generation. It does not grow up (it has no seed): it is primal creation" (PITC, 131).

Conceived of as an absolute beginning, the now has to be strictly self-identical and to exclude all difference and exteriority. In this respect, a certain discontinuity is introduced into the heart of the living present. This understanding of the impressional now is consonant with Husserl's "principle of all principles" (*Ideas I*, §24, 92–93), which establishes the interdependency between perception, interiority, self-evidence, and the punctual now. In addition to citations from *The Phenomenology of Internal Time-Consciousness*, other evidence is adduced by Derrida in support of the requirement that the primordial origin and guarantee of all epistemological value be a stigmatic now, metonymically signified by the phrase "*im selben Augenblick*" from Husserl's *Logical Investigations* (1900–01).[11]

Despite Husserl's initial avowal to exclude world time, his analysis turns out to depend on the punctuality of the instant as the primal form (*Urform*) of consciousness.[12] This is precisely why Derrida argues that, no matter how much he wishes to extricate phenomenology from a supposedly degenerate metaphysics, and however vigorously he advocates the exclusion of all metaphysical presuppositions, Husserl endorses nonetheless the form of the present now as the temporal category capable of guaranteeing the pure appearing of an object to a transcendental consciousness. Despite his vigilance and critical attitude toward the naiveté of metaphysical speculation, Husserl's discourse presupposes a temporal category grounded in the objective time of nature. The form of the now is what remains irreducible, what even the phenomenological reduction cannot do away with. The privilege of the now is not something emanating from Husserl's concrete analyses of phenomena but is grounded in a decision that defines "the very element of philosophical thought," a thought indissociable from the values of identity, evidence, consciousness, and truth (SP, 62–63).

This observation is reminiscent of Ricoeur's critique of phenomenology. However, it is here that Derrida parts ways from the discussion of *Time and Narrative* and goes farther to argue that, far from merely presupposing objective time, Husserl goes some way toward complicating it by virtue of the double necessity already discussed. Derrida's reading is structured along the lines of a reading principle differentiating between Husserl's declared intention and his actual descriptions, hence his insistence on the following aporia: the indivisibility of the living now required by the phenomenological "principle of all principles" is inevitably problematized by the fact that its appearance depends inexorably on the possibilities of difference and repetition. In addition to the exigency regarding the origination of lived experience in the absolute now, Husserl's philosophy gestures toward the fact that that stigmatic moment is divisible and essentially repeatable.

In contrast with Ricoeur, Derrida argues that Husserl's account perhaps calls into question the very identity and originarity of the actual now as the form of time. This is the case because Husserl both designates retention as a "not-now" distinct from the properly impressional now, and contends that the latter becomes possible thanks to that not-now. The *ideal* purity of the now does not even appear without being articulated with another now-point that is, paradoxically, both outside this absolute beginning and inside the primordial perceptual present. Retention, then, is not a contingency that befalls an already constituted living now *après-coup*. The appearance of that now hinges on retentional consciousness and the gross present:

> Apprehensions here pass continually over into one another and terminate in an apprehension constituting the now; this apprehension, however, is only an ideal limit. We are concerned here with a *continuum of gradations in the direction of an ideal limit*. . . . If somehow we divide this continuum into two adjoining parts, that part which includes the now, or is capable of constituting it, designates and constitutes the "gross" now, which, as soon as we divide it further, immediately breaks down again into a finer now and a past, etc. (PITC, §16, 62)

What gives rise to the intuitive source-point is the gross present, which includes the repetitious retention. Unable to constitute itself without a more originary and complex structure, the living now appears only belatedly and on condition that it give up its actual and full presence in order to present itself under the guise of the recent past.[13] Husserl affirms the necessity of retention as the possibility of repeating and constituting the living now through a differentiating movement. Retention confronts one with "the absolutely unique case," says Derrida, whereby the act of perceiving gives one to perceive something that is not present, a presentation that enables one to see a non-present, a past, or an unreal present (SP, 64).

Furthermore, Derrida underscores the necessity of retention qua repeatability, whose corollary is that both recollection and retention are anchored in the possibility of repetition.[14] If retention cannot be rigorously distinguished from memory and imagination, the radical difference between presentation and representation is vitiated, and, as a result, the primarily continuous character of the living present is undermined. The common root of retention and recollection, says Derrida, is a priori "the possibility of re-petition in its most general form, that is, the constitution of a trace in the most universal sense . . . a possibility which not only must inhabit the pure actuality of the now but must constitute it through the very movement of differance it introduces" (SP, 67).[15] This is not to say that Husserl sought to abolish the difference between presentation and representation, but merely to register a certain uneasiness about their absolute heterogeneity, and to emphasize that this chasm depends on a philosophical decision problematized by Husserl's analyses themselves.

While putting forward the continuous transition from impression to retention, Husserl's emphasis on the identity and anteriority of the primary intuition also bears witness to a necessary difference between the perceptual and nonperceptual now:

> If we now relate what has been said about perception to the *differences of the givenness* with which temporal Objects make their appearance, then the *antithesis of perception* is *primary remembrance*, which appears here, and *primary expectation* (retention and protention), whereby *perception and non-perception continually* pass over into one another. (PITC, §16, 62)

Husserl here both affirms the unity of the living present and casts doubt upon it by regarding retention and protention as *non-perceptions*. Although Derrida highlights the pivotal role of discontinuity, he does not simply take sides against the primacy of continuity. Rather, he reflects on the implications of the phenomenological account and stresses that its equivocality arises from Husserl's struggle to maintain two irreconcilable possibilities: the source of all certitude has to be the indivisible living now from where representation ought to be banished, but, at the same time, any concrete experience of that now depends on its continuous modification and representation by a nonperceptual retention.

Continuity and repetition, both instrumental in Husserl's accurate description of all temporal lived experience, entail a difference and a passivity that contaminate the nonrepresentational and foundational character of the living present. The latter's identity is complicated the moment retention is introduced into the heart of primordial perception. The inclusion of retention in the thick present inevitably undercuts the alleged unity and originarity of that present:

> As soon as we admit this continuity of the now and the not-now, perception and nonperception, in the zone of primordiality common to primordial impression and primordial retention, we admit the other into the self-identity of the *Augenblick*; nonpresence and nonevidence are admitted into the *blink of the instant*. There is a duration to the blink, and it closes the eye. (SP, 65)

That the perceptual now is not instantaneous and that the present is not simple is not something forced by Derrida upon Husserl's discourse. This nonsimplicity and the concomitant possibility of repetition are required by the concrete experience of temporality. However, the a priori synthesis involved in such experience calls into question the other philosophical exigency, the origination of presence in the punctuality of the *Augenblick*. Derrida respects those two conflicting necessities and, as Marrati suggests, plays Husserl's analysis and fidelity to phenomena off against his decision regarding the necessity of punctuality and self-identity.[16]

Derrida does not discount Husserl's declared intention to regard the divisibility of the present as a necessary but provisional aspect of the perceptual process to be eclipsed by continuity and identity. Husserl indeed stresses the ability of retention to retain and repeat, while determining difference in a negative fashion as something simply provisional and supplementary. The generation of the living present is claimed to depend on a process whereby the impressional now is affected by nothing other than itself, by nothing *essentially* different from itself, hence Derrida's portrayal of this movement as a "pure auto-affection."[17]

Simultaneously, Derrida reveals another strand of Husserl's text, according to which discontinuity and difference are irreducible and originary, and, by the same token, the present and even the now turn out to be non-simple and non-self-sufficient categories. Husserl's analyses, argues Derrida, reveal the following necessity: "The presence of the present is thought of as arising from the bending-back of a return, from the movement of repetition, and not the reverse" (SP, 68). In contrast to Ricoeur's critique that Husserl presupposes objective time, *The Phenomenology of Internal Time-Consciousness*, continues Derrida, calls upon one to conceive of time anew "on the basis now of difference within auto-affection, on the basis of identifying identity and nonidentity within the 'sameness' of the *im Selben Augenblick*" (SP, 68).

It now remains to try to understand a little better this peculiar structure that Derrida's reading has brought to light. As far as the difference between the perceptual and retentional now is concerned, he insists that it can be neither reduced nor subordinated. The possibility of difference is *absolutely* irreducible and is "in fact the condition for presence, presentation, and thus for *Vorstellung* in general" (SP, 65). If it is not a matter of a provisional or contingent difference, in what terms is one supposed to think about its absolute necessity? Can Derrida sustain the irreducibility of discontinuity without, however, simply reversing the hierarchy of continuity and discontinuity? Is there an alternative way of thinking this difference? Could one determine it without subjecting it to a logic opposing the essential to the provisional? Can one think difference and sameness in terms other than those of a dialectical opposition? In other words, can one think difference and repetition together?

The point here is not to argue in favour of a resolution of Husserl's irreconcilable possibilities. Rather, it is to show why Ricoeur's argument for continuity cannot be sustained, and to throw some light on the aporetic structure that gives rise to both perception and temporality. To this end, I will have recourse to Derrida's philosophical configuration of "necessary possibility," which, despite not being specifically deployed in *Speech and Phenomena*, can nonetheless be said to characterize his thinking about discontinuity and difference, to constitute something like a master-argument, as Geoffrey Bennington points out, from which all else flows.[18] Anticipating one of my paradoxical conclusions, the necessary possibility of difference will turn out to make perception possible while disallowing a self-identical perceptual present.

The Necessary Possibility of Difference and Syncopated Temporality

In contrast with Ricoeur's construal of difference and discontinuity as negative and provisional functions to be eclipsed by the transcendental subject's living present, Derrida draws attention not simply to the necessity of retention as distinct from primary impression, but also to the impossibility of interpreting such difference as a provisional phase. If the idea of provisionality requires some directionality from intuition toward retention, Derrida's motif of necessary possibility undermines the self-identity of these two moments and, therefore, excludes the possibility of a teleological interpretation of alterity on the basis of an envisaged presence.

The philosophical reference of the living present to an absolute beginning requires that that original *stigmē* be rigorously differentiated from all anterior and subsequent now-points. Without this a priori requirement, it makes little sense to speak of an absolute *principium*. The latter's self-identity depends crucially on its radical discontinuity with other now-points, or, in other words, on the non-presence and exclusion of other nows from the actual and living now. It follows that this diastem between an original source-point and other surrounding nows is not merely an accidental fatality but the positive *conditio sine qua non* of the perceptual now. Such a radical difference from other retentional or protentional now-points is structurally necessary and inherent in the very possibility of the intuitive now. As a result, it cannot be demoted to a contingent or empirical eventuality.

At the same time, in light of the necessity of repetition, which is not just a phenomenological necessity, this requirement of difference has to be tempered with the modality of possibility. The absolute difference between the living and retentional now does not belong to the order of actual necessity, because, in that case, the perceptual now would not even appear, but to that of *necessary possibility*. This structure alone is able to do justice to the double and apparently contradictory function of retention: it is the radical exclusion of retention that gives rise to the possibility of an indivisible now, whereas, at the same time, the ideal purity of that now depends on retention's repetitious capacity. Owing, however, to the first necessity, repetition has to be conceived here in terms rather of a *minimal* repeatability or iterability than of an ordinarily understood continuity.[19]

Not only is the impressional now unable to constitute itself independently of absence and difference, but also its very self-identity and originariness are undercut. To the extent that it emerges thanks to the necessary possibility of its difference from a retentional trace, this movement entails a principial co-implication of presence and absence, where a certain radical alterity cannot be opposed to identity. Paradoxically, this co-implication gives rise to the *possibility* of the living now, while rendering its pure and uncontaminated presence *impossible*. By determining difference as a necessary possibility, Derrida affirms its simultaneously constituting and deconstituting role.

Difference and discontinuity cannot be teleologically construed as provisional but negative necessities, for they constitute the *positive* conditions without which the ideality and identity of the now and the present would not stand a chance. What remains implicit in Husserl's account is that the possibility of presence hinges on the more originary possibility of representation, which renders the idea of a simple origin problematic. If an absolutely irreducible alterity is instrumental in the constitution of the living present, every discussion of temporality has to take this movement seriously into consideration, and its implications have to be reflected on. Derrida's line of argument in *Speech and Phenomena* seeks to do justice to the indebtedness of the present to a discontinuous synthesis as its positive and originary nonorigin.

The temporal discontinuity entailed here is thematized in "*Ousia* and *Grammē*," where Derrida discusses various philosophical approaches to time. The process of temporalization qua auto-affection is defined there as an impossible possibility. On the one hand, because of the requirement of self-identity, two nows are mutually exclusive, so they cannot be simultaneous. On the other hand, for one to be able to affirm this self-identity, the possibility of a minimal simultaneity has to be surreptitiously presupposed: "The impossibility of coexistence can be posited as such only on the basis of a certain coexistence, of a certain *simultaneity* of the nonsimultaneous, in which the alterity and identity of the now are maintained together in the differentiated element of a certain same."[20] Derrida notes that "time" is a name for this impossible possibility. Such an originary commingling of simultaneity and nonsimultaneity, which signals the complicity between the movements of spacing and temporalization, disallows the continuous transition from one now-point to the next one and, by the same token, interrupts any teleological construal of the living present. The connectedness that the Idea in the Kantian sense allegedly guarantees has to be violently interrupted by a rhythmic syncope that constitutes the only chance of a rigorous concept of "presence" and, paradoxically, of the Idea itself.

Auto-affection, for Derrida, amounts to a differential structure that produces sameness as self-relation within self-difference, that is, sameness as the nonidentical, whether the identity of the transcendental ego, the living present or the noematic content presented to consciousness is in question. Far from describing the sameness of a punctual *stigmē* and the indivisibility of the *auto*, auto-affection refers to what gives rise to that sameness by radically distinguishing it from another *stigmē*, which nonetheless has to repeat the first one minimally: "This process is indeed a pure auto-affection in which the same is the same only in being affected by the other, only by becoming the other of the same" (SP, 85). Thus, auto-affection bears witness to an a priori synthesis of difference and identity, presence and absence. This synthesis is the movement of temporalization making (im)possible the ordinary conception of time in terms of continuity and the corollary primacy of the present.

This structure reveals an economic articulation of motifs otherwise antinomically understood such as positivity and negativity, necessity and chance, the transcendental and the empirical, activity and passivity, actuality and potentiality, presentation and representation, life and death. In light of this uncanny operation that radically complicates the principle of identity, Derrida prefers to speak of *effects* of presence. The irreducible and (de)constitutive possibility of difference does not give rise to an identical present but to belated and discontinuous effects whose very possibility is inextricably bound up with non-presence and even death. What has, however, to be underlined here is that the delayed character of the present is not to be construed as a potentiality on its way to fulfilment, for this would amount to determining difference or absence, *à la* a certain Husserl and a certain Ricoeur, in a negative fashion as provisional and teleologically organized. Rather, the only possible outcome here is belated effects that appear on pain of always being marked by the essential possibility of alterity.

Derrida's neologism "*différance*" is intended to capture the co-implication of difference and repetition, the quasi-spatial difference between impression and retention, and the quasi-temporal deferral of the living present.[21] *Différance* encapsulates two a priori requirements: that of a possible difference (nonidentity) and that of a possible repetition (sameness). Here is what looks like a definition of *différance* from Derrida's 1968 essay of the same title:

> It is this constitution of the present as a "primordial" and irreducibly nonsimple, and, therefore, in the strict sense nonprimordial, synthesis of traces, retentions, and protentions (to reproduce here, analogically and provisionally, a phenomenological and transcendental language that will presently be revealed as inadequate) that I propose to call protowriting, prototrace, or differance. The latter (is) (both) spacing (and) temporalizing.[22]

Différance designates the duration of the blink of the eye, the spacing between perception and non-perception, that makes possible the actual now, its sharpness and instantaneity. There is neither presence nor perception nor identity without this primordial but divisible origin. The ideal moment of intuition, considered by Husserl as the source of all sense and evidence, owes its only chance to a logically anterior *différance*, which puts into question that moment's absolute character.

If, for Derrida, phenomenological language is inadequate, it is because the expression "*living* present" and Husserl's later concept of "transcendental *life*" occlude the positive and nonprovisional role of difference, absence, and death.[23] By determining perception on the basis of an immanent consciousness's ideal present, Husserl does not carry the reduction and the concomitant critique of metaphysics far enough, for he still privileges the ideal form of the present and transcendental life over against empirical exteriority and a merely factical death.

Derrida, on the other hand, extends the questioning power of the reduction as far as possible, thereby casting doubt upon the metaphysical security of the present, the "is," time, and life itself. Rather than defining the transcendental and the ideal in opposition to facticity, empirical existence, and contingency, Derrida points out that the provenance of ideality is a *thinking* subject reflecting on the transgression of its singular empirical life. The possibility of the present as the universal form of all experience is necessarily grounded in the thought of a finite self: "To think of presence as the universal form of transcendental life is to open myself to the knowledge that in my absence, beyond my empirical existence, before my birth and after my death, *the present is*" (SP, 54). The phenomenological certainty about the ideality of the present as the form of time that remains uncontaminated by any empirical content originates, paradoxically, in the knowledge or realization of the possibility of death. This possibility always lurks in Husserl's determination of being as presence and ideality. One can no longer say, continues Derrida,

> that the experience of the possibility of my absolute disappearance (my death) affects me, occurs to an *I am*, and modifies a subject. The *I am*, being experienced only as an *I am present*, itself presupposes the relationship with presence in general, with being as presence. The appearing of the *I* to itself in the *I am* is thus originally a relation with its own possible disappearance. Therefore, *I am* originally means *I am mortal*. (SP, 54)

If the living present and transcendental life are made possible by the logically anterior possibility of non-presence or death, this situation points toward a co-implication of life and death to which the language of phenomenology cannot possibly do justice. The realm of the transcendental is infiltrated by an originary empirical existence, finitude and facticity, all of which the *epochē* strives to exclude.[24]

Derrida's reading of *The Phenomenology of Internal Time-Consciousness* undercuts the supposed ideal interiority of the living present and introduces spacing into the heart of transcendental temporality and life. The immanence of phenomenological time is contaminated by a diastem that is its positive condition. The necessary possibility of difference implies that

> *the temporalization of sense is, from the outset, a "spacing."* As soon as we admit spacing both as "interval" or difference and as open-ness upon the outside, there can no longer be any absolute inside, for the "outside" has insinuated itself into the movement by which the inside of the nonspatial, which is called "time," appears, is constituted, is "presented." Space is "in" time; it is time's pure leaving-itself; it is the "outside-itself" as the self-relation of time. The externality of space, externality as space, does not overtake time; rather, it opens as pure "outside" "within" the movement of temporalization. (SP, 86)

It is in order to take seriously into consideration this absolute irreducibility of spacing and exteriority that Derrida refers to temporalization by having recourse to the terms *trace* and *writing*, as suggested in the passage from "Differance" above.

As a result of such an originary exteriority, retention does not simply *follow* an *anterior* intuition, does not simply take place *after* an already exist-ing impression. The very modalities of before and after are made possible by a paradoxical movement that interrupts the continuity they imply. By the same token, the identity of the present is expropriated, insofar as its only chance is a discontinuity that will always syncopate its alleged progress toward fulfil-ment. The ideal presence of transcendental life is infinitely deferred, although its deferral is grounded in finitude and the possibility of death. The corollary of *différance* is a syncopated temporality, a rhythmic discontinuity always already commingled with continuity.

In his much later *Specters of Marx: The State of the Debt, the Work of Mourning, and the New International* (1993), Derrida refers to such a syncopated temporality while discussing Hamlet's assertion "The time is out of joint," a phrase linked to the ghost's spectral appearance on stage.[25] "Dis-jointed time" encapsulates the impossible possibility that gives rise to effects of presence, to spectral moments whose otherness cannot be eclipsed by an anticipated pleni-tude of presence. Temporal disjunction is irreducible because, rather than being a provisional negativity in the service of a higher value, it constitutes the only chance of that value, whose emergence it also forestalls:

> To maintain together that which does not hold together, and the disparate itself, the same disparate, all of this can be thought . . . only

in a dis-located time of the present, at the joining of a radically dis-jointed time, without certain conjunction. Not a time whose joinings are negated, broken, mistreated, dysfunctional, disadjusted, according to a *dys-* of negative opposition and dialectical disjunction, but a time without *certain* joining or determinable conjunction.[26]

At issue in this passage is, in the final analysis, the impossibility of an *assured* joining or continuity. The discontinuity of *différance* disrupts the dialectical transition from potentiality to actuality, and renders problematic the conceptualization of the temporal process as a forward and continuous movement toward a posited *telos*.

Without denying the fact of Husserl's assertions, one should nonetheless be able to affirm that the interpretative possibilities of his discourse are not exhausted by these assertions. Throughout *The Phenomenology of Internal Time-Consciousness*, there is a discrepancy between the descriptions of temporal phenomena and Husserl's postulated "principle of all principles." Is not such equivocality symptomatic of the aporetic movement constitutive of presence and temporality, both of which have been shown to be grounded in the necessary possibilities of difference and repetition?

By insisting on these irreconcilable hypotheses, and by drawing attention to implications that undermine certain philosophical and perhaps ethical decisions, Derrida explores the more unsettling aspects of Husserl's analyses. He admits to Husserl's manifest intention to anchor the living present in the instantaneity of a punctual now. However, the possibility of a radical Husserl laying the foundations for a rigorous questioning of the "metaphysics of presence" is not excluded.[27] Hence Derrida's allusion to Heidegger's encomiastic observation that Husserl's analysis of temporality is "the first in the history of philosophy to break with a concept of time inherited from Aristotle's *Physics*, determined according to the basic notions of the 'now,' the 'point,' the 'limit,' and the 'circle' " (SP, 61).

Husserl's major insight was his affirmation of the inseparability of the source-point from the retentional instant, and his reluctance to describe transcendental life simply in terms of a self-sufficient and self-constituting present. The duration of the *Augenblick* suffices to indicate that, far from subscribing in an unreflective way to identity and immediacy, he reserved indeed a role for difference and alterity. This is why Derrida, in a note to "Freud and the Scene of Writing," points out that "the concepts of originary *différance* and originary 'delay' were imposed upon us by a reading of Husserl" (FSW, 203 n. 5). Derrida's construal acknowledges the finesse of Husserl's philosophy, a gesture that cannot be divorced from the differentiation between two reading rhythms, "commentary" and "interpretation." The complexity of this situation has to be respected if one does not want to end up with a supposedly definitive, homogenized, and therefore disrespectful version of Husserl's text.

Nevertheless, in *Speech and Phenomena*, right in the middle of the chapter on temporalization, Derrida points out that Husserl's discussion of time-consciousness "both confirms the dominance of the present and rejects the 'after-event' of the becoming conscious of an 'unconscious content' which is the structure of temporality implied throughout Freud's texts" (SP, 63). Moreover, he suggests that Freudian psychoanalysis manages to tie together the two meanings of *différance*: spacing and temporalizing, diastem and delay (SP, 149). It appears then that psychoanalysis and, more specifically, the motifs of the death drive and *Nachträglichkeit* are better suited than any phenomenological concepts to take into account the complex necessary possibility of non-presence and its delayed effects. Therefore, it is to Derrida's reading of Freud that I will now turn in order to explore how psychoanalysis negotiates the interruption of the temporal flow and its implications for presence. Such a transition is also recommended in *Freud and Philosophy*, where a certain radicalization of Husserlian themes by Freud is affirmed alongside Ricoeur's tendency to focus on the more dialectical and reflective moments of psychoanalysis.

Freud: Permeability and Impermeability, Life and Death

Freudian psychoanalysis, at least as far as Ricoeur's and Derrida's readings are concerned, can be approached in terms of three levels of analysis. Firstly, it can be seen through the prism of a more or less sharp contradistinction to phenomenology, and Freud's thought may be said to allow for a necessary and anterior non-presence at the heart of conscious presence. I have already discussed the strand of Ricoeur's reflection stressing that Freud's mechanistic hypothesis and metapsychological emphasis on drives and unconscious impulses are intended to discover an original difference that undermines the primacy of conscious perception. Derrida admits to such an archaeological tendency in Freud's thought. If Husserl concerned himself with theorizing about the eidetic structures of consciousness, absolute beginnings, and *principia*, Freud is no less of an archaeologist, obsessed with interpreting traces with a view to unearthing a more fundamental process of psychical or cultural archivization. In *Archive Fever: A Freudian Impression* (1995), Derrida notes that Freud "wants to be an archivist who is more of an archaeologist than the archaeologist," to become a "better etiologist" and "to exhume a more archaic *impression*, he wants to exhibit a more archaic *imprint* than the one the other archaeologists of all kinds bustle around, those of literature and those of classical objective science, an imprint that is singular each time, an impression that is almost no longer an archive."[28]

Secondly, psychoanalysis may be regarded as amenable to a dialectics, whereby Freud's archaeology is coupled with the possibility of reappropriating the psychical findings to the benefit of a reflective self. The dialectical opposition between the two poles of Freud's essential distinctions, says Ricoeur, reveals the necessity of yoking together an *archē* and a *telos*, an archaeologically discovered non-presence and the anticipated attainment of true meaning. This dialectical synthesis, unrealizable on the basis of a single subject, becomes possible thanks to the interaction between patient and analyst, and to the mediation of language. Although such a teleological approach does not discount the fact of difference, it seeks to place this fact into the service of a *telos*: it subordinates absence and difference to a futural presence and, therefore, denies them a radical heterogeneity. In "To Speculate—On 'Freud' " (1980), Derrida concurs with Ricoeur's teleological interpretation of Freud, whom he associates with the Hegel of the master-slave dialectic. He points out that every instance of initial displacement is seen as a provisional stage to be conveniently subordinated to a higher principle.[29]

Thirdly, Derrida's approach is complicated by a further gesture focusing not so much on Freud's theses as on the implications of his dense analyses. A rigorous construal of the latter reveals possibilities that often resist Freud's more explicit archaeo-teleological formulations. Following Derrida, I will draw attention to specific moments in the Freudian text that cast doubt upon the oppositional articulation of some of the binaries explored by Ricoeur, and that therefore disrupt their dialectical organization. Accordingly, it will be shown that Freud's archaeological quest for an allegedly primary trace is seriously hampered insofar as, by the terms of the Freudian discourse itself, any such registration is nothing other than a delayed effect of an anterior *différance*. In turn, these differential effects, irreducibly marked by non-presence and alterity, cannot be safely eclipsed by psychical life, perception, quality, consciousness, life instincts, etc.

Derrida's first detailed discussion of psychoanalysis occurs in "Freud and the Scene of Writing," where one of the points in question is the process of neuronal facilitation or breaching (*Bahnung*) as the first instance of psychical inscription.[30] From the very beginning, he points out the paradoxical fact that Freud, in spite of his intention to provide a psychology that would be as exact as a natural science, resorts to tropology and metaphor in order to express the key concept of "facilitation." It will be recalled that Freud initially distinguishes ψ from φ neurones, in between which there are other complex mechanisms, the contact-barriers, whose role is both to link and separate. The ψ system, associated with memory, is relatively impermeable and permanently altered by the passage of energy, whereas φ neurones are permeable and retain no trace of quantity. Prima facie, the impression is given that one can straightforwardly distinguish between those two systems, on whose differentiation all subsequent dichotomies of the psychical apparatus depend, such as that between perception and memory, the primary and the secondary process, the pleasure and reality principles, life and death instincts, etc. If, however, one focuses more closely on Freud's meticulous descriptions, one is bound to discover that a rigorous identity can be attributed to neither system.

Despite the centrality of perception and memory, it turns out that there are no *essential* differences between φ and ψ, which are made possible by two interdependent factors: differences in their environment and the passage of energy through undifferentiated protoplasm. The "Project" notes that ψ resistances, necessary for the faculty of memory and the accumulation of energy required by the secondary function, are actually located in the contact-barriers rather than the neurones themselves: "The resistances are all to be located in the *contacts* [between one neurone and another], which in this way assume the value of *barriers*" (SE, 1:298). And a little farther on, it is reaffirmed that "their [ψ] contact-barriers are brought into a permanently altered state," and that "this alteration must consist in the contact-barriers becoming more capable of conduction, less impermeable, and so more like those of the φ system" (SE, 1:300). Commenting on the paradoxical fact that the contact-barriers are responsible for the permeability or relative impermeability of φ and ψ, Bennington points out:

> What distinguishes *phi* and *psy* neurones is not internal quality, but the properties of their contact-barriers. In other words, the "essence" of the neurones (i.e. what makes them the neurones they are) is to be found at the points of junction between them, i.e., in their *difference*, at the point of "foreign substance." The difference between *phi* and *psy* neurones is a difference *in their difference*, in their foreign-ness.[31]

What is more, their resistance or lack of it does not depend on essentially distinct types of contact-barriers but has to do with their environment, with differences in their location. On the one hand, φ neurones and their contact-barriers do not retain any trace of excitation because, situated in the external periphery of the body, they are exposed to greater amounts of quantity, so they have to discharge them as quickly as possible. On the other hand, the ψ system and its contact-barriers are linked to the interior of the body where the stimuli are not as forceful, so the possibility of facilitation arises. As far as the provenance of the two systems and their contact-barriers is concerned, Freud, drawing upon contemporary morphology, concludes that "a difference in their essence is replaced by a difference in the environment to which they are destined" (SE, 1:304). With a view to avoiding an arbitrary *constructio ad hoc* contradicted by histology, he shifts the differentiating factor, as David Farrell Krell remarks, from the morphology of the neurones to their topology, a gesture that is no less problematic for his neurological aspirations.[32] To the extent that this "difference in the environment" is not itself an entity, it does not lend itself to traditional scientific explanation. In this respect, its introduction as the origin of neuronal identity leads to a tension between Freud's scientific intentions and actual analyses.

If neuronal difference depends on the environment to which the neurones or, rather, their contact-barriers, belong, the external world is clearly introduced into the equation. Accordingly, Freud maintains that what gives rise to this differentiation process is the passage of quantities of excitation through the nervous system:

> The path of conduction passes through undifferentiated protoplasm instead of (as it otherwise does, within the neurone) through differentiated protoplasm. . . . The process of conduction itself will create a differentiation in the protoplasm and consequently an improved conductive capacity for subsequent conduction. (SE, 1:298–99)

The fundamental distinction between the three types of neurones is the outcome of protoplasmic differentiation resulting from the passage of energy. Moreover, after the three classes of neurones have been differentiated, there is still more differentiation to come with respect to the ψ system, for it is the difference between ψ resistances that leads to the preference of a path rather than another, and finally to the production of the mysterious mnemic trace (*Erinnerungsspur*).

The division between perception and memory depends on an anterior negotiation between the nervous system as undifferentiated protoplasm and the external world. And although such a formulation might be construed as pointing toward a frontier separating two self-identical entities, this is far from being the case. In order to reach the nervous system, quantity has to be regulated and its force has to be diminished. Freud claims that, according to the discoveries of physics, the external world is the origin of "major quantities of energy" that are in violent motion which they transmit (SE, 1:304). As immediate and unhindered contact between nervous tissue and these powerful masses would be detrimental to the former, there has to be right from the beginning an irreducible diastem between the two forces. Before any amount of excitation comes into contact with undifferentiated protoplasm, it has to be diminished by cellular protective structures designated as "nerve-ending apparatuses" (SE, 1:306). These safeguard the deeper layers by reducing the pernicious effect of exogenous quantity. They function as screens granting entry to moderated amounts of energy, which they break up into quotients that become, in turn, stimuli, and it is only as such that they reach first the φ and then the ψ system, where they make a first registration. The corollary of this principial resistance is a certain impermeability of that most exposed surface of the organism.

What actually gains access to the nervous structure has already been subjected to an operation of translation, for the condition of its transference from the external world into the psyche is that it be differentiated and deferred. Psychical life is protected by means of this relative impermeability, by the creation of originary traces, even before it becomes differentiated into conscious perception and unconscious memory. This is a conviction that Freud reiterates in "A Note upon the 'Mystic Writing-Pad,' " hence the protective celluloid portion of the transparent sheet: "Experiment will then show that the thin paper would be very easily crumpled or torn if one were to write directly upon it with the stilus. The layer of celluloid thus acts as a protective sheath for the waxed paper, to keep off injurious effects from without. The celluloid is a 'protective shield against stimuli' " (SE, 19:230). Derrida stresses the significance of that initial moment of deferral, of that anterior resistance thanks to which life emerges. The possibilities of breaching, repetition and a certain memory are not processes supervenient upon an already existing life but constitute the very conditions of life and perception: "The ideal virginity of the present (*maintenant*)," says Derrida, "is constituted by the work of memory" (FSW, 226).

The distinction between φ and ψ and the emergence of life itself depend on a *différance* of quantity giving rise to a minimally permeable nervous system but excluding the possibility of the latter's pure identity. Impermeability or absolute separation between the two forces is out of the question, for the distinctive feature of life is its receptivity to and interaction with the world. At the same time, absolute contact or permeability would result in instant death, which entails that the delineation of the relation between nervous tissue and energy in terms of a simple topography is problematic. Psychical life is grounded in a necessary possibility of difference, whereby no stability or identity can be secured either on the side of the nervous system or on that of the external world. Whether the topical differences between φ and ψ or those between the system and the world are in question, Derrida observes:

> [They] are pure differences, differences of situation, of connection, of localization, of structural relations more important than their supporting terms; and they are differences for which the relativity of outside and inside is always to be determined. The thinking of difference can neither dispense with topography nor accept the current models of spacing. (FSW, 204)

According to Freud's own account, it can be hardly suggested that "the passage of energy" refers to a process where an excitation of a certain magnitude comes into contact with a self-identical and already alive nervous system. Rather, it makes sense to speak of a minimal permeability. The positive condition of life—and of all functions that Freud wishes to place at its center, such as the primary process, the life instincts, perception, the pleasure principle, etc.—is a differential movement giving rise to *effects* rather than essences or entities.

What there is in the beginning, even before a first inscription in terms of an unconscious trace takes place, is not a determinable quantity that comes into contact with the psychical structure but a negotiation of forces occurring right at the frontier between what only reductively can be designated as an inside and an outside.

That perception and memory proper emerge as belated effects of an originary *différance* is corroborated by the fact that this distinction tends not toward a greater degree of difference but, paradoxically, toward sameness. The passage of energy through ψ neurones and the creation of a mnemic trace make these neurones more permeable and, therefore, more like φ neurones. At the same time, the latter, despite their postulated permeability, belong to an environment that becomes increasingly impermeable, insofar as it needs to protect the underlying layers by setting up resistances. Perception and memory become possible thanks to an economy between permeability and impermeability, and, if either of them were to reach an absolute degree, the result would be death in both cases. If, for instance, total impermeability or memory were to take precedence, the ensuing system would be absolutely closed and, therefore, not living. If, on the contrary, there were something like permanent perception or unhindered permeability, the nervous structure would be instantly overcome by detrimental amounts of energy. In a certain sense, total memory coincides with total perception.[33]

Psychical life is defined by its capacity to receive an infinite number of impressions originating in the world, hence the priority that Freud grants to the permeable neurones, the primary process, perception, and consciousness. At the same time, such permeability depends on the necessary possibility of an anterior impermeability, memory, absence, and even death. There is no life without this a priori required diastem. The nervous system has to protect itself by setting up a reserve of traces, by a permeable-impermeable surface that constitutes the frontier between inside and outside, life and death. The movements of repetition, difference, and deferral are absolutely irreducible from this mutual co-implication of forces. The peculiar economy of permeability and impermeability brought out by this reading disallows the various watertight divisions supporting Freud's conceptual edifice, and casts into doubt the determination of the psyche and the external world on the basis of a dialectical relation between an inside and an outside.

The necessary possibilities of memory and death reveal a non-appropriable alterity, a nonnegative difference that cannot be dialectically eclipsed within the opposition of perception and memory. Rodolphe Gasché, in an illuminating account of the relation between deconstruction and dialectics, underlines the solidarity between negativity, contradiction, sublation, homogeneity, and dialectics, a solidarity that, far from excluding negativity and heterogeneity, places them under the service of the speculative unity of the totality of all oppositions:

> Hegel determines difference—that is, meaningful difference—
> exclusively as contradiction. Difference, or the relation to Other-
> ness, becomes, therefore, relation to the negative. . . . Difference,
> understood as contradiction, makes negativity one face of posi-
> tivity within the process and the system of the self-exposition of
> absolute knowledge, or of the absolute idea. As the underside and
> accomplice of positivity, negativity and contradiction are sublated,
> internalized in the syllogistic process of speculative dialectics. The
> dialecticization of negativity, by which negativity remains within
> the enclosure of metaphysics, of onto-theology and onto-teleology,
> puts negativity to work.[34]

The dialectic constructs itself out of terms that are disjoint and identifiable, as a result of which otherness is a negativity opposed to the meaningful positivity it makes possible. This oppositional determination regards negativity and positivity as interdependent, thereby affirming an initial incongruity between them while denying them a perhaps more radical heterogeneity. The negative but necessary other can always be absolutely absorbed by positivity. As Marian Hobson underlines, "[I]t is precisely this lack of independence in the negative which moves dialectical mediation and reappropriation. . . . Hegelian *sublation* is remainderless. Each stage of the dialectic has absorbed completely what has preceded it."[35] The other is a resource that remains determinable and that can be fully appropriated without excess or remainder. Negativity can be put to work, can collaborate with meaning and truth in discourse in order to bear the fruits of this teleological process.[36]

Derrida's affirmation of a nonnegative non-presence can account for the possibility of dialectical articulation, while also revealing the impossibility of a dialectical synthesis without residue. It takes into consideration both the requirement of absolute interruption and the possibility of negotiation or contact between inside and outside, which may eventually be construed as leading to a fruitful appropriation of the latter by the former. These two necessary possibilities, of radical interruption and negotiation, far from referring to two distinct movements that would be in a relation of anteriority to each other, designate a single differential process that disjoins temporality and divides the identity of the terms to which it gives rise. The ensuing non-dialectizable effects, whose "non" is both that of opposition and that of irreducible heterogeneity, is the "before" of the dialectic, the secret and originary nonorigin that, although it makes dialectics possible, excludes the possibility of a total reconciliation.

In a fine analysis of Derrida's *Glas* (1974), Hobson points out that this movement, where what is more than a dialectical exchange gives rise to dialectics, is designated by Derrida as "striction," which she goes on to define as "a tension whereby what had been excluded is put into a structuring position, and moves to a meta-level: it becomes 'transcendental du transcendental'—but, as Derrida immediately adds, it is 'false transcendental.' "[37] *Différance*, then, is not opposed to the dialectic, for to do so would be the best way to consolidate its truth and validity. On the contrary, it displaces dialectics by reaching beyond its oppositional logic toward a nonnegative and non-dialectizable alterity construed as a necessary possibility, as the quasi-transcendental condition of (im)possibility for perception and memory, life and death.[38]

On Derrida's reading, the very chance of life depends upon a porous frontier that prevents the psyche from becoming totally independent from a certain non-presence. Freud's "Beyond the Pleasure Principle" (1920) thematizes this exigency in terms of an economy of life and death.[39] The minimal impermeability of life is now explicitly linked to an originary death. The discharge of energy is associated with the pleasure principle, as was the case in the "Project," whereas the necessity of deferring satisfaction by temporarily tolerating unpleasure is linked to the reality principle. In the first pages, it is affirmed that it is incorrect to talk of the dominance of the pleasure principle, which, under the influence of the ego's instincts of self-preservation, is "replaced" by the reality principle (SE, 18:10). The word *replaced* might be slightly confusing, for it gives the impression that the reality principle and the corollary impermeability come to replace the propensity of an already existing life toward total permeability. In chapter IV, however, one comes across the following formulation:

> Let us picture a living organism in its most simplified possible form as an undifferentiated vesicle of a substance that is susceptible to stimulation. Then the surface turned towards the external world will from its very situation be differentiated and will serve as an organ for receiving stimuli. . . . It would be easy to suppose, then, that as a result of the ceaseless impact of external stimuli on the surface of the vesicle, its substance to a certain depth may have become permanently modified, so that excitatory processes run a different course in it from what they run in the deeper layers. A crust would thus be formed which would at last have been so thoroughly "baked through" by stimulation that it would present the most favourable possible conditions for the reception of stimuli and become incapable of any further modification. (SE, 18:26)

The outer crust is, strangely enough, both "permanently modified" and "incapable of any further modification," both outside and inside, both permeable and impermeable, both φ and ψ. The crust represents the system of consciousness and perception, both of which constitute points of contact between the organism and the external world, hence its permeable surface that remains forever capable of receiving fresh impressions. At the same time, insofar as it is a *crust*, this surface is characterized by impermeability and resistance to potentially pernicious amounts of excitation. On the next page, not only does Freud reiterate the irreducibility of the resistance offered by this outer layer but also closely associates it with death:

> This little fragment of living substance is suspended in the middle of an external world charged with the most powerful energies; and it would be killed by the stimulation emanating from these if it were not provided with a protective shield against stimuli. It acquires the shield in this way: its outermost surface ceases to have the structure proper to living matter, becomes to some degree inorganic and thenceforward functions as a special envelope or membrane resistant to stimuli. In consequence, the energies of the external world are able to pass into the next underlying layers, which have remained living, with only a fragment of their original intensity; and these layers can devote themselves, behind the protective shield, to the reception of the amounts of stimulus which have been allowed through it. By its death, the outer layer has saved all the deeper ones from a similar fate. . . . *Protection against* stimuli is an almost more important function for the living organism than *reception of* stimuli. The protective shield is supplied with its own store of energy. (SE, 18:27)

Although all this was already in the "Project," Freud now expressly contends that impermeability is there from the very beginning, that the outer layer retains traces of quantity and that, most importantly, a certain death is the condition of life.[40] This is a point Derrida makes much of in "Freud and the Scene of Writing" where he underlines that Freud's analyses disallow the possibility of an *already* existing life independent of an originary death. There is no anterior life that comes to protect itself against a subsequent and accidental death threat posed by unhindered excitation. The only chance of life depends on the organism's partial death whereby dangerous masses of energy are differentiated and delayed right from the start. Psychical life has to die in order to become alive, which is to say that non-presence is constitutive and absolutely ineluctable, hence Derrida's rhetorical question: "Is it not already death at the origin of a life which can defend itself against death only through an *economy* of death, through deferment, repetition, reserve?" (FSW, 202).

If one admits to an irreducible death as the corollary of the *différance* between permeability and impermeability, the primacy or anteriority that Freud sometimes grants to the primary process, permeability, perception, the pleasure principle, life instincts, etc., is complicated. Does this admission, inherent in

Freudian discourse, not undermine all the essential distinctions and dialectical oppositions of psychoanalysis? If the outermost surface of the system functions at the same time as a frontier letting in energy and as a protective shield absorbing the impact of external forces to the benefit of the underlying layers, is this not to say that there is no rigorous division between the outer and deeper layers to the extent that they are both defined in terms of permeability and impermeability? Moreover, does the idea of the crust not point toward the necessity of a trace more originary than the supposedly first inscription taking place in the unconscious? Does that differential trace not undercut the belief in a first time in general? Does Freud's acknowledgment of a principial resistance not constitute a safe criterion for concluding that psychoanalysis is indeed able to unearth a more archaic trace than the phenomenological living present?

First Inscription and *Nachträglichkeit*

In light of what has been affirmed thus far, the facilitations in the mnemic system constitute belated transcriptions of relations between forces already translated and repeated several times, transcriptions that, what is more, take place only thanks to the differences between resistances offered by the ψ neurones. The latter's contact-barriers become more capable of conduction, more like the φ system, so, notes Freud, "we shall describe this state of the contact-barriers as their degree of *facilitation* [*Bahnung*]. We can then say: *Memory is represented by the facilitations existing between the* ψ *neurones*" (SE, 1:300). However, these facilitations have to be different from one another, because if all ψ contact-barriers offered equal resistance, then memory would not emerge. If memory takes place whenever *certain* neurones are facilitated, this means that there must be some reason why some neurones rather than others are preferred for the facilitation to pass through. The reason is that the resistance offered by ψ is not everywhere equal. Thus, Freud amends his previous assertion: "*Memory is represented by the differences in the facilitations between the* ψ *neurones*" (SE, 1:300).

This, according to Derrida, is an unexpected and revolutionary claim because memory is considered to originate not in a trace left in the psyche by an amount of excitation but in quantity inextricably linked to the difference between ψ facilitations. The problem here is that Freud introduces into his description, once again, a difference that cannot become as such the object of scientific observation. Does this gesture not render problematic his declared intention to furnish a neurological or even biochemical account? Moreover, if facilitation is marked by non-presence, the ensuing trace is so heterogeneous that it resists any attempt at dialectical appropriation. Here is Derrida on the irreducibility of difference:

> We then must not say that breaching without difference is insuf-
> ficient for memory; it must be stipulated that there is no pure
> breaching without difference. Trace as memory is not a pure breach-
> ing that might be reappropriated at any time as simple presence; it
> is rather the ungraspable and invisible difference between breaches.
> We thus already know that psychic life is neither the transparency
> of meaning nor the opacity of force but the difference within the
> exertion of forces. (FSW, 201)

In view of the fact that the process of facilitation is by definition already a
difference of forces (neuronal resistance to incoming excitation), Freud's conclusion above can be rewritten as follows: memory is represented by the differences
between ψ neurones that are themselves the effects of differences as much between
the neuronal classes as between the nervous system and quantity. The mnemic
trace as the first psychical inscription depends on an originary *différance* and does
not result from the encounter between two rigorously defined entities.

To the extent that absence and difference constitute a priori required
possibilities, they split from the very beginning the identity of everything they
give rise to, such as psychical life, the neuronal classes, the unconscious trace,
external energy, and consciousness. The mnemic trace is not something permanently present that one may appropriate; it is the effect of a differential process
taking place outside a teleological horizon. Referring to the supposedly first
instance of inscription, Derrida maintains that

> there is no present text in general, and there is not even a past
> present text, a text which is past as having been present. The text
> is not conceivable in an originary or modified form of presence.
> The unconscious text is already a weave of pure traces, differences
> in which meaning and force are united—a text nowhere present,
> consisting of archives which are *always already* transcriptions. Origi-
> nary prints. Everything begins with reproduction. (FSW, 211)

The ultimate signified/signifier of psychoanalysis, far from being a self-identical
impression waiting immobile to be unearthed by an archaeologist, arises as a
trace of an anterior (im)permeability, as a deferred effect grounded in other traces, themselves the effects of a still more primordial network of forces.
Psychical writing reveals a principle of undecidability according to which it is
simply impossible for psychoanalysis to reanimate a first impression. In order to
describe the trace's deferred presence and temporality, Derrida draws attention to
Freud's "*Nachträglichkeit*" and points out its link to *différance*. *Nachträglichkeit*,
he notes, and the irreducibility of the "effect of deferral" constitute Freud's true
discovery (FSW, 203).

Nachträglichkeit, already mentioned in the section of the "Project" where Freud is dealing with hysterical repression, refers to a peculiar psychical temporality or causality that cannot be adequately represented by presence and continuity.[41] While discussing the compulsion of his patient Emma of not being able to go into shops alone, and the two memories related to that unintelligible fear, Freud introduces *Nachträglichkeit* to describe the following phenomenon: an "experience" is not experienced as such in the first instance but is revised and reworked in later life thanks to organic maturation in combination with the occurrence of an event similar to that "first" experience. The initial event, usually of a sexual nature, is not properly perceived by the subject at the time of its occurrence and has no significance, but is repressed and retained in terms of unconscious memory traces. When a similar event occurs in later life, the unconscious material of the "first" time is rearranged according to the new circumstances, and is endowed with new sexual significance and pathogenic force; in other words, it becomes traumatic only belatedly. The deferred action of the "first event" is responsible for the affective charge with which one experiences the second event, although one is not aware of this *nachträglich* process. Strangely enough, the "first event" is experienced for the first time belatedly during its quasi-repetition in the second event. The latter cannot be claimed to be a mere repetition or memory of the first one, for the first one was never really experienced, but, at the same time, it does constitute a repetition insofar as the affective charge of the first event is deferred until that later occurrence.[42]

The temporality of *Nachträglichkeit* cannot be accounted for by the continuous and flowing time of consciousness. Rather, it implies a necessary possibility of discontinuity that constitutes the positive condition of the second experience while complicating its self-identity by regarding it as a first experience in a certain sense. Derrida describes this strange temporality by alluding to the meaning of the term *Nachtrag* in epistolography and its unsettling implications for the value of presence in general:

> *Nachtrag* has a precise meaning in the realm of letters: appendix, codicil, postscript. The text we call present may be deciphered only at the bottom of the page, in a footnote or postscript. Before the recurrence, the present is only the call for a footnote. That the present in general is not primal but, rather, reconstituted, that it is not the absolute, wholly living form which constitutes experience, that there is no purity of the living present—such is the theme, formidable for metaphysics, which Freud, in a conceptual scheme unequal to the thing itself, would have us pursue. (FSW, 212)

This formulation calls upon one to rethink the role of repression qua borderline between the unconscious and consciousness, a dichotomy considered to be "the fundamental premiss of psycho-analysis" (SE, 19:13). In light of *Nachträglichkeit*, the frontier between those two psychical "regions" can be regarded neither as a point of continuous transition, nor as a barrier preventing entry altogether. Rather, it has to be approached as a permeable-impermeable borderline, as a result of which unconscious traces *must* remain, in principle, unreadable, although not totally unreadable.

On the one hand, unconscious experience becomes accessible by virtue of a minimal contact with consciousness. Hence Freud's assertion that repressions that have failed will have more claim on his interest, as the successful ones will for the most part escape examination.[43] In the case of Emma's hysterical repression, the second experience becomes possible on the basis of the phenomenalizability of the anterior event repressed into the unconscious. The trace has to give up its absolute exteriority with respect to consciousness, so it has to be minimally repeatable by the subsequent *nachträglich* experience. On the other hand, a certain unreadability is required if the unconscious is not to become a mere modality of consciousness. If it is to be a rigorous concept worthy of its name, the unconscious has to hold on to its necessary possibility of difference from consciousness and to retain a minimal secrecy that should not be construed as a negative or provisional necessity.

The separation between the unconscious and consciousness does not constitute a conveniently bridgeable gap but a differential diastem where distance and alterity are bound up with a minimal repeatability. *Nachträglichkeit* points to a lack of transparency that opens the way for psychoanalysis and interpretation, while complicating the stability of the unconscious trace and disallowing the certainty of any interpretative venture.[44] It does not seem preposterous to suggest that Freud at least gestures toward such a paradoxical situation, when he describes the relation of consciousness to the unconscious as "the first shibboleth of psycho-analysis" (SE, 19:13).

The necessary possibilities of absence, difference, and repetition entailed by *Nachträglichkeit* reveal a discontinuous "relation without relation" (*rapport sans rapport*).[45] Such conceptuality undercuts the ordinary teleological (topographical, dynamic, or economic) understanding of that relation, for, by adding a differential twist to it, it excludes the dialectical opposition of presence to absence. *Nachträglichkeit* and its temporality can be said, by extrapolation, to be as inconceivable as *différance* is "if one begins on the basis of consciousness, that is, presence, or on the basis of its simple contrary, absence or nonconsciousness. It is also inconceivable as the mere *homogeneous* complication of a diagram or line of time, as a complex 'succession' " (SP, 88). The notions of the "unconscious" and "consciousness" remain essentially unable to do justice to the rhythmic discontinuity at issue here because they partake in a conceptuality that understands absence and difference, in the best-case scenario, as provisional and negative necessities on their way to plenitude. I have already indicated the extent to which Ricoeur favors such a dialecticized version of psychoanalysis.

Nachträglichkeit, which is applicable not only to the unconscious trace whose pathogenic force emerges only belatedly but also to the very production of that trace, complicates the logic of dialectics. To the extent that the mnemic trace appears belatedly as the effect of another more originary trace—the differential co-implication of permeability and impermeability—it does not assume the status of a *first* inscription to be excavated by Freudian archaeology. The trace arises as the deferred effect of an anterior weave of traces, something that undermines the idea of presence in general the very moment it gives rise to its only possibility and chance. *Différance* and *Nachträglichkeit* point as much to the porous boundary between consciousness and the unconscious as to the (im)permeable frontier between life and death. Derrida underlines that the verb "to defer" (*différer*) involved in these motifs

> cannot mean to retard a present possibility, to postpone an act, to put off a perception already now possible. That possibility is possible only through a *différance* which must be conceived of in other terms than those of a calculus or mechanics of decision. To say that *différance* is originary is simultaneously to erase the myth of a present origin. Which is why "originary" must be understood as having been *crossed out*, without which *différance* would be derived from an original plenitude. It is a non-origin which is originary. (FSW, 203)

The so-called first inscription does not constitute a present possibility but the *nachträglich* outcome of an uncanny commingling of presence and absence. This commingling casts doubt upon the idea of a simple origin or a first time, and divides the identity of unconscious experience right from the beginning. No origin and no first time, then, but also no presence and no plenitude.

In order to respect the nonappropriable alterity of this originary nonorigin, Derrida occasionally has recourse to the figure of the "absolute past." In a different context, in a discussion of Hegel's *Erinnerung* and *Gedächtnis*, he couples the absolute past to a memory that excludes a dialectical transition from absence to presence. Such memory directs one toward the immemorial or the unrememberable, toward a past that no archaeological, archival, or psychoanalytical endeavour, however assiduous, could successfully or conclusively recover. This originary memory, which conditions the mnemic faculty that Freud associates with the unconscious, "stays with traces, in order to 'preserve' them, but traces of a past that has never been present, traces which themselves never occupy the form of presence and always remain, as it were, to come—come from the future, from the *to come*" (MPM, 58).[46]

Nachträglichkeit gives rise to the unconscious trace while preventing one from conceptualizing its relation to consciousness in terms of a before and an after. By drawing attention to its syncopated temporality, Derrida tries to think difference outside an archaeo-teleological horizon. The outcome of his reflection is that the past and the future cannot be regarded as modifications of a present but, rather, have to be thought of on the model of an absolute past infiltrated by an unmasterable future.[47] The psychical trace belongs to an absolute past whose radically promissory nature disallows the possibility of future actualization or arrival. Even the idea of progress toward an infinite and nonrealizable *telos* is violently interrupted by the discontinuous and economic character of *Nachträglichkeit*, although "economy" here refers to an unstable differentiation rather than a dialectical articulation.[48]

Freud was arguably unable to think through, at least as straightforwardly as Derrida does, this originary conjunction of presence and absence as the arche-trace (de)constitutive of the first psychical inscription. This is the case, first and foremost, because Freudian concepts, in the words of Derrida, "without exception, belong to the history of metaphysics" (FSW, 197). I indicated in the first chapter the extent to which the terms *unconscious* and *consciousness*, for instance, lend themselves to an ethico-teleological understanding of absence and presence. However, Derrida acknowledges that Freud nonetheless *invites* one to think, especially by virtue of *Nachträglichkeit* and its rhythmic discontinuity, the trace that makes presence possible while complicating its purity and identity. Derrida is beguiled by psychoanalysis because of Freud's devotion to something like an absolute past and the thought that the present is always already *re*-constituted.

But, it will be objected, this was already the case with Husserl, whose gross present and retention point toward a differential reconstitution at the very heart of transcendental life. Is it not by virtue of this difference that Husserl describes the living present, on the basis of a Kantian Idea, as an infinitely deferred *possibility* that never phenomenalizes itself? Freud's originality, nevertheless, consisted in that he took more seriously into account this originary complication and ventured to think its implications for presence a little more explicitly than Husserl did. As a result, not only does Freud call upon one to reflect on the non-simple character of the present but also goes some way toward admitting to the *impossibility* of thinking or perceiving this non-simple and originary nonorigin. In this light, Bennington identifies a difference between Husserl and Freud, stressing that psychoanalysis provides the resources to think the unlimited possibilities of, say, science in terms of an impossibility.[49] In support of his claim, Bennington cites a passage from "Beyond the Pleasure Principle," where Freud, commenting on the openness of biology to infinity, notes that "we may expect it to give us the most surprising information and we cannot guess what answers it will return in a few dozen years to the questions we have put to it. They may be of a kind which will blow away the whole of our artificial structure of hypotheses" (SE, 18:60). The idea that his hypotheses may be blown away by future developments suggests that Freud had considered, to a certain degree, the impossibility of gaining access, securely and definitively, to a present being, whether that be the psyche, the unconscious trace, or the external world.

Bennington's observation is corroborated by Derrida's remark that Freudian discourse is not "exhausted" by belonging to a metaphysical and traditional conceptuality (FSW, 197–98). Derrida's reading maintains the tensions of the Freudian text and takes into account the originality of Freud's thinking and the precautions he took vis-à-vis conventional concepts. At the same time, Derrida recognizes that Freud did not sufficiently reflect on the historical and theoretical sense of these precautions. This is why Krell remarks that deconstruction pursues Freudian psychoanalysis "both to dismantle it and to enter under its spell."[50] Freud's scriptural metaphorics will help me clarify further these tensions emanating from the double necessity inherent in psychoanalysis: that of borrowing all of its concepts from a metaphysical tradition and that of displacing the same concepts.

Scriptural Metaphorics

Ricoeur likens the working of the psyche and, more specifically, of the unconscious to a linguistic operation, even though he specifies that it functions along lines analogous to rhetoric rather than ordinary language. Derrida, by contrast, underscores Freud's tendency to represent the perceptual apparatus in terms of traces, marks, and writing, a metaphorics that became more and more refined over the years, until the "Note" where the psychical system is compared to a writing machine.

In the "Project," Freud conceived of memory on the model of neuronal facilitation, which clearly amounts to a process of effraction. About a year after this work had been written, notes Derrida, Freud, in a letter to Fliess, describes the psychical system for the first time in terms of writing and inscription, and his discourse is dominated by terms such as "sign" (*Zeichen*), "registration" (*Niederschrift*), and "transcription" (*Umschrift*) (FSW, 206).[51] The same metaphorics is systematically deployed in *The Interpretation of Dreams*, where dreaming is compared to a type of writing, and dreams to texts to be interpreted. In addition, in a text from 1913, Freud asserts that "it is even more appropriate to compare dreams with a system of writing than with a language. In fact the interpretation of dreams is completely analogous to the decipherment of an ancient pictographic script such as Egyptian hieroglyphs."[52] If the corollary of this metaphor is that the content of dreams or unconscious activity in general is comparable to a text, and if one pays heed to Freud's suggestion in the "Project" that dreams follow old facilitations, then this psychical text has to be understood on the model of the palimpsest: a text superimposed upon another, the marks of the former following, to a certain extent, anterior traces preserved in the unconscious. The task of the hermeneut, accordingly, would be to decode the superimposed and ciphered script in which the dream-content consists. Dream interpretation constitutes a decoding method seeking to bring to light the meaning of an encrypted message.

Freud's scriptural metaphorics reaches its crescendo in the "Note," where the psychical apparatus is represented by the *Wunderblock*. The analogy of breaching and the tracing of a trail introduced in the "Project" is transformed into a metaphorics of the written mark, spacing, and *graphē*. Freud's descriptions have now become much more rigorous. However, the reference to pathbreaking and traces is maintained across this gap of thirty years, and so is a metaphorics of the machine. The main framework of the neurological conception of the perceptual process is replicated in the "Note": ψ neurones become a slab of dark brown resin or wax, while the φ system takes the form of the transparent piece of celluloid that constitutes the upper layer of a sheet. The latter's bottom layer, which represents the ω neurones, is made of a thin translucent waxed paper that lightly rests on the upper surface of the wax slab when the machine is not in use (SE, 19:228–31).

What is at stake here? In the final analysis, there is nothing dramatically new about this scriptural analogy and the association of the psyche to a certain typography. Plato had already instigated a long-standing imagery of impressions and iconography by introducing in *Theaetetus*, in the famous discussion of perception and memory, the metaphor of the imprint on a slab of wax.[53] Why is Freud's comparison of psychical processes to inscription so vital, and why does Derrida devote such a large part of "Freud and the Scene of Writing" to a discussion of these graphic analogies? What does the act of inscription ultimately entail and what is one to understand from the representation of psychical content by text? Does Freud conceive of the stratified writing taking place across the different levels of the psyche in a traditional way? Is transcription understood as a continuous transference of content from one place to another, or is there something more complex involved therein? Is the aforementioned instability of the mnemic trace not contradicted by Freud's scriptural metaphor, inasmuch as writing ensures the durability of the mark?

In trying to address some of the above issues, I will refer to Derrida's double reading gesture, whose first strand is not dissimilar to the second tendency of Ricoeur's double reading of Freud. On the one hand, the emphasis is placed on mundane writing and the functioning of the psyche is reduced to a continuous operation, whereby a signified content remains largely stable and essentially recoverable. On the other hand, attention is drawn to the fact that Freud's analyses point toward an originary psychical writing affirmative of a necessary possibility of difference. In this case, the expression "psychical writing" is not a simple metaphor presupposing what writing is but signifies a strange infiltration of the proper by the metaphorical, where the "essence" of writing is paradoxically revealed on the basis of a reflection on the psyche.

According to the first gesture, insofar as Freud's scriptural metaphors introduce an element of spatiality and topography into the psyche, they can be said to consolidate the belief in the permanence of the unconscious trace. Given that one of his main concerns from the very beginning was to provide an explanation of the aptitude of the nervous system for retaining traces, writing was an obvious candidate as a representative of this aptitude. After all, the distinctive feature of the written mark is precisely its durability. In the "Project," Freud even attempts to depict the different systems of neurones and the facilitation process in terms of graphic, spatial drawings, hence Derrida's suggestion above that no thinking of difference can radically dispense with topography.

It will be recalled that Ricoeur too insists on Freud's association of the mnemic faculty with durability and permanence. Unconscious experiences are unforgettable and available for transcription into consciousness, he asserts, adding that the trauma remains the same even though it may be inaccessible: "In particular circumstances, entire sections of the reputedly forgotten past can return. For the philosopher, psychoanalysis is therefore the most trustworthy ally in support of the thesis of the unforgettable. This was even one of Freud's strongest convictions, that the past once experienced is indestructible" (MHF, 445).[54] On this reading, "psychical writing" constitutes a metaphor presupposing, faithful to the spirit of a dominant *scripta manent* tradition, the spatial stability and durability of the text qua product of the scriptural act. Psychical content is analogous to a largely immobile text lending itself to interpretation.

Admittedly, unhappy with a rigid construal of spatiality and writing, Freud sought to radicalize it by means of his dynamic model. As a consequence, he challenged the fixity and generality of the code at work in unconscious activity but also in interpretation and analysis, and acknowledged that there is no self-identical locality where one could reach in order to recover a signified content or an original experience.[55] And yet, even if the dynamic model displaces a simplifying understanding of writing and translation, even if it allows for some instability or mobility, still, it is compatible with the dialectical structure usually assigned to a written mark and its meaning. Although Ricoeur recognized that the unconscious and instinctual impulses cannot be portrayed as belonging to a reservoir of readily accessible traces, he nonetheless affirmed that they are essentially representable and, therefore, amenable to the hermeneutic work of the analyst. Even Freud's dynamic model is congruous with the analogy between psychical content and a script or a text that, however unstable or cryptographic, allows for interpretation. The scriptural representation of the psyche is not completely abandoned. Rather, the model of writing used as one of the terms of the analogy is becoming more and more refined.

Derrida does not discount such a dialectical reading and admits to Freud's commitment to the possibility of recovering primary impressions. He alludes, for instance, to Freud's ambition, despite his denigration of popular dream-books for their simplicity, to come up with a largely fixed key of interpretation, and to his temptation to compile a complicated "dream-book" (SE, 5:351).[56] Despite accepting the necessity of instability or non-presence, Freud considers this necessity to be a phase subordinated to the demand for meaningfulness.

Derrida contends that a similar logic is at work in the penultimate paragraph of "Beyond the Pleasure Principle," just before the moment I discussed at the end of the previous section, where the relation between scientific observation and theoretical language is at issue. Freud recognizes the exigency of having recourse to the figurative and inaccurate language of psychology in order not only to describe but even to perceive whatever it is that one observes. However, he appears optimistic that one day such inaccuracy or deficiency may be removed if one were to deploy "physiological" or "chemical" terms (SE, 18:60), which are less figurative than the psychological ones. Freud defines this necessity of borrowing from a figurative language in terms of a provisional and empirical eventuality. In Derrida's words, he "often describes this structural necessity as an external and provisional fatality, as if the provisional were only what it is, provisional. A very classical logic: suspense is provisional, the borrowing supposes a proper fund, the notes and the coins must be guaranteed in the final judgment" (SF, 384–85). A large part of Freud's conceptuality is governed by a teleological structure germane to the *possibility* of meaningfulness. The latter does not have to be conceived on the basis of actual presence, but may be seen, as Ricoeur argues, through the prism of an infinite task, a thought that introduces the Kantian Idea into psychoanalysis. Meaningfulness is not posited as an attainable *telos* but as an idea regulating a horizon of infinite psychological, cultural, or scientific progress. Psychical content is thought to be homogeneous to interpretation. Therefore, its comparison to a more or less durable text persists and the analogy between psychical processes and mundane writing is upheld. Freud's scriptural representation of the psyche gives rise to psychoanalytical hermeneutics and opens up a horizon of truth within which this hermeneutics operates.

According to an alternative reading gesture, Derrida refrains from subscribing unequivocally to the conclusions of a certain Freudianism focusing exclusively on Freud's declarations. Rather, he underscores that other strand of psychoanalysis, whereby the accounts of psychical processes can be shown to call for an originary type of writing radically resistant to the idea of the trace's availability and even dynamic permanence. The interest of Freudian metaphorics, for Derrida, lies not in its ability to illuminate the unknown (the psyche) by having recourse to the known (writing), but in the demand it makes on one to reflect on the difference itself between the known and the unknown, the explicit and the implicit, presence and representation, signifier and signified, consciousness and the unconscious, perception and memory.[57] In seeking to shed light on the psyche's complex functioning, Freud's scriptural metaphors have implications that exceed the ordinary conception of inscription and textuality. If the psychoanalytical gesture is radical, it is because, taking nothing for granted, it invites one to think what a text is and what the act of writing ultimately implies. Freud's analogy between the psyche and writing, far from simply endorsing a given model of inscription, renders the latter enigmatic by comparing it to the *nachträglich* functioning of the nervous system. Psychical inscription amounts to an originary writing that complicates the more or less unproblematic scene of interpretation described above.

In light of *Nachträglichkeit*'s differentiating and deferring movement, if the unconscious trace cannot be reduced to a signified content to be translated, it is because its simple presence is always already problematized. To the degree that the unconscious text is ineluctably marked by difference, psychical writing cannot be understood in terms of conventional writing, which presupposes not only a clear-cut distinction between signifiers and signifieds, but also a *certainty* that the latter can be reached by means of the former. The necessary possibilities of non-presence and repetition imply that no certainty is possible, for the value of presence itself is made possible by differential traces. Derrida points out that Freud's break with tradition consisted in that he construed psychical functions on the basis of a writing incompatible with motifs associated with mundane writing, such as the sensible signifier, an intelligible content, permanence, communication, etc. As a result of the (im)permeable frontier between two complementary necessities, those of life and death, there is no such thing as a self-identical experience that the hermeneut could unearth once and for all, something that complicates the teleological organization of signifier and signified.

If the movement and temporality involved in this *nachträglich* writing are other than those of mundane writing, why does Derrida insist on the term *writing*? Because the latter, whose corollary is a certain exteriority, resists the determination of unconscious activity on the basis of a content enclosed within the interiority of the psyche. Writing is bound up with exteriority and spatial difference. By deploying this term, Derrida seeks to indicate that it is a quasi-exteriorizing process that constitutes the condition of the supposedly interior unconscious trace. He grounds the very interiority of the psyche in an exteriority that is not simply that of a spatial outside, thereby questioning the originariness, ideality, and sovereignty of the psychical signified. The scriptural analogy conjoins interiority and exteriority, whose paradoxical relation is upheld not only by Freud's metaphorics but also by his use of the quasi-spatial word *memory trace*. In this light, the signified of psychoanalysis, the unconscious trace, is placed in the position of a signifier, and it is precisely this reversibility of roles that renders problematic any teleological organization of the psyche, and that prevents the assimilation of originary writing to an ordinary scriptural act. As Derrida notes in *Of Grammatology*, the consequence of what he calls in that book "arche-writing" is that "the signified is originarily and essentially . . . trace, that it is *always already in the position of the signifier*."[58]

Originary writing, then, refers to a movement distinct from the smooth transition from a sensible and durable signifier to a signified content. The outside of the psychical signified does not describe a spatial entity, an absolute exteriority that the interiority of the psyche can always appropriate. Rather, it refers to a differentiating and spacing process that constitutes, for Derrida, the sine qua non of writing in general: "Diastem and time becoming space; an unfolding as well, on an original site, of meanings which irreversible, linear consecution, moving from present point to present point, could only tend to repress, and (to a certain extent) could only fail to repress" (FSW, 217). At issue here is a spacing of time and a temporalizing of space, a movement reducible neither to a merely spatial differentiation nor to the interior process of a temporal deferral. The *nachträglich* temporality of originary writing refers, as Krell puts it, to a "silent, spacing *periodicity* [that] would displace the *Nacheinander* of time, letters, quality signs, reality signs, and all such durable traces in wax."[59] Inasmuch as this movement entails a co-implication of presence and absence, it undoes the marks it produces at the very moment of producing them.

In view of *Nachträglichkeit* and the problematic frontier between perception and memory, the primary and secondary processes, the permeable and impermeable neurones, life and death, the psyche and the external world, one can claim, with Derrida, that Freud complicates the logic of dialectical opposition by, at least, pointing toward an alternative thinking about the borderline between the terms of these binaries. Freud may be said not only to affirm the *provisional necessity* but also to allow for the *absolute irreducibility* of non-presence and difference, thereby calling for a thinking that would undermine that other commitment of his to the possibility of decipherment. Hence Derrida's remark that Freud's discourse is not *exhausted* by belonging to a traditional conceptuality.

This construal brings out the strange tension inherent in Freud: there is the obsession with delving deep into the psyche with a view to discovering and interpreting archaic traces and impressions, but simultaneously the nature of such traces is admitted to be so complicated that the project of analysis is rendered not just difficult but impossible. Freud's texts invite one to take into account the radical forces of resistance disallowing, right from the beginning, recuperation or reactivation. They bear witness to a thinking of the trace in terms of an absolute past, which has serious implications with respect to the possibility of reawakening an unconscious inscription to presence. Accordingly, Derrida speaks of a principle of undecidability or interminability that reveals an internal resistance of psychoanalysis to psychoanalysis and that problematizes the attribution to Freud of a predominantly teleological structure.[60]

Now, in response to the demands that my initial contention about the improbable encounters between Ricoeur and Derrida makes upon me, I would like to put forward the following paradoxical hypothesis: the deconstructive effects of undecidability, interminability, and the impossibility of acceding to the force of unconscious activity, as revealed by Derrida, haunt Ricoeur's interpretation of Freud too. In spite of what the first chapter affirmed regarding the dialectics of Freud's essential distinctions, there are certain moments in Ricoeur that cast doubt on his hermeneutic declarations and insistence on dialectics.

Despite appearances, these moments do not have so much to do with the admission, right in the middle of the chapter on the archaeology of the subject, to the *impossibility* of a totally successful interpretation: "Perhaps, we said, the possibility of moving from force to language, and also the impossibility of completely recapturing that force within language, lies in the very emergence of desire" (FP, 440). Although Ricoeur will never cease extolling the merits of interpretation, he affirms the impossible adequation between instinctual force and psychoanalytical meaning, and accepts that the unconscious refers back to "a substrate that cannot be symbolized" as it imposes a limit on any *finite* construal that claims to be without remainder (FP, 454). No doubt, the word *impossibility* tempers the possibility of *completely* capturing the mystery of the unconscious within language and thought. An infinite tension is introduced between the recognition of this impossibility and the belief in the possibility of an infinite progress toward a Kantian Idea never to be in fact attained, but also between the two readings of Freud examined in chapter 1. Without denying that an unequivocal interpretation by a finite being is impossible, still, Ricoeur associates this impossibility with an empirical and negative finitude that has to be articulated with the demand for a transcendental and positive meaningfulness. In consequence, impossibility and all the concepts attendant upon it, such as the unconscious, force, drives, etc., are seen through a teleological prism that denies them a radical independence.

A more disruptive maneuver occurs in another context, where Ricoeur comments on the discrepancy between, on the one hand, the psychoanalytical reading of the Oedipus story stressing the impossibility of reappropriation, and, on the other, a hermeneutic one postulating a possible meaningfulness: "Despite the affirmation of the dissymmetry of interpretations," he notes, "the 'positive' interpretation has never finished evening the score with the 'negative' interpretation."[61] Firstly, this sentence appears to recognize the *absolutely* excessive character of Freud's negative interpretation, which was intended to reduce the illusion that meaning might be finally restored. Notwithstanding the positive-negative dissymmetry and Ricoeur's wish to assign an eminently positive role to the reading that aims to restore meaning, his text now confirms an absolute limit imposed on every attempt at reappropriation. What might the provenance of such a limit be if not a radically heterogeneous impossibility? As a result of this heterogeneity, the score between the two interpretations will never be even, and, as he remarks on the same page, one is prevented from "placing oneself comfortably in the triumphant position of hermeneutics."

Secondly, it is of the utmost significance in the above sentence that the words *positive* and *negative* are placed within inverted commas. The latter bear witness to a hesitation about determining possibility and impossibility on the model of the opposition between positivity and negativity. Ricoeur's use of inverted commas bespeaks an uneasiness about construing the inaccessibility of the trace and the corollary interpretation as merely *negative* stages. The possibility of ascribing a positive value to this inaccessibility is left open, which entails the reversibility of these terms and complicates the teleological directionality from a negative toward a positive construal. In this sense, Ricoeur's text calls upon one to take seriously into account the role of this ineluctable impossibility as the very condition of interpretation and psychoanalysis.

A similar moment occurs in "The Question of the Subject." I have argued that Ricoeur's archaeology of the subject endorses a Hegelian teleology of spirit that dialectically relates a negative instinctual ground to a positive intersubjective aim. And yet, one comes across the following phrase: "This apparent loss, of the *cogito* itself and of the understanding belonging to it, is required by the strategy of the work of mourning applied to the false *cogito*. . . . The loss of the illusions of consciousness is the condition for any reappropriation of the true subject" (QS, 244). If the only chance of such a reappropriation is predicated upon an anterior loss, is this not to say that this loss assumes the role of a *positive* condition of possibility? To the extent that loss is instrumental in the emergence of a true self, it is associated not only with necessity and originarity but also with positivity. Does Ricoeur's text not problematize here the clear demarcation line between the positive and the negative, the essential and the contingent? The attribution of a transcendental status to loss appears to be converging with Derrida's identification of a certain death as the only chance of life, consciousness and reflection.

Finally, in *Freud and Philosophy* too, Ricoeur's teleological arrangements are undercut when his text admits that the analogy between rhetoric and the unconscious collapses in light of the fact that unconscious traces occupy the position of both signifier and signified *at the same time*. He claims that the reversibility of roles intrinsic to this situation has no linguistic parallel and goes on to wonder: "Can one treat as a linguistic element an image that would be in the position of both the signifier and the signified? What linguistic character is left in the imago if the latter functions indifferently as signifier or signified?" (FP, 404). Both rhetorical questions gesture toward an undecidable co-implication of roles that disallows the self-identity of each element and excludes the continuous transition from signifier to signified, from the external to the internal, from the world to the psyche. All these oblique moments, dispersed within Ricoeur's discourse, outflank a teleological interpretation that strives to suppress the irreconcilable tensions in Freud. They also complicate his relation to Derrida and invite one to regard the encounter between the two thinkers as a " 'singular' dialogue" rather than simply a confrontation.[62]

Chapter 3

Ricoeur's Hermeneutics of the Self

The discussion of Ricoeur's readings of Husserl and Freud indicated the extent to which his philosophy, while resisting the belief in an immediately available perceptual present, favors the idea of a mediated and reflective self posited as a task rather than as a datum. With a view to displacing and reinterpreting subjectivity, Ricoeur has reflected on the intricate and multifaceted problem of present consciousness, and has been willing to take on board, up to a point, the challenge posed by Freudian psychoanalysis to the so-called philosophies of the subject. In this light, he has not only reformulated the concept of subjectivity but also wrested it from transcendental subjectivism.

This chapter will focus on other ways in which Ricoeur's thinking, mainly in *Oneself as Another* but also in other works, allows for a certain difference within the very heart of identity. This difference appears under the guise of numerous mediations whose outcome is a self that has passed through various phases of dispossession. The first section will examine one of the major contributions of Ricoeur's theory of discourse: the mediating role of language and the singularity of the speaking subject. The second section will be devoted to a discussion of the relation between *idem*-identity and *ipse*-identity, which instantiates the mediation of selfhood by time and change, and which will lead to the dialectic of the narrative and the ethical self. In the third and fourth sections, I will explore the responsible self as this emerges from Ricoeur's account of the ethical intention of the good life and the notion of "benevolent spontaneity," both of which are intimately bound up with the overarching dialectic of selfhood and otherness. These thematic axes will serve as guiding threads into Ricoeur's development of a hermeneutics of the self, whose main virtue is that, in his own words, it provides access to a self "that will neither be exalted, as in the philosophies of the cogito, nor be humiliated, as in the philosophies of the anti-cogito" (OA, 318). In assessing Ricoeur's success in negotiating such a position, I will try, throughout this chapter, to understand a little better his characterization of his philosophy as a return to Kant via Hegel and to draw attention to some of the tensions that such a perspective entails.[1]

83

The Singularity of the Speaking Subject

In "The Question of the Subject," Ricoeur proposes to negotiate a point of contact between reflective philosophy and the objections raised to it by psychoanalysis and structuralist linguistics. What these two schools of thought have in common is "a consideration of *signs* which questions any intention or any claim that the subject's reflecting *on* himself or the positing of the subject *by* himself is an original, fundamental, and founding act" (QS, 237).

Structuralist linguistics, according to Ricoeur, questions the specifically Husserlian correlation of the transcendental ego to a theory of meaning. If every being is to be described, for Husserl, as a phenomenon, as appearance, and, consequently, as the intended meaning of one's lived experience, then meaning, whose bearer is the subject, constitutes the most comprehensive category of phenomenological description. Meaning functions as the universal mediation between the subject and the world. To the extent that meaning is inseparable from a linguistic theory, Ricoeur subscribes to Merleau-Ponty's observation that Husserl moved language into central position, and maintains that "one can present phenomenology as a generalized theory of language. Language ceases to be an activity, a function, an operation among others: it is identified with the entire signifying milieu, with the complex of signs thrown like a net over our field of perception, our action, our life" (QS, 247).

The criticism leveled by structuralism at such coupling of subjectivity and signification is that it subordinates the latter to the former. For phenomenology, language "loses itself as it moves toward what it says, going beyond itself and establishing itself in an intentional movement of reference. For structural linguists, language is self-sufficient: all its differences are immanent in it, and it is a system which precedes the speaking subject" (QS, 251). Structuralism, for Ricoeur, defines signification as an essentially autonomous process, thus it refuses to place it under the aegis of intentionality. It regards language not as a mere medium at the disposal of the conscious subject and directed toward an intended reality, but as a self-sufficient system, as the structural unconscious presupposed by the idealism germane to phenomenology.

In response to the structuralist objections to Husserl's supposed solipsism, Ricoeur wishes to maintain a balanced stance. On the one hand, he takes into account the challenge of structuralism, thereby keeping at bay the Husserlian idea that meaning and signification emanate from a self-sufficient consciousness. On the other hand, he does not subscribe unreservedly to such a critique, for his intention is to reinscribe subjectivity having assimilated the lessons of structuralism. Accordingly, he allows for both the structuralist challenge and the insights of phenomenology with a view not to unearthing, following Husserl, a primordial sphere of subjective experience as the origin of language, but to achieving a return to the self by way of its other on the basis of a rigorous dichotomy between semiotics and semantics.

Ricoeur endorses the distinction introduced by the French Sanskritist Émile Benveniste between three hierarchized levels of linguistic analysis: the phonological, the lexical, and the syntactical one. Each of these levels, to which different linguistic units correspond (the phoneme, the word, and the sentence respectively), functions according to different laws.[2] Depending on whether one's attention is turned toward words or phonemes, or toward words situated within a sentence or a text, Benveniste's theory identifies two types of linguistics: semiotics or semiology and semantics.[3] With respect to the first two levels, Ricoeur acknowledges that the units involved constitute indeed differential and oppositional elements in a system, so he subscribes for the moment to Saussure's famous adage that language is a system of differences without positive terms.[4] He also accepts that this structure of oppositional values is necessarily presupposed by his theory of discourse to the extent that a speaker, in order to make himself or herself understood, has to draw upon a preexistent reservoir of lexical units.

Although the insights of structuralism are indispensable at the semiotic level of *langue*, says Ricoeur, they teach one nothing when one turns to a concrete act of discourse, an utterance or a sentence intended to signify or represent something. He adds that "the symbolic function, that is, the possibility of designating the real by means of signs, is complete only when it is thought in terms of the double principle of difference and reference, thus in terms of an 'unconscious' category and an 'egological' category" (QS, 261). What is at stake is a dialectical articulation of structuralist linguistics and phenomenology, a dialectics whereby the necessary conditions of language discovered by semiotics are both preserved and negated in order to give rise, at a higher level, to the function of reference and a reappropriated concept of subjectivity.

For Ricoeur, the semiological level has to be sharply distinguished from the semantic one, and it would be a mistake to apply to the latter the necessary conditions that give rise to the former. If the negative linguistic unconscious resulting from the study of the transcendentals of semiology can adequately account for the possibility of an ahistoric and potential system of language, it is unable to provide a satisfactory explanation for a situation where a specific agent takes the initiative to actualize an anterior potentiality by saying something to somebody about something. The differential and taxonomic system of *langue*, considered by structuralism to constitute the origin of every speech situation, is determined by Ricoeur as a negative condition that alone cannot explain what is living and actual in speech. One must take into account the passage from language to discourse, from the system of signs to the signifying act. This passage is marked by the transition from the negativity of a *differential* principle to the positivity of a *referential* principle:

> One can no longer remain within its negative dimension of variation, of distance, of difference; one must reach its posi-

tive dimension, namely, the possibility for a being who is torn away from intranatural relationships by difference to turn toward the world, to direct his attention toward it, to apprehend it, to grasp it, to understand it. And this movement is entirely positive. (QS, 260)

Ricoeur notes that referentiality is indissociable from subjectivity to the extent that a sentence refers simultaneously to a speaking subject and to the world. As soon as one leaves behind the semiological order and the negative relations between abstract signs, one enters the semantic realm of discourse where the salient factor is a positive reference that gives rise at the same time and symmetrically to the positing of an ego and the showing of a world.

By way of riposte to the ahistoricity of structuralism, Ricoeur adopts Benveniste's expression "instance of discourse" (*instance de discours*), which grants priority to the *act* or utterance as dialectically opposed to the *fact* of a preexistent and potential system of language.[5] Shifting the focus of attention from static oppositions to the dynamism of linguistic acts, the instance of discourse refers not to lexical units antinomically determined but to subjective speech acts. The linguistic unit proper here is the sentence, which is the outcome of a dynamic operation instigated by a speaker. Ricoeur draws upon Plato's and Aristotle's philosophies of language in order to establish that the sentence alone, the synthetic unity of a noun and a verb, constitutes a proper assertion because it brings forth a predicative link. In this respect, it is held to carry a meaning and to be able to lay claim to truth.[6]

Inasmuch as every discursive instance is an event that has an actual, temporal existence, the emphasis is placed on the act by means of which someone takes the initiative to deliver a message to somebody else. By assigning a temporal existence to this event, Ricoeur underlines its intimate link to the temporal category of the present. In *The Rule of Metaphor*, in a brief discussion of verb tenses, he goes as far as to declare that "the present is the very moment at which the discourse is being uttered. This is the present of discourse. By means of the present, discourse itself qualifies itself temporally" (RM, 86).[7]

The affirmation of the realization of discourse in the present not only underlines its dynamic and temporal character but also yokes this event to all presences organizing the moment of enunciation: the presence of its producer, its context, its reference, and its receiver. Hence Ricoeur's insistence that "discourse" designates the whole situation whereby someone communicates something to someone else. By means of shifters or indexicals, such as personal pronouns, adverbs, verb tenses, etc., a speech act is a singularized event that always refers back to its producer, to a world outside language, and to an interlocutor to whom it is addressed, right here, right now. Here is a passage from Benveniste that Ricoeur endorses: "A sentence is always embedded in the here and now. . . . Every verbal formation without exception, no matter what the idiom may be, is always linked to a particular present, thus to an always unique combination of circumstances."[8]

Obviously, the speaker has to make use of a repeatable code in order to make his or her message comprehensible. However, "the instance of discourse" is intended to grant a certain primacy to the *actual* existence of the message over against the *virtual* existence of the code. Ricoeur contends that an "onto-logical priority" should be accorded to the actuality of a discursive event to be contrasted to the "mere virtuality" of the system of language (IT, 9). It is in this sense that he seeks to overcome what he claims to be an epistemological weakness of structuralism, namely, its one-dimensional emphasis on the structure of systems and its inability to account for the temporal nature of a speech act.

By virtue of its temporality, discourse exists in duration and succession, hence its fleeting, vanishing, and dynamic character as opposed to the stable existence of systems that remain.[9] This dynamism, in turn, results in the necessary instability of the event-aspect of the message, in a minimal distance or disarticulation between the virtual system and the speech act. The event-hood of discourse opens up a gap between the message and the code upon which the speaker should nonetheless draw. Without denying the salience of the code, Ricoeur certainly seeks to undermine its domination over the whole scene of communication. Consequently, he introduces the idea of a certain distance between code and message, and affirms the latter's significance and essential dynamism, which are linguistically marked by self-reference. Actuality and singularity take precedence over against the virtuality and generality of the Saussurean *langue*, hence Derrida's characterization of Ricoeur as "a man of speech [*l'homme de la parole*]" (W, 168–69).[10]

Every sentence refers, before anything else, to the speaking subject. The speaker is the determinate subject who actualizes discourse, who takes the initiative to communicate something here and now. Although some types of sentences refer back to their singular speaker implicitly (constatives), others such as promises, threats, etc., involve an "I" in a more explicit way (performatives). Here is what Ricoeur contends in *Interpretation Theory*:

> The inner structure of the sentence refers back to its speaker through grammatical procedures, which linguists call "shifters." The personal pronouns, for example, have no objective meaning. "I" is not a concept. It is impossible to substitute a universal expression for it such as "the one who is now speaking." Its only function is to refer the whole sentence to the subject of the speech event. It has a new meaning each time it is used and each time it refers to a singular subject. . . . There are other shifters, other grammatical bearers of the reference of the discourse to its speaker as well. They

include the tenses of the verb. . . . The same thing is true of the adverbs of time and space and the demonstratives, which may be considered as egocentric particulars. Discourse therefore has many substitutable ways of referring back to its speaker. (IT, 13)

Ricoeur subsumes personal pronouns, deictics or demonstrative pronouns (this, that, etc.) and adverbs of place and time (here, now, etc.) under the category of "shifters" or "indicators." The essential feature of such indexical signs is that they do not signify a class of objects but designate the present occurrence of discourse. They do not name but indicate the relation of a speaker to an audience or a situation. These grammatical elements do not have a more or less objective meaning outside the sentence as most signs do, but acquire a singular meaning each time a speaker uses them. Ricoeur does not contest the universal applicability of these words but places it under the service of the unique referential capacity of the sentence.[11] The singular character of the event of discourse depends on the designation by grammatical lexemes of a determinate person as the speaking subject.

By underlining that these indices are indispensable for the self-referential function of a sentence, for singularizing the individual who speaks, Ricoeur aims at killing two birds with one stone: firstly, he reintroduces the question of reference in order to rectify the unilateral concern of structuralism with the intralinguistic relation between signifier and signified; secondly, by stressing the role of discourse in the emergence of the speaking subject, he claims to have evaded Husserl's tendency to regard the ego-cogito as the constituting principle of language. It appears, then, initially at least, that Ricoeur wants to distance himself as much from the phenomenological idea that one's ability to posit oneself as subject is the extralinguistic presupposition of the personal pronoun, as from the linguist's rejoinder that the reality of the ego is a creation of language alone.[12] In his own words, "the postulate *I* and the expression *I* are contemporaneous" (QS, 256).

Their contemporaneity, however, does not amount to equivalence, and the following passage suggests that Ricoeur's ties with structuralism and phenomenology are far from symmetrical:

The expression *I* as little creates the postulate *I* as the demonstrative pronoun *this* creates the spectacle of this world toward which the deictic indicator points. The subject posits itself, just as the world shows itself. Pronouns and demonstratives are in the service of this positing and this showing; they designate as clearly as possible the absolute character of this positing and this showing. . . . Language is no more a foundation than it is an object; it is mediation; it is the *medium*, the "milieu," in which and through which the subject posits himself and the world shows itself. (QS, 256)

To the extent that he asserts that the use of the pronoun "I" does *not* create the subject that it designates, and that the subject manipulates the linguistic *medium*, Ricoeur refuses to take an equal distance from phenomenology and structuralism. Even though a large part of this essay and of his philosophy as a whole is devoted to arguing against a radical subjectivism and the concomitant privileging of a self-constituting consciousness, one should not rush to conclude that Ricoeur distrusts subjectivity as such. On the contrary, the distance he takes from Husserl's postulation of a transcendental subject constitutes a strategic move made with his sight always set on a reappropriation that would amount to a "true 'return to the subject' " (QS, 261). Although Ricoeur resists Husserl's interpretation of language as accidental and nonessential, still, he regards it as a necessary but provisional medium.

The objective of Ricoeur's reflective philosophy is not to unearth an independent phenomenological principle but to mitigate such an archaeology by relating it to a teleology: "This polarity of the *archē* and the *telos*, of the origin and the end . . . can alone tear the philosophy of the *cogito* from abstraction, idealism, solipsism, in short, from all the pathological forms of subjectivism which infect the positing of the subject" (QS, 244–45). In order to disencumber phenomenology from its excesses, he adopts *some* of the insights of structuralism while also appealing to a Hegelian model. If structuralism convincingly establishes the mediation of the subject by language, a true "return to the subject" becomes possible on the basis of

> a meditation [on language] which does not stop short, a meditation which crosses the threshold separating the semiological from the semantic. For this way of thinking, the subject founded by reduction is nothing other than the beginning of signifying life, the simultaneous birth of the spoken being of the world and the speaking being of man. (QS, 261)

The outcome of such a dialectical gesture is not a transcendental consciousness but a mediated subject determined by his or her act of speaking. It is a return to the self by way of its other, hence the inverted commas of the expression "return to the subject." Three points might usefully be made with respect to this reinscription of subjectivity on the basis of a singularizing speech act.

Firstly, in his reflection on the singular self, Ricoeur endorses the structuralist mediation of the subject by language. By insisting on the priority of a differential code over against any individual act of discourse, structuralist linguistics constitutes an anti-idealist and anti-phenomenological trend, revealing a moment of disappropriation and humility. Taking into account these insights, Ricoeur subscribes to the idea of a structural linguistic unconscious that Husserlian phenomenology cannot help presupposing. Hermeneutics, he maintains, encounters structuralism as a support and not as a contrast.[13]

Secondly, Ricoeur's attempt to arrive at a singular self by way of the personal pronoun accompanying every instance of discourse is grounded in the dialectical opposition between code and message, difference and reference, negativity and positivity, *langue* and *parole*, generality and singularity, passivity and activity. Accordingly, the moment of structuralist dispossession turns out to be a provisional one that ought to be subordinated to the singular event of discourse. The first term of the pairs above is teleologically construed as a necessary negativity looking forward to the positivity of a self-reference claimed to remain largely uncontaminated by generality. The poles of these binaries never cherish the peaceful coexistence of a vis-à-vis but are always governed by a hierarchy, and, as Ricoeur explicitly states, the negative and differential conditions of semiology must be sublated by the singularizing referential capacity of discourse. In light of such determination of all structuralist principles as provisional moments, Stephen H. Clark's characterization of Ricoeur as one of the "most vigorous upholders" of structuralism appears to me a little exaggerated.[14] Rather, I would like to pose the following questions in anticipation of some of the issues I will discuss in the rest of this study: If the *only* chance of the speaker's singularity depends on the use of a *generalizable* language, can one legitimately qualify the latter as something simply negative, potential or virtual? Isn't the relation between the singularity of the personal pronoun and the generality of an iterable linguistic system more aporetic than Ricoeur would recognize?

Thirdly, although Ricoeur wishes to take on board the challenge of semiology to the philosophies of the subject, his retention of the term *subject*, in that early essay at least, indicates the degree to which his discourse is indebted to a traditional conceptuality. No matter how much one wishes to stress the mediation of subjectivity by language, the recourse to the concept of the "subject" cannot be disengaged from the belief in a substratum or an *hypokeimenon* defined in terms of an underlying substance, stability, and identity. This claim is consolidated by the lack of reference to the other as the hearer of discourse. Although the speech event is a situation where the speaker says something to *somebody else*, there is very little mention of the other person in the works I have cited, where Ricoeur focuses almost exclusively on the speaker's monadic experience. Might this conspicuous oversight be anchored in Ricoeur's tendency to subscribe to Husserl's subjectivism more readily than he wants to admit? Aware of this objection, Ricoeur remedies this imbalance in later work, where the semantics of self-reference is thought to be indissociable from a pragmatics of language taking the interlocutor's role into account too.[15] The pragmatic analysis of the speech act introduces the otherness of the other person into the scene of signification. However, reference first has to be made to another type of alterity revealed by the distinction between *idem-* and *ipse*-identity.

Idem and *Ipse*: From Narrative Identity to the Ethical Self

The dialectic between *idem-* and *ipse-*identity, introduced in the third volume of *Time and Narrative* and more explicitly thematized in *Oneself as Another*, constitutes another crucial contribution of the hermeneutics of the self.[16] Ricoeur's meditation on subjectivity during the eighties and nineties is dominated by the conceptual triad of description, narration, and prescription. The dialectical articulation of the two types of identity, which is mediated by the function of the narrative self, occupies the middle ground between description and prescription, between a merely descriptive account of the self by semantics and pragmatics, and the prescription involved in a theory of ethical responsibility.

On the one hand, sameness or *idem*-identity (Latin *idem*, German *Gleichheit*, French *mêmeté*) is a concept of relation and a relation of relations that is associated to a particular modality of "permanence in time." Ricoeur identifies three criteria on whose basis an individual's sameness can be affirmed: numerical identity (oneness as opposed to plurality), qualitative identity (extreme resemblance), and the uninterrupted continuity between the first and the last stage in the development of the same individual (for instance, an oak tree is the same from the acorn to the fully developed tree). Time proves to be a destabilizing factor threatening to play havoc with one's attempt to identify an individual, and Ricoeur refers to cases where the process of ageing, by introducing dissemblance, renders identification risky and uncertain. In order to overcome these uncertainties, one would have to appeal to the permanence, for example, of the genetic code of a biologic individual. Accordingly, Ricoeur has recourse to Kant's reformulation of "substance" as a category of relation,

> as the condition of the possibility of conceiving of change as happening to something which does not change, at least not in the moment of attributing the accident to the substance. . . . The entire problematic of personal identity will revolve around this search for a relational invariant, giving it the strong signification of permanence in time. (OA, 117–18)

On the other hand, Ricoeur differentiates sameness from selfhood or *ipse*-identity (Latin *ipse*, German *Selbstheit*, French *ipséité*) by trying to respond to the following question: "Does selfhood imply a form of permanence in time that is not reducible to the determination of a substratum or substance, even if the latter is a relational one?" There are two models of permanence in time with respect to selfhood: one is linked to character and is similar to that involved in sameness,[17] whereas the other, which is the most pertinent to my discussion, refers to keeping one's word.

Keeping one's word in faithfulness to the word that has been given entails a distinct type of stability: "[It] expresses a *self-constancy* [*maintien de soi*] which cannot be inscribed, as character was, within the dimension of something in general but solely within the dimension of 'who?'. . . . The continuity of character is one thing, the constancy of friendship is quite another" (OA, 123). The difference between these two modes of permanence arises from the fact that keeping a promise implies a sense of selfhood that does not have to be interpreted as unchangeability: one can keep the word given to the other even if one's character, opinion, or belief have significantly changed with time. This is the case because the self-constancy germane to keeping one's word is rooted not in the perseverance of character traits but in one's obligation to abide by the institution of language and to respond to the trust the other has placed in one. Such an ethical justification of keeping one's word develops

> its own temporal implications, namely a modality of permanence in time capable of standing as the polar opposite to the permanence of character. . . .
>
> This new manner of opposing the sameness of character to the constancy of the self in promising opens *an interval of sense* which remains to be filled in. This interval is opened by the polarity, in temporal terms, between two models of permanence in time—the perseverance of character and the constancy of the self in promising. It is therefore in the sphere of temporality that the mediation is to be sought. Now it is this "milieu" that, in my opinion, the notion of narrative identity comes to occupy. (OA, 124)

Oddly, Ricoeur affirms the "polar opposition" between character and keeping one's word, and, at the same time, subsumes both modalities under the category of selfhood. Henry Isaac Venema draws attention to this tension in Ricoeur's discourse, so I need not linger on it here.[18] However, I would like to point out that this situation is reminiscent of that other peculiar relation between intuition and retention, both in Ricoeur and Husserl, discussed in the first two chapters: they have to be kept apart while, simultaneously, they are brought together under the aegis of perception. The polar opposition between sameness and the self-constancy of the individual who keeps his or her word is expedient as it leads to the introduction of "narrative identity." The latter, elucidated in the sixth study of *Oneself as Another*, is the agent able to bridge the gap between the two modes of permanence in time.

Initially, Ricoeur embarks on an analysis that picks up the threads of his account, in *Time and Narrative*, of "configuration" as the art of narrative composition that mediates between concordance and discordance. Configuration consists in a poetic synthesis of the heterogeneous: the plot must bring about a mediation between the diversity and discontinuity of events, intentions, causes, etc., and the temporal unity of the story recounted. The same dialectical function is ascribed to a character in a story, whose identity can be understood on the model of the narrative plot. Characters are themselves plots, claims Ricoeur, for there is an internal dialectic to them which is akin to that of concordance and discordance involved in the emplotment of action: a character draws his or her singularity from the unity of a life considered to be a temporal totality that is itself singular and distinguished from all others; at the same time, this totality is threatened by the disruptive effects of the unforeseeable events that punctuate it. The dialectical synthesis of concordance and discordance, or necessity and contingency, is intrinsic to a character's identity, which is not regarded as immobile and stable but as a dynamic entity that can potentially mediate between sameness and selfhood.[19]

If in everyday experience sameness and selfhood tend to overlap, in fiction writers have the chance to explore the whole gamut of relations between them. At one end of the spectrum, one finds narratives whose characters have a definite identity that renders them identifiable as the same, as is the case in fairy tales. At the other end, there are literary works, such as the stream-of-consciousness novel, where character identity, by escaping the control and ordering principle of the plot, is destabilized sometimes to the point of entirely disappearing.[20] Despite describing these latter cases as "fictions of the loss of identity" and pointing to the detrimental effect that such loss has on the plot and the narrative form as such, Ricoeur seeks to reappropriate them: they may take away the support of sameness by casting doubt on a character's *total* identifiabilty but they foreground the significance of selfhood and self-constancy. This reappropriating gesture, which leads from narration to prescription, is predicated upon the dialectical opposition between narrative identity and the ethical self.

In the first place, Ricoeur acknowledges that a character's self-constancy cannot be guaranteed on the level of the literary. In the final pages of *Time and Narrative*, he concludes that narrativity renders self-constancy plural and unstable. In light of the fact that the imaginary variations involved in literature are by definition absolutely open and unforeseeable, fiction may always disrupt identity and self-constancy: "Narrative identity is not a stable and seamless identity. . . . [It] continues to make and unmake itself. . . . [It] thus becomes the name of a problem at least as much as it is that of a solution" (TN, 3:248–49).

The same view is expressed even more powerfully in *Oneself as Another*, where Ricoeur discusses, in addition to the aforementioned instances of the loss of identity, science fiction. The latter presents unsettling cases that treat identity in an impersonal way by violating the corporeal and terrestrial conditions of human existence and by focusing on technological manipulations of the brain such as bisection, transplantation, reduplication, teletransportation, etc.[21]

These extreme cases demonstrate the disturbing extent to which the order of the imaginary, insofar as it cannot and should not be censured, can undercut and even abolish both identity and selfhood. This is why the properly ethical question the other addresses to me, "Where are you?," cannot be adequately dealt with on the literary level.

In the second place, Ricoeur points toward a watertight division between, on the one hand, the self-constancy of narrative identity, which fiction cannot guarantee, and, on the other, the true self-constancy of ethical identity, which requires that one be unequivocally accountable for one's acts. An unbridgeable chasm is opened up between fictional narration and ethical prescription, between the imaginary responses to the question "Who am I?" and the ethical responsibility to reply "Here I am!" (*Me voici!*) to whoever needs my help. In *Oneself as Another* as much as in *Time and Narrative*, Ricoeur considers one's response "Here I am!" to be indissociable from the singular identity of an agent who decides and acts. "Here I am!" and "Here I stand!" (*Ici je me tiens!*) signal the non-narrative sphere of action where the genuine self-constancy and ethical responsibility required of an acting subject put an end to the plurality the imaginary variations of fiction allow for.[22]

Is there any way of bridging the gulf between the plurality of narrative identity and the singularity of ethical selfhood? At first sight, it looks as if the two sides of the gap are mutually exclusive to the extent that literature is incompatible with the principle of prescription required in the domain of ethics. Nevertheless, if authorial configuration cannot guarantee their proximity, the refiguration of the story by the reader provides an opportunity for yoking together narrativity and ethical responsibility. The process of refiguration, also designated as "mimesis$_3$,"[23] constitutes the middle ground where narration and prescription intersect.

Refiguration is bound up with "appropriation," which refers to the application of textual meaning to the situation of the reader here and now.[24] In one of his definitions of this hermeneutic-existential function, Ricoeur contends that "to 'make one's own' what was previously 'foreign' remains the ultimate aim of all hermeneutics. Interpretation in its last stage wants to equalize, to render contemporaneous, to assimilate. . . . This goal is achieved insofar as interpretation actualizes the meaning of the text for the present reader" (IT, 91–92). This link between refiguration and appropriation constitutes the final stage of the hermeneutic process, where the transition is being made from the fictive "world of the text" to the real "world of the reader" (TN, 3:157–79 and TA, 84–88). This transition is regarded as a productive transformation whereby the potentially unstable narrative configuration is eclipsed by the reader's responsible refiguration, which has a revealing and transforming power: "Revealing, in the sense that it brings features to light that were concealed and yet already sketched out at the heart of our experience, our praxis. Transforming, in the sense that a life examined in this way is a changed life, another life" (TN, 3:158). Thanks to such a dialectics, the reader's selfhood may be transformed after having assimilated the difference embedded in the text.

Ricoeur illustrates this dialectical process by alluding to the unreliable narrator. The latter, who foils the expectations of readers by leaving them uncertain and plunging them into confusion, is symptomatic of the tendency of contemporary literature to criticize conventional morality and to lay bare the illusions of blindly accepted norms by provoking and insulting. "There is no denying," exclaims Ricoeur, "that modern literature is dangerous" (TN, 3:163).[25] Yet the unreliability of these allegedly "poisonous" (*vénéneuse*) and threatening texts is compensated for by the emergence of a responsible reader on the level of refiguration. The thought experiments conducted in the sphere of the imaginary, even though they may problematize responsibility by robbing identity of all support, do not lead to the dissolution of identity. Rather, when they return to life through the reading act, "the narrative can finally perform its functions of discovery and transformation with respect to the reader's feelings and actions" (OA, 164).[26] Although the reader may indeed be confronted with cases that undermine subjectivity, selfhood does not disappear. Ricoeur argues that even a nonsubject is not nothing:

> As fiction returns to life, the readers in quest of identity find them-
> selves confronting the hypothesis of their own loss of identity, con-
> fronting this *Ichlosigkeit*. . . . The self refigured here by the narrative
> is in reality confronted with the hypothesis of its own nothingness.
> To be sure, this nothingness is not the nothing of which there
> is nothing to say. . . . The sentence "I am nothing" must keep its
> paradoxical form: "nothing" would mean nothing at all if "nothing"
> were not in fact attributed to an "I." But who is *I* when the subject
> says that it is nothing? A self deprived of the help of sameness, I
> have repeatedly stated. (OA, 166)

Faced with the possibility of such a loss, the reader's identity, far from being dissipated, may be positively transformed after passing through "the crucible of this nothingness." The empty response to the question "Who am I?," notes Ricoeur, "refers not to nullity but to the nakedness of the question itself" (OA, 167). The potential disappropriation brought about by literature poses the question "Who am I?" to the reader, thereby inviting him or her to link this question with the ethical injunction to respond "Here I am!" to the call of the other.

The tension between narrative and ethical identity is rendered fruitful by a reader who transforms the initial discord into a fragile concordance. Ricoeur's valorization of the "Here I am!" or "Here I stand!" of a singularly responsible self is not denying that literature explores a whole gamut of possible patterns of behavior. He is arguing that among those possibilities some are more beneficial than others and that, anyway, one finally has to make a choice: "There is no doubt that the 'Here I am!' by which the person recognizes himself or herself as the subject of imputation marks a halt in the wandering that may well result from the self's confrontation with a multitude of models for action and life, some of which go so far as to paralyze the capacity for firm action" (OA, 167). A responsible self ought to be able both to take into account those possibilities and to decide what to do on the basis of the other's ethical primacy over the self.

The ethical selfhood that Ricoeur's hermeneutics prescribes for the reader is not a stable and preexisting entity but a dialectical category mediated by the text. In this sense, the relation between reader and text is not dissimilar to that between the speaker and the linguistic code described in the last section. Ricoeur qualifies the reading self that ought to be the outcome of such a dialectical articulation by deploying the terms *correction* (*correction*), *rectification* (*rectification*), *purification* (*épuration*), *clarification* (*clarification*), *enlargement*, and *transformation*, processes that he often refers to the Aristotelian catharsis. The self is claimed to attain a degree of self-knowledge while escaping the substantialist illusion about a self-identical and narcissistic ego. The mediated self "is the fruit of an examined life, to recall Socrates' phrase in the *Apology*. And an examined life is, in large part, one purged [*épurée*], one clarified [*clarifiée*] by the cathartic effects of the narratives, be they historical or fictional, conveyed by our culture" (TN, 3:247).[27]

Similarly, in *From Text to Action*, the reading process is believed to result in an enlarged self involved in an act of self-understanding in front of the text: "To understand is *to understand oneself in front of the text*. It is not a question of imposing upon the text our finite capacity for understanding, but of exposing ourselves to the text and receiving from it an enlarged self" (TA, 88).[28] Thanks to this anticipated rectification of the reader's selfhood, the potentially irresponsible instability of narrative identity is sublated and the transition is made from the fictional realm of literature to the actual world of the reader.

What guarantees the smooth and continuous transition from narrativity to ethical and responsible action? Is the outcome of this process, consistently portrayed by Ricoeur as productive and fecund, certain? What is the origin of the certainty about the enlargement of the reading self? For Ricoeur, all the processes and acts described above ought to take place within a horizon opened up by a Kantian Idea, whether that of successful communication, of a single humanity, or of the good life with and for others in just institutions.[29] Already in his early work, Ricoeur points out the asymmetry between, on the one hand, the Idea, which functions as a limiting concept prescribing for reason and science infinite tasks, and, on the other, a human finitude that must give up the pretension of absolute knowledge and certainty.[30] In light of this oppositional determination of the finite and the infinite, Ricoeur admits to the impossibility of achieving, actually and unequivocally, something like an authentic self-constancy. Nevertheless, this impossibility is teleologically construed as an empirical limitation subordinated to and considered to be progressing toward an ideal possibility. One of the problems here concerns the uneasy relationship between the demand that the ethical self be *singularly* responsible for his or her actions, and a certain *generality* involved in the phrase "Here I stand!" said within a horizon regulated by the Idea. "Here I stand!," despite Ricoeur's conviction that it guarantees the singularity required in the domain of ethics and politics, is not only compromised by generality but also made possible, as I will argue in the next chapter, by an originary *generalizability* that splits its identity right from the beginning.

Benevolent Selfhood

In the seventh study of *Oneself as Another* entitled "The Self and the Ethical Aim," Ricoeur turns to the ethical dimension of selfhood with a view to clarifying the "ethical intention" defined as *"aiming at the 'good life' with and for others, in just institutions"* (OA, 172). Ricoeur's reflection now moves from the realms of description and narration into those of ethics and prescription, although it will not be until the eighth study that the discussion will focus on the properly deontological perspective resulting from the obligation to follow a norm. The first two sections of the seventh study are the most relevant to my exploration of his ethical determination of selfhood, inasmuch as they reveal a new type of mediation, a new limitation forcing the self to start anew, once again, along the return path toward itself.[31] The first section is devoted to the idea of the "good life" founded on the notion of "living well" as developed by Aristotle in *Nicomachean Ethics*.[32] Ricoeur subscribes to the belief that the "good life," whose counterpart is what he designates as "self-esteem," constitutes the object of the ethical aim. He stresses that it can only be a question of the good *for us*, which is to say that Aristotelian ethics presupposes a nonsaturable use of the predicate "good," hence the quotation marks in the definition above.

From the very beginning, ethical selfhood is yoked together, in a more straightforward way than narrative identity is, with action, deliberation, decision, and volition. This gesture is also evident in the third volume of *Time and Narrative*, where Ricoeur's account of historical consciousness and the historical present focuses on the acting agent's aptitude for taking initiative and on the experience of the "I can."[33] But even before that, in *Freedom and Nature: The Voluntary and the Involuntary* (1950), one of Ricoeur's earliest works, the deliberative process of decision and action is presented as forming the nexus of the voluntary and involuntary dimensions of the cogito.[34] It is by virtue of such emphasis on agency that Ricoeur's philosophy has been characterized as a "hermeneutics of action."[35] Only an ethics of agency can supply an unequivocal answer to the question "Who am I, so inconstant, that *notwithstanding* you count on me?" (OA, 168). Similarly, the proud declaration "Here I stand!" can originate in the voluntary act of the ethical self alone. Venema, then, is right when he affirms that Ricoeur always frames the question of selfhood "within a philosophy of action that revolves around the determination of 'who?' is acting by means of key terms such as agency, power, activity and passivity."[36]

Accordingly, the exploration of Aristotle concentrates on the concepts of *praxis, proairesis, methodos, poiēsis,* and *boulēsis,* and, with a view to setting up a teleology internal to praxis as the structuring principle for the aim of the good life, Ricoeur draws upon the complex model of deliberation presented in Book 6 of the *Nicomachean Ethics.* Deliberation is defined there as the path that the person of practical wisdom (*phronēsis*) follows to guide his or her life. This formulation, which links a singular action to the ultimate end pursued, is crucial for Ricoeur's argument considering that his goal is to contemplate the *acting* self from an ethical point of view, and that the aim of ethics has already been described as the good life.

Every action or decision can be subsumed under a cooperative activity called "practice," such as a profession, art, or even a game, while these practices are themselves integrated into broader unities designated as "life-plans," such as professional life, family life, community and political life (OA, 153–58). In turn, these hierarchized levels of praxis are ethically integrated under the idea of the good life that serves as an ultimate goal never to be actually achieved. Ricoeur contends that "the action-configurations that we are calling life plans stem, then, from our moving back and forth between far-off ideals, which have to be made more precise, and the weighing of the advantages and disadvantages of the choice of a given life plan on the level of practice" (OA, 177). In this way, he maintains both that each praxis has an "end in itself" and that all action tends toward an "ultimate end," thereby resolving the conflict between the two types of deliberation Aristotle identified. Here is how those two kinds of ends can be dialectically articulated:

> Once it is chosen, a vocation confers upon the deeds that set it
> in motion this very character of an "end in itself"; and yet we
> never stop rectifying our initial choices. Sometimes we change them
> entirely, when the confrontation shifts from the level of the execu-
> tion of practices that have already been chosen to the question of
> the adequation between the choice of a practice and our life's ideals,
> however vague these may be, and yet at times even overriding the

rules of a profession we have considered up to that moment to be invariable. (OA, 178)

Singular actions, decisions, practices, and life plans constitute intermediary stages taking place within a horizon opened up by the limiting idea of the good life, which should be conceived in terms not of a possible completion but of an infinite, asymptotic approximation:

> With respect to its content, the "good life" is, for each of us, the nebulus of ideals and dreams of achievements with regard to which a life is held to be more or less fulfilled or unfulfilled. It is the plane of "time lost" and of "time regained." In this sense, the "good life" is "that in view of which" all these actions are directed, actions which were nevertheless said to have their ends in themselves. This finality within finality, however, does not destroy the self-sufficiency of practices as long as their end has been posited and continues to be so. This opening, which fractures practices otherwise held to be closed in upon themselves when doubts arise about the direction of our life, maintains a tension, most often a discreet and tacit one, between the closed and the open within the global structure of praxis. (OA, 179)

Ricoeur underlines that the good life opens up a horizon of unending work of interpretation as far as the good life itself, action, and the self are concerned. The hermeneutic point of view results from the back-and-forth motion between the good life and the most important decisions of our existence.[37] Insofar as the content of the good life remains a nebulous ideal, an infinite and ever-changing aim, one has to interpret and reinterpret ceaselessly one's finite choices. Moreover, to the extent that interpretation is always undertaken by someone, interpreting the meaning of specific actions leads to self-interpretation, which on the ethical plane becomes self-esteem. The latter always remains subject to interpretation and can provoke controversy. Ricoeur brings this section to a close by affirming that the adequation between our life ideals and specific actions always "involves an exercise of judgment which, at best, can aspire to plausibility in the eyes of others" (OA, 180). Hence the necessity of linking self-esteem to another component of the ethical aim, solicitude.

Ricoeur goes on to focus on the phrase "with and for others" from his definition of the ethical intention, and, for fear that his meditation might be taken to lead to a solipsistic self that moves in a direction other than that of openness, he hastens to stress the importance of solicitude and friendship. The first point made is that the self implied in his discussion of self-esteem is indissociable from the role that others play in the self's constitution. In order to explicate the necessary mediation of selfhood by otherness, he draws upon Aristotle, for whom friendship "serves as a transition between the aim of the 'good life,' which we have seen reflected in self-esteem, apparently a solitary virtue, and justice, the virtue of human plurality belonging to the political sphere" (OA, 182).[38]

Why is friendship so crucial and why is it that the self needs friends in order to be happy? The answer Aristotle provides is grounded in the distinction between capacity and realization, act and power. If man is a being capable of aiming at the good life and of acting accordingly, the realization of his or her actions on the ethical plane will be evaluated not only by himself or herself but also by others. The others' mediation is necessary along the route from capacity to realization, and Aristotle's treatise on friendship in *Nicomachean Ethics* celebrates precisely this mediating role. The gap between potentiality and realization draws attention to a lack at the core of one's self-esteem, thereby giving rise to the indispensability of others who will assess the self's actions. Paraphrasing Aristotle, Ricoeur points out that this lack brings to the forefront the otherness of the other self whose role is to provide what one is unable to procure by oneself:

> If the good and happy man needs friends, it is because friendship is an "activity" (*energeia*), which is obviously a "becoming" and hence simply the incomplete actualization of a power. It is therefore lacking with respect to the act, in the strong sense of *entelekheia*. The door is therefore open for a rectification of the intellectualist conception of friendship developed up to now. Under the aegis of need, a link is made between activity and life and, finally, between happiness and pleasure. Friendship, therefore, works toward establishing the conditions for the realization of life, considered in its *intrinsic goodness and its basic pleasure*. (OA, 186)

The ideal of the good life can only be realized, for Aristotle, in living together (*suzēn*), whereby one becomes conscious of and takes pleasure not only in one's own being but also in the existence of one's friends. It is due to this essential lack, which constitutes the provenance of the phenomenon of friendship, that the self has to link up with the other in a relation of mutuality and equality. Ricoeur cautiously points out that Aristotle's admission to the necessity of other selves does not amount to a straightforward conception of otherness.[39] Nevertheless, if he commends Aristotle's ethics of reciprocity and sharing, it is because such an ethics is able to make a contribution to self-esteem without taking anything away: "What it [this ethics] adds is the idea of reciprocity in the exchange between human beings who each esteem themselves. As for the corollary of reciprocity, namely equality, it places friendship on the path of justice" (OA, 188).

Conceiving of friendship as a mutual relationship, Ricoeur stresses, throughout this section, the significance of reciprocity, thanks to which friendship borders on justice. His meditation on the phrase "with and for others" reveals that friendship and solicitude should be "based principally on the exchange between *giving* and *receiving*. Friendship, even when it is released from the sociocultural limitations of *philia*, appears to me to constitute a fragile balance in which giving and receiving are equal, hypothetically" (OA, 188). This coupling of friendship, solicitude, and symmetrical exchange is disrupted by the philosophy of Emmanuel Lévinas.

According to Ricoeur, Lévinas puts forward the idea of the other's exclusive initiative in the intersubjective relation and banishes the possibility of mutuality. By virtue of the fact that the Lévinasian other, in *Totality and Infinity*, "appears" in the face of a master of justice who instructs and summons the self to responsibility, the other represents absolute exteriority, and, as a result, neither friendship nor reciprocity is possible.[40] Such a reading of intersubjectivity as dissymmetry and irrelation is, for Ricoeur, highly unsatisfactory, for it grants absolute priority to the other. His objection to Lévinas is that, if the other indeed summons the self to responsibility, this summons should be compensated for by the self's ability not only to hear and receive the other's injunction but also to respond to it. The other's call, in order to be meaningful and effective, has to be followed by the self's capacity for responding and giving to the other something in return. With respect to the origin of such capacity, Ricoeur answers with the following rhetorical question: "Now what resources might these be if not the resources of *goodness* which could spring forth only from a being who does not detest itself to the point of being unable to hear the injunction coming from the other?" (OA, 189).

In response to the Lévinasian positing of a totally exterior other at the origin of ethics, Ricoeur regards the loving self who sympathizes with the suffering other and who takes the initiative to help him or her as the apex of the ethical relation. He does not deny the primacy of the other's call that Lévinas so powerfully evokes. He wishes dialectically to articulate this call with the self's regard for others and to affirm a relation of reciprocity. The moral obligation to obey the other's call must be eclipsed by the self's goodness and benevolent spontaneity:[41]

> Our wager is that it is possible to dig down under the level of obligation and to discover an ethical sense not so completely buried under norms that it cannot be invoked when these norms themselves are silent, in the case of undecidable matters of conscience. This is why it is so important to us to give solicitude a more

fundamental status than obedience to duty. Its status is that of *benevolent spontaneity*, intimately related to self-esteem within the framework of the aim of the "good" life.[42] (OA, 190)

The affirmation of benevolent spontaneity does not contest the anteriority of the other's call. Ricoeur admits that the origin of the ethical relation is the call of the suffering other or, more precisely, of the other who has been denied the ability to act. This initial dissymmetry, however, is compensated for by the self's benevolence, which does not constitute a *purely* active and empowering quality. To the extent that benevolence is motivated by the weakness of the suffering other, it is bound up with the human condition of mortality and, therefore, with vulnerability. Tempered with the finitude the self shares with the other, the power to act cannot attain an absolute degree. The outcome of this operation is alleged to be a certain equality between the self and the other reestablished "through the shared admission of fragility and, finally, of mortality" (OA, 192).

The self's realization of his or her fragility gives rise to solicitude, which not only complements and mitigates the moment of self-esteem but also prevents the possibility of a closed self by forcing one to perceive oneself as another among others. The ensuing equality is seen through the prism of three distinct modalities: reversibility, nonsubstitutibility, and similitude. The first one refers to the reversibility of roles as epitomized in the exchange of personal pronouns between interlocutors, whereas nonsubstitutibility is understood on the model of the irreplaceability of one's experience by that of another. Similitude is a synthetic function that mediates between reversibility and nonsubstitutibility:

> [It] is the fruit of the exchange between esteem for oneself and solicitude for others. This exchange authorizes us to say that I cannot myself have self-esteem unless I esteem others *as* myself. "As myself" means that you too are capable of starting something in the world, of acting for a reason, of hierarchizing your priorities, of evaluating the ends of your actions, and, having done this, of holding yourself in esteem as I hold myself in esteem. (OA, 193)

Ricoeur's discussion of "with and for others" concludes on this quite optimistic note with the analogizing concept of "similitude" and the *fruitful* dialectic of self-esteem and solicitude, selfhood and otherness, activity and passivity. All these dialectical relations are regarded as ineluctably marked by finitude, and are teleologically construed as looking forward to and regulated by the infinitely removed Idea of the good life with and for others in just institutions. According to Ricoeur's post-Hegelian Kantianism, the unity and continuity between the terms of these dialectics is assured by the ethical intention, which functions as the ultimate aim providing this conceptual set-up with direction and meaning. Ricoeur underlines the orienting role of the Kantian Idea in various contexts, whether the dialectic between signifier and signified or that between horizon of expectation and space of experience is in question.[43]

Oneself as Another

Ricoeur returns to the dialectic of selfhood and otherness in the tenth study of *Oneself as Another*, entitled "What Ontology in View?," where the question under scrutiny is "What sort of being is the self?"[44] My main focus here will be the third section of this study, which "concerns the specific dialectical structure of the relation between selfhood and otherness. . . . [This dialectic] best allows the speculative dimension of an ontological investigation into the mode of being of the self to appear" (OA, 298). Ricoeur affirms the fundamental character of this dialectic over against all other dialectical relations dealt with so far, and stresses the exigent and mediating role of otherness: "The fact that otherness is not added on to selfhood from outside, as though to prevent its solipsistic drift, but that it belongs instead to the tenor of meaning and to the ontological constitution of selfhood is a feature that strongly distinguishes this third dialectic from that of selfhood and sameness" (OA, 317). The main virtue of such a gesture, as already mentioned, is that it keeps the self from occupying the place of foundation, thereby achieving a mediation between the philosophies of the cogito and those of the anti-cogito.

Ricoeur's working hypothesis is the polysemic character of otherness or passivity, which is said to take on three distinct forms: the otherness represented by the experience of one's body as the mediator between one and the world, the otherness implied by the self's relation to the foreign or other self and, finally, the passivity of the self's relation to itself, which is designated as "conscience" in the sense of *Gewissen*. It is the otherness of other people that I will investigate with a view to shedding some light on Ricoeur's mediation between Husserl's derivation of the alter ego from the ego and Lévinas's belief that the assignment of responsibility to the self lies exclusively with the other.

The account of Husserl's "Fifth Cartesian Meditation" begins with pointing out his methodological decision to exclude from the sphere of ownness all objective predicates indebted to intersubjectivity.[45] The delimitation of a realm of primordial experience is indissociable from an ontology of the flesh; the latter is the pole of reference of all bodies belonging to such experience. The essential features of the flesh, as what properly belongs to the sphere of ownness, are described by Ricoeur as follows: "The flesh is most originally mine and of all things that which is closest . . . its aptitude for feeling is revealed most characteristically in the sense of touch" (OA, 324).[46] At the same time, in addition to being the provenance of my primordial experience, my flesh is a body among bodies, hence Husserl's strategic dichotomy between flesh (*Leib*) and body (*Körper*). Here is a passage from the *Cartesian Meditations* that Ricoeur does not fail to cite:

> Among the bodies belonging to this "Nature" and included in my peculiar ownness, I then find my *animate organism* as *uniquely* singled out—namely as the only one of them that is not just a body but precisely an animate organism: the sole Object within my abstract world-stratum to which, in accordance with experience, I ascribe *fields of sensation* . . . the only Object "in" which I "*rule and govern*" *immediately*. (CM, §44, 97)

The significance of the flesh lies in that it constitutes a body too. It can, therefore, become the point of transition from my flesh or the body that is properly mine to other bodies and other selves: since the flesh that belongs to me is a body among bodies, it is a part of the world, and it is on this basis that a connection can be established between ego and alter ego. The flesh makes possible both the derivation of the objective aspects of the world from the nonobjectifying primordial experience of the ego, principally by means of intersubjectivity, and the pairing of one flesh with another. Ricoeur, however, critically observes that the phenomenological reduction to the sphere of ownness cannot be thought otherwise than dialectically, and that Husserl cannot help presupposing the other even if he strives, in a quasi-Cartesian way, to suspend this common knowledge.[47]

For Ricoeur, Husserl's "authentic discovery," namely, the paradoxical character of the other's mode of *givenness* designated as "appresentation" (CM, §50, 108–11), is grounded in the crucial distinction between *Leib* and *Körper*:

> Husserl gave the name "appresentation" to this givenness in order to express, on the one hand, that unlike representations in signs or images, the givenness of the other is an authentic givenness and, on the other hand, that unlike the originary, immediate givenness of the flesh to itself, the givenness of the other never allows me to live the experiences of others and, in this sense, can never be converted into originary presentation. (OA, 333)

Appresentation differs from representation in that it constitutes an operation whereby the self perceives the other or, more accurately, the body of the other in an original fashion in the living present without the interference of any expression or image. Nevertheless, appresentation and intuition are not equivalent: whereas the former consists in an unparalleled passive synthesis, in a primitive and prereflexive operation intertwined with all the other passive syntheses, the latter refers to the originary and unmediated perception of what belongs properly to my primordial sphere, to my own animate organism or flesh. If one attempts, notes Husserl, to analyze the paradoxical situation where a body within one's primordial sphere and similar to one's body is apprehended as likewise a living body, one encounters

> first, the circumstance that here the *primally institutive original* / is *always livingly present*, and the primal instituting itself is there-fore always going on in a livingly effective manner; secondly, the peculiarity we already know to be necessary, namely that what is *appresented* by virtue of the aforesaid analogizing can never attain actual presence, never become an object of perception proper. (CM, §51, 112)

While acknowledging an initial dissymmetry between appresentation and originary presentation, Husserl defines the former in the positive terms of an "apperceptive transfer" from my flesh or of an " 'analogizing' apprehension" whose origin lies in the perception of the other's body "over there" (CM, §50, 110–11). Ricoeur uses once again the phrase "genuine discovery" to refer this time to Husserl's *positive* portrayal of appresentation as an analogizing func-tion. Appresentation signifies that the other's body is also apprehended as flesh, on which basis an analogy or pairing can be established between my and the other's apprehension of our respective bodies as flesh. Although Husserl recog-nizes that the ego's movement toward the alter ego amounts to a transgression of the sphere of ownness, this transgression is nonetheless qualified as a transfer of *sense*: "The sense of ego is transferred to another body, which, as flesh, also contains the sense of ego" (OA, 334). In this light, Ricoeur affirmatively points out that "appresentation" valorizes assimilation while downplaying the role of difference:

> If it [appresentation] does not create otherness, which is always presupposed, it confers upon it a specific meaning, namely the admission that the other is not condemned to remain a stranger but can become *my counterpart*, that is, someone who, *like* me, says "I." The resemblance based on the pairing of flesh with flesh works to reduce a distance, to bridge a gap, in the very place where it creates a dissymmetry. That is what is signified by the adverb "like": like me, the other thinks, desires, enjoys, suffers. (OA, 335)

The discussion of Husserl concludes with the observation that the phrase "alter ego" reduces the sense of alterity and prioritizes that of ego, and with the admission that, at the gnoseological level, the movement from the ego toward the other maintains indeed a priority. Far from renouncing Husserl's belief in the "authentically productive operation" of analogical transfer (OA, 335), Ricoeur is merely pointing out that, as soon as one's focus of attention shifts from the gnoseological to the ethical dimension, the emphasis has to be placed on the other's movement toward the self, as sketched out in Lévinas's work.

By placing at the origin of this movement a radical break, Lévinas criticizes the phenomenological concept of "intentionality" for subscribing unreflectively to the dogma of representation, and, therefore, for falling into the traps of idealism and solipsism. Here is the criticism that Ricoeur imagines Lévinas would level at Husserl: "To represent something to oneself is to assimilate it to oneself, to include it in oneself, and hence to deny its otherness. The analogical transfer, which is the major contribution of the *Cartesian Meditations*, does not escape this reign of representation" (OA, 336). Contrary to Husserl's commitment to the other's phenomenalizability and assimilation by the ego, the Lévinasian "face" makes the other appear, but what appears is not a spectacle. Rather, it is described in terms of epiphany and a voice that prohibits murder by commanding "Thou shall not kill." "Epiphany" or "revelation" express something other than a phenomenon, something whose words, although placed at the origin of the self's acts, are not uttered by an interlocutor. Here, it is the other that constitutes the self as capable of responding, as responsible.[48] To the extent, however, that the other's face is not a spectacle and does not have a sensible voice, it remains unrepresentable and untotalizable, absolutely exterior to the self: "The Other absolves itself from relation, in the same movement by which the Infinite draws free from Totality" (OA, 336). Ricoeur attributes the portrayal of the ethical relation as a break to Lévinas's hyperbolic philosophical argumentation.

What necessitates this construal of the other as absolutely other is, for Ricoeur, Lévinas's understanding of the self as an ego stubbornly closed in on itself, as an essentially separate ego marked by the desire to form a circle with itself. The ego is a being unable to relate to the other, hence the latter's exteriority. If the separation of the ego is the dominant figure of hyperbole on the side of identity, the equivalent on the side of otherness is the idea of epiphany, which points to the absolute alterity of the other who cannot become the object of representation. Ricoeur notes that the other, in *Totality and Infinity*, is a paradigmatic figure of the type of a master of justice: at once elevated and absolutely exterior to a self that is summoned from above always in the accusative. According to Lévinas's hyperbolic formulations, initiative lies wholly with the other, so "no middle ground, no between, is secured to lessen the utter dissymmetry between the Same and the Other" (OA, 338).

In *Otherwise than Being*, hyperbole is alleged to reach the point of paroxysm. Lévinas's argumentation opens up the era of "Retraction" (*Dédire*), in whose name the assignment of responsibility withdraws from the language of manifestation, from its expression and from its theme. Ricoeur points out that the assignment of responsibility adopts the figure of hyperbole and withdraws back to a past more ancient that any past memory, while drawing attention to the increasingly excessive character of Lévinas's language.[49] Such "paroxysm" results from "the extreme—even scandalous—hypothesis that the Other is no longer the master of justice here, as is the case in *Totality and Infinity*, but the offender, who, as an offender, no less requires the gesture of pardon and expiation" (OA, 338). Lévinas's dual hyperbole—of separation on the side of the same and of absolute alterity on the side of the other—is unable to conceive of selfhood in terms of its openness and capacity for discovery. In this respect, it necessarily leads to an impasse.

In the last few pages of his discussion of the otherness of other persons, Ricoeur puts forward the idea of a dialectic between Husserl and Lévinas. He contends that the latter's obsession with exteriority does not reach "the end of its trajectory" without some implicit reference to the self's capacity for reception, discrimination, and recognition (OA, 339). Firstly, Ricoeur discredits Lévinas's approach to the ego as a separate and closed self, for, if this were the case, how could one ever hear a word addressed to one? The other's call presupposes the self's capacity to hear and understand this call, thus the self must be defined in terms of openness rather than isolation. Secondly, the ego has to be able to distinguish the master from the offender, the master who calls for a disciple from the master who requires a slave. Now, once the self has identified the other as the master who teaches, he or she, claims Ricoeur, has to internalize the other's order "Thou shall not kill" and turn it into a personal conviction. The self should be able to transform his or her initial accusative response to the other "It's me here!" into the nominative of the conviction "Here I stand!" Thirdly, the opening of the same onto the other and the internalization of the other's call are processes mediated by language, which contributes its resources of communication toward the bridging of the gap between self and other. By virtue of his view that exteriority, in order to avoid remaining incomplete, presupposes that the initial chasm between self and other is essentially bridgeable, Ricoeur affirms the dialectical coupling of Husserl and Lévinas:

> From this confrontation between Husserl and Lévinas results the suggestion that there is no contradiction in holding the movement from the Same toward the Other and that from the Other toward the Same to be dialectically complementary. The two movements do not annihilate one another to the extent that one unfolds in the gnoseological dimension of sense, the other in the ethical dimension of injunction. The assignment of responsibility, in the second dimension, refers to the power of self-designation, transferred, in

accordance with the first dimension, to every third person assumed to be capable of saying "I." (OA, 340–41)

Two points deserve to be emphasized with respect to these key moments of *Oneself as Another*. In the first place, wishing to avoid promoting a solipsistic interpretation of selfhood and to formulate an ethics that would *not* place the self under the control of the voluntarism of the ego-cogito, Ricoeur assigns a prominent position to the value of mutuality and defines friendship, despite Aristotle, as equality.[50] In this way, and in response to Lévinas's presentation of the ethical relation as a radical imbalance, he claims to have placed sufficient emphasis on reciprocity. What is one to make of this largely economic model on whose basis Ricoeur conceives solicitude and friendship? No doubt, as Cohen notes, it is indicative of Ricoeur's Parmenidean-Hegelian tendency to limit his analysis to "internal" or "dialectical" relations "whose terms do not in any irreducible sense exceed their relationality."[51] Accordingly, self and other are dialectically linked terms operating within a horizon opened up by the Idea of the good life. There are two implications involved in Ricoeur's discourse.

Firstly, as a consequence of his endorsement of mutual exchange and reciprocity, the other's *radical* alterity is inevitably reduced. The notion of mutuality, by uniting two persons aiming at more or less the same good life, excludes a rigorously conceived heterogeneity. As Cohen puts it, "[T]hus conceived, mutuality is not an affirmation of the alterity of the other person . . . but rather a social or shared confirmation of the primacy of each person's correct aim or moral character."[52] By contrast, it is Lévinas's thought that, in allowing for the possibility of an external relation or "irrelation" between self and other, takes seriously into account not only the other's irreducible alterity but also the self's ethical responsibility emanating from this originary "irrelation."

Secondly, Ricoeur's ethics of exchange demotes responsibility to a calculative and programmatic enterprise, thereby excluding a rigorous understanding of the ethical. According to Derrida, one's decision to respond to the other's call has to be absolutely singular in order to be responsible, so it should result neither from calculation nor from one's obligation to pay back the debt one owes to the other. If one responds with a view to returning a favor or to receiving something in return, if, in a nutshell, "decision-making is relegated to a knowledge that it is content to follow or to develop, then it is no more a responsible decision, it is the technical deployment of a cognitive apparatus, the simple mechanistic deployment of a theorem."[53] In chapter 4, I will discuss how Derrida's writings allow for a radical thinking of responsibility, singularity, and alterity.

Venema also reproaches Ricoeur for basing his approach to friendship on the premise of a quasi-economic exchange. He designates such commerce of friendship by the term *reciprocity*, which he denigrates in the following way: "Does one give in order to receive, and receive in order to give? Is the reciprocity of acting with equal capacity an attestation of mutual selfhood or an attempt to keep the tally sheet balanced and remain out of debt?"[54] Venema distinguishes reciprocity from mutuality, which amounts not to a calculation of passivity and activity but to a nonoppositional difference or an economy of love: "[This economy] does not worry about a balance of power, but simply gives, and '[i]n giving to the other, I, paradoxically, in being received, am enlarged and enhanced—receiving, in the words of Lévinas, "inspiration." In receiving the other, I expand, and paradoxically through my receiving, give.' "[55] By laying bare Ricoeur's insistence on an economics of exchange, Venema's notion of mutuality gestures to a more complex and promising thinking of the ethical relation and selfhood.

In the second place, despite Ricoeur's stated intention to highlight balance, and despite being at pains, in the words of Venema, "to open voluntary selfhood to the affect of loss and suffering in the other,"[56] his dialectics grants a certain primacy to the self's benevolent and spontaneous act. As Ricoeur himself accepts, what distinguishes his approach from Lévinas's is that the sympathy for the suffering other constitutes a case where "the initiative comes from the loving self" and extends to the other (OA, 192). Consequently, although he acknowledges that benevolent spontaneity, to the extent that it is mediated by the other's passivity and the self's own finitude, does not function as a simple origin, he goes on to argue that both types of otherness ought to be eclipsed by the benevolence of the self. This argument is symptomatic of his wish to place passivity under the service of the self's benevolent act, thereby consolidating the crucial link between selfhood and action.

While describing various cases of a supposedly reciprocal relation, Ricoeur identifies two possibilities: the other either summons the self to responsibility and instructs him or her to act, or is a suffering being whose capacity for acting has been totally destroyed.[57] The self is regarded either as being enjoined *to act* benevolently, or as *acting* out of sympathy, whereas the other either instructs the self to *act* in a benevolent manner or is the occasion for the self to *act* in a sympathetic manner. As Venema cogently puts it, "[T]he self always acts from a position of power, whereas the power of the other seems to be situated somewhere between calling me to action and being purely receptive to my action."[58] Ricoeur's account of the ethical relation ends up describing selfhood in terms of a dialectical teleology of passivity and activity.

There is nothing surprising here insofar as from the very beginning of *Oneself as Another* Ricoeur determines selfhood on the basis of agency: Who is speaking? Who is acting? Who is telling or reading a story? Who is responsible? By answering these questions, he equates the self with the subject of action and prioritizes agency as a constitutive and essential property of selfhood. More specifically, he identifies four distinct modes of power: power-to-do and act, which is an agent's capacity to constitute himself or herself as the author of action and is germane to the benevolent behavior of the ethical self; power-over, whereby power is exerted over one will by another will and which can be the occasion par excellence of the evil of violence; power-in-common, which describes the capacity of a historical community to exercise their desire to live together, and which is distinct from domination; and finally, power-as-productivity, which he determines by having recourse to Spinoza's notion of "*conatus*."[59] Selfhood originates in the coupling of the first and the last modalities: it is defined as the power-to-do that is positively and essentially creative in its action.

Ricoeur, however, admits that the borderline between, on the one hand, creativity and power-to-do, and, on the other, the evil epitomized by power-over is a treacherous one: "It is difficult to imagine situations of interaction in which one individual does not exert a power over another by the very fact of acting" (OA, 220). In order to safeguard this fragile balance and to keep the possibility of violence at bay, he seeks to create as many safety catches as possible, hence the construal of selfhood on the basis of the Idea of the good life with and for others in just institutions, and the necessity of a moral framework saying no to all figures of evil.[60] This is a perfectly justified project, and Ricoeur's attempt to thematize the ethico-moral self with a view to limiting the infelicities that threaten to destabilize the ethical relation appears wholly legitimate.

Nevertheless, no matter how many safety catches one puts into place, and however effective these may be, there is an absolute limit that will always prevent selfhood from unequivocally reaching a satisfactory degree of good will and productive activity. This limit has to do with a radical alterity that introduces an irreducible passivity into the heart of the self's benevolent act. By dialectically articulating activity and passivity, Ricoeur considers the latter to be a necessary but provisional element subordinated to a largely benevolent and active selfhood. Such a coupling of selfhood to agency and volition seems to me significantly problematic in light of an originary passivity that alone can make possible the dialectical pairing of self and other, but that paradoxically prevents any conclusive identification of an act as benevolent or otherwise. Cohen remarks that Lévinas's philosophy takes seriously into account such alterity, whose corollary is the fundamental passivity of the self. He criticizes Ricoeur for his inability to understand the significance of the other in Lévinas, whose thought allows for a passivity that escapes the opposition active-passive and that is " 'more passive than any receptivity,' 'more passive than any passivity.' . . . The moral self arises as pure subjection to the other, as a subjectivity irreplaceably subject, hence as 'elected' by the other."[61]

Concluding Remarks

After the exposition of several of Ricoeur's reflections on selfhood, I would like to assess his aforementioned claim that the main virtue of his dialectics is that it keeps the ego from occupying the place of foundation, insofar as it points toward a self that is neither exalted, as in the philosophies of the cogito, nor humiliated, as in the philosophies of the anti-cogito. I will evaluate this claim by considering the following crucial question, to which admittedly there is no straightforward answer: Does Ricoeur's hermeneutics of the self succeed in keeping sufficient distance from the philosophies of the cogito, which he purports to amend by allowing for various types of non-presence at the core of subjectivity?

Ricoeur's project appears to be successful, considering that he has managed to resist the self-founding certainty of the Cartesian cogito. I have pointed out, on many occasions, his intention to dissociate himself from the belief in the ability of the conscious subject to constitute all reality, as this belief is epitomized, for Ricoeur, in Husserl's work. His response to the supposed solipsism of the Husserlian ego-cogito is a polysemic self that, ineluctably mediated and inscribed by difference, has given up the illusion of immediate consciousness, certainty, and pure identity. I will quickly recall four of the instances bearing witness to the polysemic nature of selfhood.

Firstly, in his early essay on subjectivity, Ricoeur expresses his uneasiness, from a linguistic perspective, about the privilege phenomenology confers upon a self-constituting consciousness. As far as structuralism is concerned, the emergence of a singular subject capable of saying "I" depends on a preexistent linguistic code that functions as a quasi-unconscious category presupposed by speech. Inasmuch as Ricoeur takes into account this category as the sine qua non of the speaking subject, he resists Husserl's conviction about the subject's anteriority in relation to discourse. Therefore, far from interpreting the speaking self as a principle or an origin, he allows for an original non-presence that gives rise to a mediated subject and that exposes the illusion of self-sufficiency and immediacy.

Secondly, the self's identity is interrupted by the introduction of temporality into the sphere of sameness. Not only does Ricoeur differentiate *idem* from *ipse* but also contrasts the immutability of the former to the self-constancy of the latter. Although there is a dialectical link between the two types of identity, one has to recognize that the self-constancy of *ipse*-identity successfully incorporates a certain degree of dynamism and change, on which basis it cannot be reduced to the self-identity and permanence of an immobile subject.

Thirdly, as soon as the transition is being made from description and narration to ethics, the motif of benevolent spontaneity calls for another type of passivity: finitude and vulnerability. Clearly, Ricoeur's discussion of ethical action, responsibility, and initiative does not subscribe to the voluntarism and omnipotence of an unmediated ego. On the contrary, he stresses the plight of the suffering other, whose call gives rise to benevolence and a symmetry between self and other in light of their shared mortality. It is, therefore, recognized that the act of the ethical self is limited by finitude, as a result of which benevolence and power can never reach an absolute degree. Nevertheless, the act of the finite self is teleologically construed as always taking place within a horizon regulated by the Kantian Idea of the good life with and for others in just institutions, for it is this Idea alone that can ensure the dialectical continuity between passivity and activity.

Fourthly, Ricoeur underlines the primordiality of the self-other dialectic not merely on the ethical level but on that of gnoseology too. Accordingly, with a view to making intersubjectivity the foundation of selfhood, he discerns in Husserl's distinction between flesh and body a more original intertwining of the self with the other. The problem with Husserl's distinction is that the status of the foreign is derived from the sphere of ownness and that everything is believed to originate in the ownness of my flesh. Even the constitution of objective nature and reality is claimed to take place in and through consciousness, a constitution of a piece with the philosophies of the cogito: in Husserl, he notes, "we are in a self-proclaimed egology and not in a philosophy of the self" (OA, 323). In response to this reduction of otherness, Ricoeur argues that the other's alterity, far from relating *après coup* to the otherness of the flesh that I am, must be held to be prior to the constitution of the self: "My flesh appears as a body among bodies only to the extent that I am myself an other among all the others, in the apprehension of a common nature, woven, as Husserl says, out of the network of intersubjectivity—itself, unlike Husserl's conception, founding selfhood in its own way" (OA, 326). Although Ricoeur endorses the belief in the primordiality of the flesh serving as the ground for all human activity,[62] he reproaches Husserl for making the *leibhaft selbst* the constituting origin of intersubjectivity and objective nature, and for thinking only of the other than me as another me, and never of the self as another. Due to his inability to regard intersubjectivity as prior to the constitution of the self, Husserl, for Ricoeur, can neither understand nor adequately explain how my flesh is also a body.

In this light, Ricoeur underlines the dialectical mediation of selfhood by various types of otherness. Thus, priority is granted to the relational character of selfhood as opposed to an immediate and self-positing subjectivity. What Ricoeur affirms about the anteriority of unconscious impulses can be applied *mutatis mutandis* to the originary non-presence that makes possible the speaker, the narrative self, and the acting self of the ethical domain: the ontic plane is always anterior to reflection, speech, awareness, volition and action. The *I am* is prior to the *I think*, so the self is simultaneously the certainty and affirmation "*that* I am" and the open question or suspicion as to "*what* I am" (QS, 244 and 265). By allowing for alterity and passivity at the core of selfhood, Ricoeur has successfully incorporated some of the insights of a Nietszchean, Freudian, and structuralist critique, thereby avoiding an idealistic conception of subjectivity. Commenting on this radical aspect of his philosophy, Kathleen Blamey remarks that, "from what was assumed to be best known, consciousness has become an enigma, a problem for reflection," and wonders: "Having passed through the rigors of dispossession—which, as we recall, Ricoeur describes in terms of the wounded, humiliated cogito—what is left of the ambition of reflection, of the desire for self-understanding?"[63]

And yet, it is one thing to acknowledge this affirmation of a necessary moment of distance and dispossession, it is quite another to claim, as Madison does, that "Ricoeur's contribution is, in effect, to have 'desubjectivized' subjectivity," and to insist on the "deconstructive" and "antimetaphysical" character of such a gesture.[64] On account of Ricoeur's dialectics, what needs to be cautiously established is that what he is casting doubt on is not subjectivity as such but the positing of the subject at the very beginning of intersubjectivity and even reality. Ricoeur's reservations vis-à-vis the philosophies of the cogito is not so much that they draw upon a metaphysical concept of subjectivity as that they interpret subjectivity as a pure and absolute principle, as a self-sufficient value that can be the source of all knowledge. Hence his reluctance to accept the terms "post-" and "antimetaphysical" that Madison attributes to his thought.[65] By conceiving of selfhood as a polysemic function dialectically articulated with alterity, Ricoeur seeks neither to eliminate subjectivity nor to do away with the phenomenological belief in origin or *archē*. Rather, he wants to problematize the purity of this *archē* and to relate it to a teleology, according to which the self is a task or a cultural aim yet to be achieved. The task of reflective philosophy is to resolve the conflict between archaeology and teleology in a fruitful synthesis.

Blamey metaphorically portrays this transition from a largely Cartesian ego to a hermeneutic reading of the self in terms of an itinerary or a journey. Blamey explains that this journey does not refer to a program of conceptual development in Ricoeur's own thinking over the years but to the transformation that this thinking has brought about.[66] If selfhood is the end-station or terminus, Ricoeur's contribution is to have argued in favor of the anterior phase of disarticulation. The latter, which is always thought of as a necessary but provisional negativity, has taken various forms such as the unconscious, the generality of the linguistic code, temporal change, human finitude, the passivity of the flesh, and the other's alterity. Similarly, the self qua terminus appears in several hierarchized guises such as the speaking agent, narrative identity, and the ethical self. It is clear that the coupling of those two stages is marked by a directionality from a dispossessed self toward a reappropriated one, where the former is teleologically determined as always in view of the latter.

What guarantees the transition to a positively defined selfhood is the fact that this process is believed to take place within a horizon opened up by the infinite idea of the good life. The directionality from disarticulation toward reappropriation presupposes a limiting idea regulating ethical behaviour. Because the Idea constitutes an infinite aim never to be actually attained, it has to prescribe the concrete task of ethical selfhood for fear of remaining alien to present experience and effective history. In *Time and Narrative*, Ricoeur thematizes the prescriptive character of the Idea, which, despite consisting in a nebulous transcendental function, becomes regulative by setting tasks and demanding strategic action.[67] One of the essential features of this conceptual set-up is that it endorses an infinite asymptotic progress toward something that remains, by definition, out of our reach. Another one is the acknowledgment of the limitations that finitude imposes upon human action, which is thereby determined in opposition to the infinity of the Idea.

As Ricoeur underlines in the early discussion of the Idea in "What Does Humanism Mean?," the pretensions of absolute knowledge are shattered by the realization of mortality: "Man is man when he knows that he is *only* man. The ancients called man a 'mortal.' This 'remembrance of death' indicated in the very *name* of man introduces the reference to a limit at the very heart of the affirmation of man himself."[68] It will also be recalled that in the "Conclusion" to *Time and Narrative*, the third aporia of temporality—the inscrutability of time—points precisely to the failure of human thought to master time. Here Ricoeur alludes to the Proustian characterization of time as "the artist," vis-à-vis which one finds oneself buffeted back and forth between resignation and the grief arising from the contrast between human fragility and the destructive power of time.[69] If, in *Time and Narrative*, the background against which the inevitability of mortality emerges is an invincible time, in *Oneself as Another* infinity appears under the guise of an ethical aim that remains unrealized but also unrealizable.

Accordingly, the dialectic between selfhood and otherness, marked by finitude and consisting in an incomplete mediation, takes place within a horizon regulated by the infinite idea of the good life that serves as the ultimate guide providing human action with meaning and direction. By virtue of this essentially limited mediation, Ricoeur admits that the teleological process he is describing is a fragile one and that risk is always a factor that has to be reckoned with. This risk, however, is always linked to the realm of finite and empirical action, whereas the infinite idea is coupled to rational thinking and ideal universality. I have already referred to the extent to which this teleological process and the corollary dialectic between selfhood and alterity constitute operations fraught with difficulties. I will return to these difficulties in more detail in chapter 4. However, one point needs to be emphasized in this context.

Ricoeur's approach is complicated by the following uneasy relationship. On the one hand, during the descriptive stage of his analysis, he insists on the preeminence of the singularity of the speaking subject as opposed to the virtual generality of *langue*. Similarly, when the discussion moves on to the domain of ethics, he valorizes the singularly responsible self who decides and declares "Here I stand!," who takes a stance and puts an end to the wandering that results from the self's confrontation with a multitude of models for action. The phrase "Here I stand!" allegorically represents the ethical self's singular decision to designate himself or herself as the subject of imputation and to assume responsibility before the other who is counting on him or her.

On the other hand, the same self is simultaneously inscribed within the horizon of a general ethics, according to which one's ethical intention *ought to* be the idea of the good life with and for others in just institutions. Ricoeur's account of the ethical aim requires that we pursue the good life not as monads but collectively, hence the generality of the injunction. In addition, the eighth study of *Oneself as Another*, devoted to the moral law, examines the necessary link between the ethical intention and the universality of moral obligation. Ricoeur reiterates here even more forcefully the requirement that the teleological conception of ethics should assume a certain generality and submit itself to a deontological principle, which alone can keep inscrutable evil at bay: "Because there is evil, the aim of the 'good life' has to be submitted to the test of moral obligation" (OA, 218).

Does the generality entailed by the ethical intention and the recourse to the concept of "duty" not compromise the singularity of an individual who declares "Here I stand!"? One of the paradoxes of Ricoeur's reflection on selfhood is this tension between his portrayal of the self in terms of *singular* responsibility and the more or less explicit valorization of *universally* applicable ethical ideals and laws. While acknowledging his carefully constructed arguments and valuable insights into the structure of selfhood, one has to point out that his prescriptive demands detract from a rigorously conceived singular responsibility, and that, in consequence, the ensuing self cannot lay claim to a genuinely ethical behavior. One is faced here with the following aporia: whereas the Idea of the good life, which should regulate the horizon of our actions and decisions, is intended to exclude indifference and hostility by prescribing benevolence, at the same time, it deprives the self of any singularly assumed responsibility.

A similar argument can be made with respect to the selfhood-otherness dialectic, which, by pointing toward an internal relation between these two terms, reduces alterity to a provisional necessity. It is, however, one thing to say that Ricoeur downplays the radical character of alterity and quite another to argue that he collapses the other into the identity of the same. Venema appears to be a little too harsh when he concludes that

> perhaps Ricoeur's ontological reflections should be seen as an ontology of identity rather than of selfhood. How does Ricoeur distinguish the *being* of selfhood from that of sameness? On the basis of the correlation between the question "who?" and the questions "what?" and "why?" And how does Ricoeur distinguish the *meaning* of selfhood from that of sameness? On the basis of universal and individual descriptions of identity that collapse selfhood or *ipse* identity (Who?) into sameness or *idem* identity (What?).[70]

There is no need to repeat here the various ways in which Ricoeur displaces the authority of the subject. The hermeneutic self is a polysemic value whose stability and identity is always mediated, and therefore limited, by the alterity of other people and also by other forms of passivity. Moreover, insofar as dialectics presupposes and requires difference, one cannot convincingly argue that Ricoeur prioritizes identity at the *complete* expense of alterity, but has to credit him with allowing for some otherness at the heart of ownness and with admitting to a disappropriated ego that cannot function as the foundation of intersubjectivity and reality.

If Ricoeur's dialectics does not seek to exclude alterity *altogether*, it envisages a state of reconciliation where otherness will be sublated by ethical selfhood. The latter is then determined not as an absolute and independent *archē* but as a task necessarily mediated by alterity and grounded in the infinite idea of the good life. Although passivity and the otherness of other people are not negated, they are nonetheless placed under the service of selfhood, with which they purportedly communicate in relations of mutuality, similitude, friendship, and symmetrical exchange. The other may be different from me, still, he or she must also be essentially homogeneous to me.[71] By promoting such a dialectical tie, Ricoeur's reflection underestimates the possibility of radical alterity, which is conveniently interpreted as just stimulating the already ethically inclined solicitude or benevolence of the self.[72]

A final problem that one encounters here arises from the fact that what ensures the dialectical transition from otherness to selfhood is its teleological construal on the basis of an infinite aim never to be actually realized. In other words, the continuous transition within the dialectic is guaranteed by a certain continuity between the dialectic and the Idea of the good life. Paradoxically, it turns out that the very infinity of the Idea requires that the progress toward this ultimate aim be interrupted. On the one hand, the smooth transition from a disarticulated to a reappropriated self is possible within a unified horizon of sense opened up by a limit idea. On the other hand, if this idea is to remain infinite and out of reach, the same horizon has to be discontinued and the supposedly safe and progressive movement from alterity to selfhood has to be interrupted for reasons that are essential rather than contingent. This is the ultimate aporia inherent in Ricoeur's endeavor to produce a philosophy that would constitute a return to Kant via Hegel.

Chapter 4

Secret Singularities

The thematic organization of this chapter reflects my discussion of Ricoeur's writings, on the one hand, on the interdependence between singular selfhood, speech, and responsibility, and, on the other, on the ethical relation itself. In the first two sections, I will explore how Derrida's account of signification and, more specifically, of the personal pronoun goes beyond a dialectics of semiotics and semantics, *langue* and *parole*. One of my major concerns here is the link between generality and singularity, compromised responsibility and absolute responsibility. Derrida's thinking provides the resources for grasping together the demand, here and now, for a rigorously conceived singularity and the requirement that such a demand be always articulated with a certain exemplarity. As a result, singular speech will be shown to be grounded in an originary secrecy, in a principial possibility of perjury which, far from being a negative, provisional, or empirical eventuality, constitutes the positive condition of truthful speech and a genuinely responsible self. Although this commingling of truthfulness and perjury, or singularity and generalizability, is far removed from Ricoeur's manifest declarations, I will point to specific moments in his texts that bring him closer to deconstruction when he appears to be getting farther away from it.

The last three sections will concentrate on the relation between self and other, as this is approached in Derrida's early reading of Lévinas but also in more recent writings. I will explore the reasons why Derrida sides with Lévinas, against Ricoeur, in affirming the exigency of the absolutely other, while simultaneously underlining with Ricoeur, against Lévinas, some ineluctable contact between self and other. Derrida maintains both the impossibility of the other appearing as such and the possibility of a minimal phenomenalizability, and insists, unlike Ricoeur, on the non-teleological, non-dialectical character of this configuration. The advantage of this structure is that, by introducing a new thinking about the border or the limit, it allows, inasmuch as it resists dialectics, for the possibility of a singular self and an other worthy of its name, although it also expropriates the effects of presence to which it gives rise.[1] Throughout this chapter, I will seek to explicate Derrida's peculiar "less is more" logic, according to which the chance of the better depends on the irreducible possibility of the worst, and which, moreover, upsets the teleological organization of impossibility and possibility, the finite and the infinite.

Spacing, Iterability, Signatures

Ricoeur puts forward the singularizing power of the personal pronoun and the instance of discourse with respect to the speaker. The dichotomy between, on the one hand, narrative identity, whose ethicality is destabilized by the plurality of imaginary variations in literature, and, on the other, the singular responsibility of the ethical self is grounded in the requirement that the latter should declare "Here I stand!" Speech and the use of the pronoun are claimed to condition a speaker's singular selfhood and self-constancy.

What is one to make of this coupling of deixis and singularity? Is there a direct and safe passage from the personal pronoun to the singular self without any need to pass through the circuits of meaning? How certain is the ensuing singularity and, therefore, genuine responsibility of the self who says "I"? How does Derrida's account of deictics and the personal pronoun compare to Ricoeur's dialectics of the generality of the code and the referentiality of the speech act?

Derrida's argument is marked by the following gestures. Prima facie, by stressing that the provenance of all signification is the possibility of repetition, he links language to generality, thereby subscribing to the idea that the singularity of the "I" is always minimally contaminated. Jean-François Lyotard, in light of his own interest in the referential singularity of deixis, complains that, in *Speech and Phenomena*, by placing too much emphasis on repetition, Derrida assimilates deictics to other elements of language and reduces singularity to the differential negativity and generality of *langue*.[2] Derrida, then, is reproached for subordinating the singular actuality of the now of a sentence to its transcendental conditions of possibility. However, far from seeking to assimilate deictics to other words, Derrida is concerned, as much as Lyotard himself is, with demonstrating that the relation between the empirical and the transcendental should be negotiated in ways other than those promoted by approaches that accredit their simple or dialectical opposition. The aporetic outcome of this argument is that *stricto sensu* there is no singularity and no generality as such but a peculiar non-dialectical co-implication of the two.

Derrida discusses the personal pronoun in *Speech and Phenomena*, where Husserl's distinction between expression and indication is at issue. Husserl subsumes the pronoun under a category of expressions that he designates as "essentially occasional," whose actual meaning depends on the occasion, the speaker, or the situation.[3] The distinctive feature of such expressions is that one cannot replace them by a conceptual meaning or a general definition without deforming the referential meaning of the utterance in question. It would be absurd, for example, to replace "I am happy" with "Everyone now speaking designates himself or herself as happy." The meaning of essentially occasional expressions, for Husserl, is carried off to indication, exteriority, and generality whenever one makes use of them in discourse addressed to an interlocutor. However, insofar as they are being used in solitary speech, there is no exteriority involved. In this respect, the meaning of the pronoun *I*, for instance, coincides with the immediate and individual idea of one's own personality.

Derrida stresses that the word *I* and any other linguistic element, even in soliloquy, in order to be functional and meaningful, have to presuppose a certain repeatability. The latter and the concomitant ability of signs to represent or designate cannot be construed simply in terms of continuity. With a view to shedding some light on the link he establishes between repeatability, the presence-representation binary and discontinuity, I will briefly summarize the continuist presuppositions intrinsic to most theories of signification.

The substitution in which the sign is involved, remarks Derrida in "Differance," is "both *secondary* and *provisional*: it is second in order after an original and lost presence, a presence from which the sign would be derived. It is provisional with respect to this final and missing presence, in view of which the sign would serve as a movement of mediation" (SP, 138). By definition, the sign arises in order to represent a thing or an experience of the world in their absence. The signifying act presupposes a meaning, a referent or a reality that, albeit absent from the addressee's mind the moment this act is taking place, is linked to an anterior intuition, in relation to which the sign is considered to be *secondary*. Derrida goes on:

> A sign is put in place of the thing itself, the present thing—"thing" holding here for the sense as well as the referent. Signs represent the present in its absence; they take the place of the present. When we cannot take hold of or show the thing, let us say the present, the being-present, when the present does not present itself, then we signify, we go through the detour of signs. We take up or give signs; we make signs. (SP, 138)

In order to make up for that initial absence, the sign must be able to conjure up an intelligible presence. Therefore, its sensible form provides access to a signified content that stands in for the absent referent. The process of signification compensates for the latter, as it originates in an act of intending or aiming at a relation to an object. This intention would be fulfilled as soon as the addressee could have a present intuition of the intended object. Nevertheless, in that case, the need for signification would disappear, insofar as this need depends on the non-presence of the referent. The sign is essentially representational and supplementary, and, moreover, it *must* look forward to the presence of the referent in full intuition, it *must* be in view of a presence that one intends to reappropriate. In this sense, the sign is *provisional* in relation to that instant of reappropriation. If language is grounded in the intention to signify in the absence of the object from present perception, its aim is to eliminate this distance between intention and intuition.[4]

As a result of this classical interpretation, firstly, the referent's absence is often construed as an empirical eventuality that is essentially reparable by the intelligible presence of meaning, where the sensible form would serve as the point of transition. The sign constitutes the bridge eliminating the distance between an anterior intuition of reality and an envisaged intuition intended by the act of meaning. Thus conceptualized, the relation between absence and presence is determined on the basis of homogeneity or continuity, as it is believed that it is always possible to transform the initial absence into presence, to appropriate and somehow reduce the referent's absence, if not to a mere accident, to a provisional and negative necessity. The essence of language, then, is defined in terms of its *telos*, which is the coincidence of meaning-intention and fulfilled intuition. The conviction about such coincidence is epitomized by Ricoeur's belief in the ability of the personal pronoun to provide access to the speaker's singular presence.

Secondly, the sensible presence of form and the intelligible presence of meaning are the two indissociable aspects of the sign, and it is often thought that one can more or less easily reach the latter on the basis of the former. The sign has always been regarded through the prism of a dialectical opposition between the sensible and the intelligible, and cannot be conceptualized otherwise.[5] The initial absence and the subsequent presences are organized according to a hierarchy where the sensible form is believed to refer to "the concept which refers to the world, allowing us a grasp of the world which is other than chaotic and evanescent."[6]

Derrida breaks with this continuist conceptuality by putting forward the idea of a "breaking force" (*force de rupture*) interrupting the supposedly smooth and unproblematic transition from absence to presence (SEC, 9). This breaking force is applicable to the complex network of relations between the three types of presence (referent, signified, signifier). If one focuses on the link between the referent and the act of signification for the moment, the motif of spacing qua necessary possibility of absence will have to be recalled, according to which the *possibility* of the absent thing is *necessarily* inscribed in the structure of a repeatable sign. "Necessary possibility" describes the apparently paradoxical situation where absence is a possibility rather than a certainty, but one that is absolutely irreducible rather than a matter of contingency or provisionality. Because the sign remains functional irrespective of the actual presence of the thing itself, this absence belongs to the order of possibility; simultaneously, this possibility, because it *alone* can give rise to a repeatable sign, is absolutely necessary. Qualifying absence as a necessary possibility does not mean that the thing *has to* be absent for the message to be identifiable; it means that the message *has to* be functional even if its referent is absent. This essential possibility is the provenance of the act of signification, which is why Derrida claims that absence leaves an indelible mark in all aspects of the trace it produces.

The functionality of the sign turns out to be independent of the *full* presence of its referent. Signification requires a priori the noncoincidence or distance between, on the one hand, the present sign and its meaning-intention, and, on the other, the referent: "The fulfilment of the aim by an intuition," notes Derrida, "is not indispensable. It belongs to the original structure of expression to be able to dispense with the full presence of the object aimed at by intuition" (SP, 90). One cannot appeal to the referent in order to be able to identify a sign because the emergence of the latter is grounded precisely in the former's absence from the addressee's present perception. Derrida draws upon the *Logical Investigations*, whose originality consists in Husserl's acknowledgment that a sign or syntagm of signs is comprehensible even if the thing or the reality to which it refers is false or absent from one's field of perception. In order for the body of the signifier to be animated, the speaker's intention to mean is a sufficient condition and does not have to fulfil what is intended. Even in the case of no objective reference (*Widersinnigkeit*), a spoken or written expression is still somewhat functional: if one wishes to reject a small or large unit of discourse as false, one would *first* have minimally to identify it in order *then* to decide that the intended referent is empirically (a golden mountain) or a priori (a square circle) impossible.[7]

The same discontinuous structure, which points toward the infiltration of the realm of language by referential exteriority, is also applicable to the sensible and intelligible presence. Meaning or the intention to signify has to be portrayed in terms of an ideality to be confused neither with the act of intending nor with the referent. Ideality, however, is compromised by difference inasmuch as it depends on the necessary possibility of repetition and absence. This peculiar temporalizing movement, which I described in chapter 2, introduces an element of non-presence that is both constitutive and deconstitutive of meaning. The corollary nonplenitude, once again, does not debilitate the functionality or repeatability of the sign, as attested to by cases where the absence of meaning does not prevent *some* comprehension. Derrida remarks that even when the act of meaning involves no intention or relation to an object, as in the case of nonsensical (*sinnlos*) expressions ("the green is either" or "abracadabra") and mathematical symbolism, still, these expressions or symbols retain a minimal functionality. Even a nonsensical sentence signifies "nonsense," which is to say that it is identifiable.[8] This implies that the *full* presence of meaning, of the desire to say what one means, in which most theories of signification anchor the act of speaking, is not essential to the functioning of the sign.

A similar paradox emerges if one turns to the sensible presence of the signifier, which also obeys the law of ideality. On the one hand, the recognition of a sign presupposes the identifiability of a signifying form. There would be no language and no communication without the possibility of recognizing a spoken or written form as the same. Whether by sensible form one understands the hard stone of a tablet or the pixels of a computer screen, all signs involve some material presence, whose sensibility makes intuition possible. On the other hand, the identifiability or ideality of the signifier depends on the possibility of its being repeated as *minimally* the same through significantly different variations of accent, tone, voice, graphism, or context. What gives rise to an ideal form is the spacing between its nonidentical repetitions, which means that the identity of form is always already contaminated by non-presence and repetition.[9] Indispensable as materiality may be, the ideal signifier arises thanks to the possibility of repetition, which is indissociable from the alterity inherent in the temporalizing movement of spacing. The system of differences that language is and the nonidentical repetitions contribute indeed to the identifiability of a material form but entail that this form does not amount to a *purely* material presence. One would never be able to recognize a word or a sentence as the same if one relied on the materiality of the signifier alone. Materiality cannot be conceived in terms of a full and actual presence, nor can it *single-handedly* account for the identity of the sign, for which one always needs to have recourse to other nonsensible criteria.

Derrida has in mind the unsettling consequences of spacing for a material or intelligible presence when he notes that the materiality of the sign "does not fit the classical philosophical definitions of metaphysical materialisms any more than the sensible representations or the images of matter defined by the opposition between the sensible and the intelligible. Matter, a matter without presence and without substance, is what resists these oppositions" (MPM, 52). What is a matter without substance and a meaning without meaning*ful*ness if not the *effects* of presence to which spacing gives rise? The essential possibilities of non-presence and difference render signification possible while excluding the possibility of a full presence. Spacing reveals the inadequacy of the oppositional but continuous determination not only of form and content but also of reference and language. By allowing for an originary commingling of presence and absence, spacing gives rise to the sign as a repeatable mark, a structure intended to replace the plenitude of presence not with absence but with effects of presence, with effects of sensibility, intelligibility, and referentiality.

What are the implications of spacing for the sign's repeatability? The latter is not *annulled* but is certainly *affected* by the necessary possibility of absence. If a repeatable sign always presupposes absence, its form, meaning, and referent cannot attain an absolute degree of presence. Considering that the *concepts* of "repetition" and "repeatability" entail sameness and continuity, the disjunctive term *iterability* is introduced in order to allow for an irreducible difference, as a result of which the unity of the sign will always and originarily be dissociated from itself. "Iterability," whose root "iter" comes from the word *itara* meaning "other" in Sanskrit (SEC, 7), captures the "logic" of spacing thanks to its ability to conjoin repetition and alterity.[10] In light of this terminological clarification, repeatability cannot be assimilated to an iterability that, resistant to meaningfulness and identity, will always gesture toward a differential and repetitious trace. Commenting on the difference between the two terms, Gayatri Chakravorty Spivak notes that "whereas repetition presupposes a full idealization (repeatability as such), iterability entails no more than a minimal idealization which would guarantee the possibility of the re-mark. . . . This is an impure idealization, a contradiction in terms, which cannot be caught within the either-or logic of non-contradiction."[11] Hence Derrida's preference for a "graphics" rather than a "logic" of iterability (LI, 48).

To what extent is iterability applicable to "occasional expressions" such as the personal pronoun? According to Derrida, even these expressions do not continuously and transparently represent the situation or the person they designate; rather, they function, as much as all other words do, in terms of a certain ideality. Their sensible form is recognizable as minimally the same and they signify something thanks to iterability, even in the absence of what they are supposed to designate. The word *I* is identifiable and expresses something independently of the full presence of the speaker who utters it. Its functionality originates in the necessary possibility of its being repeated as minimally the same in the radical absence or death of the person who says "I," or, to put it differently, its iterability is inseparable from an originary noncoincidence of meaning-intention and intuition. Just as the minimal meaningfulness of a statement about perception does not depend on the actuality or possibility of this perception, the signifying function of "I" does not depend on the full living presence of the speaking subject.

The pronoun *I*, notes Derrida, has to be capable of "remaining *the same* for an I-here-now in general, keeping its sense even if my empirical presence is eliminated or radically modified. When I say "I," even in solitary speech, can I give my statement meaning without implying, there as always, the possible absence of the object of speech—in this case, myself?" (SP, 95). Extrapolating from a formula deployed above, this essential possibility does not mean that the speaker *has to* be absent or dead for "I" to be functional, but that "I" *has to* be understandable even if the speaker is dead, and his or her speech is reproduced, for example, with the help of a tape recorder. Life and self-presence, therefore, are only contingent; they constitute the *telos* of the pronouncement of the pronoun rather than its *eidos*.

This construal has two serious implications. Firstly, iterability introduces an element of generalizability into the supposedly singularizing act whereby a speaker says "I." Even Husserl himself, underlines Derrida, despite maintaining that the meaning of the word *I* is the *individual* concept of one's personality, could not help recognizing that "since each person, in speaking of himself, says 'I,' the word has the character of a universally operative indication of this fact."[12] Iterability prevents discourse from constituting a medium the speaker manipulates in order to indicate his or her singularity. Inasmuch as the *Bedeutung* of "I" functions as an ideality, the possibility of repetition attendant on the latter effaces the de facto singularity of any speech event. The difference of this account from Ricoeur's dialectics of generality and singularity consists in that generalizability, rooted in an irreducible absence, excludes the possibility of a purely singular presence, while also constituting the only chance of a rigorously *thought* singularity here and now. This is why iterability and death do not function as transcendental conditions but as the quasi-transcendental moments that make singularity (im)possible. What is being affirmed here about the personal pronoun applies for exactly the same reasons to the proper name, whose sharp distinction from the common noun is rendered questionable.[13]

Secondly, to the extent that this generalizability cannot be divorced from the referent's absence, Derrida's account of the personal pronoun is not confined within a purely linguistic order closed in on itself. By stressing the irreducibility of spacing, death, and alterity, and by regarding this structure as the sine qua non of any signifying element, Derrida infiltrates the linguistic sphere with a type of "reference" that cannot be determined in opposition to sense and that has to be conceived of in terms other than those of presence or identity. Iterability is so intimately bound up with a certain exteriority that it cannot be dialectically opposed to a referential realm; it functions, therefore, as a nonnegative structure that defies reappropriation. The domain, then, of the Saussurean *langue*, associated by Ricoeur with a negative transcendentality, is essentially commingled with a quasi-exterior deconstructed referentiality. This commingling disallows the purity of either the transcendental or the empirical, meaning or reference. Defending Derrida against Lyotard's criticism, Bennington maintains that, by insisting on the iterability of the pronoun,

> Derrida is less assimilating an indexical item to a lexical item, than infiltrating lexical items in general with indexicals. . . . But if lexical items are thereby indexed, then it would follow that far from reinforcing too unitary a view of *langue* in Saussure's sense, . . . Derrida is opening any such system, and in fact any transcendental realm whatsoever, to the contingency, eventhood and "mere probability" attendant on Husserl's notion of the index.[14]

The use of the pronoun "I" refers, for Derrida, to a network of intra- and extralinguistic traces—although the very distinction between an inside and an outside of language has to be seriously questioned—and is caught up in the differential co-implication of absence and presence, generalizability and singularity. This argument prevents me, in the final analysis, from subscribing to Ricoeur's hierarchized and watertight division between semiology and semantics, between the general virtuality of the system and the singular act of discourse.

J. L. Austin claims that the signature guarantees the tie between the signatory and his or her text in the same way that the word *I* and the utterance guarantee the smooth transition from an oral statement to its singular human origin,[15] so let me clarify further the non-dialectical negotiation of the transcendental and the empirical by alluding to Derrida's account of the signature. The last section of "Signature Event Context" points to a conundrum: on the one hand, the event and form of a signature, in order to be able to guarantee the self-presence of someone as the origin of a singular decision or commitment, have to be essentially and absolutely singular themselves; on the other hand, inasmuch as one needs to countersign at least once for a signature to be valid, there is no such thing as an absolutely singular signature, for the latter always presupposes absence and repetition.[16] Iterability and the necessary possibility of the signatory's death constitute the quasi-transcendental conditions of a singular signature. Although the possibility of a unique signature guaranteeing one's undivided commitment remains an infinite demand, this possibility has a chance thanks to a certain death that paradoxically contaminates singularity with generalizability and interrupts the teleological organization of finitude and infinity.

Iterability gives rise to *effects* of signature that are usually mistaken for absolutely singular events providing access to the signatory's intention. The minimal sameness of iterability corrupts the identity and uniqueness of the signature, divides its seal and undermines the full presence of the origin of this seal. Strictly speaking, there is no signature as such but only *signatures*, as every signature presupposes iteration and, therefore, the event of a countersignature. Alterity is introduced not only into the signature itself, insofar as it is always a matter of nonidentical repetitions, but also into the signatory's identity to the extent that this depends on the indivisibility of his or her signature. In this way, the form of a signature and its signatory or referent are yoked together in a differential relation where the very terms *referent* and *signature* are slightly inappropriate in light of their displacement by the aforementioned conditions of (im)possibility. The mark that identifies me by differentiating me from everybody else also expropriates me by announcing my death, something that does not affect, in principle, the functionality of my signature. The signatory's unicity is expropriated, which is why it is always the other who countersigns, be that other myself.[17] Strangely, the "logic" of the countersignature, by refusing to subordinate alterity and absence to the principle of identity, constitutes the only chance of something like a singular self and an *ethical* relation to the other.

The processes of signing and deixis are infiltrated with what Ricoeur would designate as "referential exteriority." Derrida, however, displaces the identity of the referential and linguistic domains which cannot be construed any more in terms of an inside-outside relation of representation. In view of his emphasis on non-presence and alterity, is it not clear that Derrida cannot be reproached for inadvertently drawing singularity into the sphere of a generalized conceptuality, as Lyotard claims? Always implying a "non-present remainder [*restance non-présente*]" (SEC, 10 and LI, 50–54), iterability gives rise to a dissemination of events of signature and speech that are perhaps always different and singular, but only to the extent that such singularity can be subsumed by a certain rule, for it is always commingled with generalizability.

Far from restricting his discussion of the pronoun within the confines of language and conceptuality, Derrida puts forward the co-implication of "sense" and "reference," thereby deconstructing, against Ricoeur, their oppositional determination, and, by the same token, questioning, with Ricoeur, the possibility of a purely transcendental realm of *langue* unaffected by contingency and eventhood. The supposed contingency of the referent's absence becomes the quasi-transcendental on which the so-called transcendental ineluctably depends, which is why the conditions of possibility for the personal pronoun and for any other word are conditions of impossibility too.

The following aporia is revealed at the heart of deixis: a deictic word is singular only to the extent that it has to refer minimally to its own iterability before designating a worldly referent that is divided from itself. "In so far as iterability entails non-identity," argues Bennington, "each event really is singular, . . . but singular only through the iterability that can also always allow its singularity to be reduced, as philosophy has always done, to the status of exemplification of an ideality, or a case subsumable by a rule."[18] The singularity of the personal pronoun presupposes its own iterability before being able to designate an individual who is expropriated the moment he or she is constituted by uttering the word *I*. Paul de Man's playful paraphrase of Hegel's expression "*kann ich nicht sagen was ich nur meine*" into the paradoxical proposition "I cannot say I" amounts to an attempt to take into account this structure which, (de)constitutive of a rigorous singularity, gives rise to the endless demand for the singular or the idiomatic.[19] The only chance of the latter is predicated upon an ineluctable and differential movement that disallows the possibility of a de facto absolutely idiomatic speech act.

On this reading, Ricoeur's subordination of difference to reference and the belief that "Here I stand!" constitutes a more or less safe criterion providing access to one's identity and singular responsibility is cast seriously into doubt.

Inasmuch as the word *I* has been shown to be already caught up in a network of iterable traces, its supposed singularity will never acquire the status of a fulfilling presence but will always remain entangled with iterability, difference, and death. Whoever speaks and says "I" cannot avoid the risk of compromising one's responsibility by using the language of the other. As Derrida maintains, he who says "I" "feels himself to be irresponsible when he commits himself, making a promise in the language of the other" (MPM, 101).

And yet, this essential divisibility of a singular speech act and the concomitant infiltration of singularity by generalizability occasionally irrupt into Ricoeur's text and interrupt his philosophical convictions. One such occasion concerns his adoption of Benveniste's phrase "*instance* of discourse" in order to designate the singular *instant* of speech. On the one hand, every utterance is bound up, for Ricoeur, with the present and even punctual instant in which discourse is actualized by the speaking subject, hence the characterization of speech as a transitory, fleeting and instantaneous event. Simultaneously, "instance" clearly points to an exemplarity and temporal extension incompatible with the instantaneity of the actual I-here-now. This difference in meaning between "instant" and "instance" is evident in English. In French too, specific uses of the word *instance* entail a temporal density incongruous with the punctual instant: the expression "*en instance*," for example, indicates imminence and deferral, and the juridical sense signifies a legal process, a sequence of events rather than an indivisible act. "Instance" announces a distension and a universalizability that inevitably compromise the *stigmē*.[20]

If the singular here and now of speech is portrayed as an instance, is this not because it must minimally participate in the generality of a code according to a necessity already discussed? Ricoeur's designation of the instant of discourse as an "instance" calls upon one to contemplate the primordial contamination of singularity by generality as a result of which the instant's identity is originarily divided. Despite Ricoeur's declared intentions, his text complicates the punctuality of the speech event by articulating it with repeatability, thereby attesting to the irreducible co-implication of sameness and difference involved in Derridean iterability.[21] This structure, however, excludes the possibility of a dialectic between the event and meaning of discourse for the event does not enjoy a simple and stigmatic identity that could be opposed to meaning as its contrary. If the appearance of the discursive instant depends on it being always already an instance, is this not to say that the allegedly singular speech act is divided in a way for which no dialectics could account? Does this commingling of instant and instance in Ricoeur's text not bear witness to a reversibility of singularity and generality that no teleology could tolerate?

The point here is not to suggest that there is an unintentional strand in Ricoeur according to which he may be claimed implicitly to admit to many or some of Derrida's configurations. Such a claim would still be indebted to a teleological conception of the implicit and the explicit, the unintentional and the intentional. The point is to draw attention to the differentiated moments of Ricoeur's text, moments that may be at variance with one another and whose alterity can be thought of in a non-teleological way. Such a thinking of alterity alone, by refusing to prioritize one reading at the expense of another and to return a conclusive verdict regarding Ricoeur's dialectics or otherwise, can do justice to the singular richness and finesse of his philosophy. My claim is that a reading of Ricoeur that resists simplification and is attentive to the irreconcilable possibilities of his thought *will have been* fairer than one ascribing to it an unequivocal position, whether hermeneutic or post-structuralist.

It is one thing to affirm the impossibility of the absolutely singular presence of the speaking self, and quite another to denigrate the quest for singular responsibility. The endless desire for idiom is not a matter of choice; it is an exigency one cannot just choose to do away with. Nevertheless, in light of the fact that this desire is rooted in the impossibility of its accomplishment, any discourse on identity, subjectivity, and responsibility should take the interruptive character of this impossibility seriously into consideration instead of endorsing the continuous passage from linguistic generality to a singular selfhood.

Secrets of Speech

One of the focal points of Ricoeur's reflection on selfhood is the demand that one should declare "Here I stand!" in order to assume responsibility and be accountable before others. What this formulation presupposes is the trite link not only between singular responsibility and speech, but also between the latter and phenomenalization. It would not be difficult to identify thinkers or tendencies within the Western tradition that have accredited the coupling, on the one hand, of linguistic expression to responsible behavior, and, on the other, of silence or secrecy to irresponsibility.

In his *Heretical Essays on the Philosophy of History* (1990), Jan Patočka refers to Platonism as an early attempt to break with the secrecy of orgiastic mystery in order to make room for a conscious experience of responsibility.[22] According to Patočka, the heterogeneity between these two dimensions is graphically described by Plato in terms of the opposition between the radiant sun of "the Good," which tolerates no secrecy, and the subterranean darkness of the demonic cavern.[23] In his detailed reading of this book in *The Gift of Death*, Derrida points out that Patočka himself endorses a similar correlation between the secrecy of demonic rapture and irresponsibility, and maps out the subtle differences between Patočka's Christian thinking and Platonism.[24] Furthermore, as Søren Kierkegaard observes in *Fear and Trembling* (1843), Hegelian philosophy, taking for granted that the ethical is the universal and the disclosed, and that the individual who remains in concealment sins and is in a state of temptation, assumes that there is no justified secrecy and demands disclosure and public expression.[25] Here is how Derrida synopsizes this dominant tendency: "There are no final secrets for philosophy, ethics, or politics. The manifest is given priority over the hidden or the secret, universal generality is superior to the individual; no irreducible secret that can be legally justified . . . nothing hidden, no absolutely legitimate secret" (GD, 63).

Although Derrida nowhere denies the seriousness or urgency of this ethico-philosophico-political demand for manifestation and public expression, he draws attention to an irreducible irresponsibility at the heart of speech, thereby complicating the routinely affirmed coupling of silence and irresponsible behavior. In *The Gift of Death*, he refers extensively to how Kierkegaard's commentary on Isaac's sacrifice undermines the link between speech and responsibility. Kierkegaard underscores that Abraham, in contrast with the tragic hero who speaks and complains, remains silent about what God has ordered him to do, so he does not talk to Sarah, Eleazar, or Isaac about the sacrifice. By keeping this secret, Abraham undoubtedly betrays ethics, which demands that the individual should unwrap himself or herself by speaking out. He refuses to become disclosed in the universal; accordingly, his behavior is ethically unjustifiable. Ethics condemns Abraham, for it dictates that one must acknowledge the universal, and one does that by speaking.[26]

Nevertheless, by choosing not to speak, Abraham also refuses to compromise his singularity. For Kierkegaard, it is precisely his silence that prevents Abraham from entering a domain of generality, phenomenality, and, as a result, diminished responsibility. He assumes responsibility as an irreplaceable individual and retains his unmediated singularity: "Abraham cannot be mediated, which can also be put by saying he cannot speak. The moment I speak I express the universal, and when I do not no one can understand me."[27] Speech relieves to the extent that it translates me into the universal, so Abraham does not relieve his merciless solitude by sharing the responsibility of deciding.[28] As Derrida affirms, "[T]o the extent that . . . Abraham doesn't speak, he assumes the responsibility that consists in always being alone, entrenched in one's own singularity at the moment of decision. . . . But as soon as one speaks, as soon as one enters the medium of language, one loses that very singularity" (GD, 59–60). Abraham does not have the comfort of sharing responsibility with others, nor does he relieve himself by crying, which is why he is not a tragic hero. He assumes a singular responsibility and exhibits a courage that is far greater than that of somebody who compromises the absoluteness of his experience by giving reasons.

Derrida draws upon Kierkegaard's exegesis of the Abraham story in order to problematize the link between speech, public expression, and responsible behavior, and to highlight a dissymmetry between absolute and general responsibility. He cites Kierkegaard's extraordinary claim that the ethical and speech, far from indicating courage, constitute a temptation.[29] Abraham does not give in to this temptation and assumes the absolute responsibility resulting from his solitude. By remaining unintelligible and by refraining from giving his reasons in a convincing manner, he does not submit to an ethical generality that would have rendered him, in a sense, irresponsible.[30]

The whole point of this argument is not to take sides in favor of silence and concealment to the detriment of speech and accountability. Derrida makes it clear that the account of an excessive and singular responsibility is not intended to authorize or justify silence. Rather, it aims to complicate the mechanical and perfunctory compulsion toward sententious discourse and strategic exploitation. In "Passions: 'An Oblique Offering' " (1992), he outlines the risks of silence or non-response that always threaten to undermine, theoretically and practically, the concept of responsibility.[31] Similarly, reflecting elsewhere on Heidegger's silence on Auschwitz, he states that such silence "will never be justifiable; [but] nor is speaking about it in such an instrumental fashion and in order to say nothing, to say nothing about it that does not go without saying, trivially, serving primarily to give oneself a good conscience, so as not to be the last to accuse, to teach lessons, to take positions, or to grandstand."[32] The discussion of Abraham's singular responsibility emanating from his absolute relation to God reveals the paradox that speech compromises a radical responsibility, whence the differential coupling of speech to a certain silence. How is one to understand this apparently contradictory co-implication of expression and secrecy, response and non-response, truth and non-truth? Where does the ability of speech to silence and dissimulate originate?

There are two types of dissimulation related to speech. Firstly, Abraham does not remain completely silent when Isaac asks him where the sacrificial lamb is to be found; he replies that God will provide. Although his response is neither false nor non-true, it does not reveal the secret between himself and God. Therefore, he still remains silent about the sacrifice. In speaking without revealing the essential thing, Abraham responds without responding. In question here is a content one consciously dissimulates precisely by speaking, a content that nonetheless could be revealed or become manifest if Abraham so wished. If one follows the ordinary portrayal of secrecy in terms of the optical dimension, this kind of secret belongs to what Derrida terms "visible in-visible," namely, something that can be concealed but that remains essentially within the order of the visible (GD, 90). This is a first indication that speech and secrecy are not opposed to each other to the point of being mutually exclusive. On the contrary, Derrida argues that "speaking in order not to say anything is always the best technique for keeping a secret" (GD, 59).[33]

Ricoeur certainly recognizes that speech cannot automatically guarantee the sincerity of the speaker, as conscious dissimulation often poses a threat to phenomenalization and disclosure. This is why "historical consciousness" in *Time and Narrative* and "selfhood" in *Oneself as Another*, both of which he associates with the expression "Here I stand!," do not point to a given reality or a fait accompli but to a task prescribed by the Kantian Ideas of one humanity and the good life respectively. In other words, Ricoeur envisages the possibility of an infinite asymptotic progress toward an Idea that opens up a horizon of univocity and rational endeavor, although he acknowledges the impossibility, because of human finitude, of ever acceding to the infinite content of that Idea. There is always the factical risk that "Here I stand!" may not represent the speaker's sincere conviction. This risk, however, is attributed to an empirical finitude whose acts take place within a horizon unified by the Idea. What this teleological formulation presupposes is the continuity of this infinite movement punctuated by finite acts. Despite his recognition that "misunderstanding finally prevails," the process of communication is nonetheless claimed to tend toward the *telos* of univocity.[34]

Secondly, iterability points toward a radically heterogeneous secrecy. Let me suppose a situation of spoken discourse between two interlocutors where one declares "Here I stand!" On the one hand, this phrase, in order to be able to guarantee the genuine commitment of the speaker, has to take place in a present instant that remains singular. The legitimate association of this phrase with responsibility requires the full and undivided presence of the person committing himself or herself before the other. This requirement refers first and foremost to the presence of the speaker's intention, attention, sincerity, or conviction. If the instant in which such a declaration is made is divided, if the full presence of the speaker's intention is contaminated by absence, then he or she cannot lay claim to truth or reliability. On the other hand, this requirement of self-identity is tempered by a generalizability without which "Here I stand!" would be incomprehensible. The iterability of this phrase cannot be disengaged from the necessary possibility of absence of the speaker's intention from the hearer's mind. This entails that "Here I stand!" remains functional even if one does not fully mean what one says, or does not intend to do what one says one will. The meaning-intention of this expression is independent of the speaker's fulfilled and actualized intention. Here is Derrida on this essential impossibility of saturation:

> Intention or attention . . . will strive or tend in vain to actualize or fulfill itself, for it cannot, by virtue of its very structure, ever achieve this goal. In no case will it be fulfilled, actualized, totally present to its object and to itself. It is divided and deported in advance, by its iterability, towards others, removed [*écartée*] in advance from itself. This re-move makes its movement possible. . . . Intention is a priori (at once) *différante*: differing and deferring, in its inception. (LI, 56)

Even in the case of testimony, where the person testifying is supposed to give publicly a truthful account of the events, this account presupposes iterability and non-presence, hence the inextricable link between testimony and secrecy. In *The Instant of My Death / Demeure*, Derrida maintains that iterability constitutes the common provenance of testimony and literature, truth and fiction. Not only when I am telling the truth but also when I am deliberately lying, I am speaking and the other understands what I am saying: "Even a lie presupposes the structure 'I am speaking,' 'we are speaking the same language.' . . . I could not lie if I did not presuppose that the other understands what I am saying to him *as* I am saying it to him, *as* I want to say it to him. There is no lie otherwise."[35] What makes testimony possible is the generalizability of the speaker's non-present experience, without which there is neither truthful communication nor perjury. As soon as one speaks, there is no way of conclusively ruling out the possibility of non-truth, the possibility of the worst.

By insisting on the pervertibility of speech as the secret provenance of both truthfulness and perjury, Derrida acknowledges the irreducibility of a non-present intention, that is, of lying, and reverses the teleological relation of priority between truth and non-truth. The possibility of non-presence or perjury is not an accidental negativity that *may* empirically contaminate the purity of truthful speech but a necessary possibility without which there is no speech. In order to stress that perjury is ineluctable, Derrida often contends that this possibility of the worst has to be presupposed if truthful speech is to be worthy of its name, if one wishes to avoid reducing speech to the effect of a cause, to a predictable and compromised operation. The possibility that one always might be lying or hiding something the very moment one is claiming to tell the truth, constitutes the a priori requirement without which ethical behavior and fidelity do not stand a chance. Without the structural possibility that one always might not be telling the truth, without this "perhaps not" or "possibly not," truthful speech would be tantamount to a banal transition from potentiality to actuality.

The aporia one encounters here is that the only chance of a speech act originates in a logically prior secrecy that excludes the possibility of purely truthful speech. This is the quasi-transcendental condition that complicates the watertight division between phenomenality and silence. This originary secret belongs to an order other than that to which Abraham's conscious silence about the sacrifice does. It is an absolute secret that does not have any content and that, therefore, cannot become the object of interpretation, revelation, thematization, or phenomenalization.

Its absolute character may be captured more effectively by the phrase "*There is something secret [il y a là du secret]*" than by the noun "secret," underlines Derrida, as it is not "a question of a secret as a representation dissimulated by a conscious subject, nor moreover of the content of an unconscious representation, some secret motive that the moralist or the psychoanalyst might have the skill to detect, or, as they say, to de-mystify."[36] This secret does not belong to an interior realm waiting to be confessed or brought into public view. Despite giving rise to the distinction between the public and the private, revelation and dissimulation, unveiling and veiling, speech and silence, it is itself nonphenomenalizable, for it emanates from an order of "absolute invisibility" (GD, 89–90). If Derrida has chosen the word *secret* to designate the "origin" of speech that remains resistant to phenomenality, it is because this term points, not least due to its etymology, toward detachment, separation, and non-belonging.[37]

By thus grounding speech in a principial secrecy that involves alterity and non-belonging, a strange bond is disclosed between speech and silence, an undecidable commingling that effectively undercuts any belief in speech as the medium of sincere and reliable expression. The paradoxical consequence of this structure is that, although speech and phenomenality constitute conditions of responsibility, they are grounded, at the same time, in a necessary possibility of perjury they cannot absolutely exclude. The acknowledgment of such a co-implication does not amount to a suggestion that the effort of communication is *totally* dysfunctional. Rather, in order to take seriously into account secrecy as the sine qua non of speech, Derrida announces a suspicion about the possibility of *appropriating* the intention conveyed by a discursive act. In fact, the teleological desire for a relatively univocal and recoverable meaning is predicated upon the impossibility of a rigorous distinction between secrecy and manifestation.

Insofar as all speech is marked by secrecy with respect to the speaker's intention, it follows that it contains a tacit promise of truth or veracity. In addition to a constative or descriptive content, every utterance implies the speaker's commitment to the effect that "I promise that what I say is the truth." Ricoeur admits to this performative and promissory aspect of speech when he maintains that "I cannot assert something without introducing a tacit clause of sincerity into my saying it, in virtue of which I effectively signify what I am saying, any more than I can do so without holding as true what I affirm" (TN, 3:232).[38] He goes on to refer explicitly to promises, clarifying that the speaker always promises not only to do something in the future but also to keep this promise.

Prima facie Derrida affirms something similar when he designates such a tacit claim to sincerity as an irreducible "promise of truth." Subsequently, however, he highlights Paul de Man's transformation of Heidegger's well-known phrase "*Die Sprache spricht*" into "*Die Sprache verspricht (sich)*," that is, "language promises (itself)" instead of "language speaks."[39] Commenting on de Man's gesture, Derrida notes that "the essence of speech is the promise, that there is no speaking that does not promise, which at the same time means a commitment toward the future through what we too hastily call a 'speech act'" (MPM, 97). It is this last phrase of vigilance that marks a difference between how Ricoeur and Derrida construe the promissory nature of language.

Ricoeur is happy to portray this implicit promise in terms of one's task to act, take initiative, and commit oneself in what he calls "the historical present," thereby prioritizing the ethical *demand* for responsible and truthful discourse. Without denigrating this demand, Derrida argues that the only chance of a responsible speech act depends, in principle, on the structural necessity of a secrecy that excludes, de jure and de facto, the possibility of a purely responsible and phenomenalizable promise. If "speech act" does not do justice to the essentially promissory mark, it is because this phrase, by presupposing an array of concepts indebted to the values of presence and identity (action, selfhood, will, decision, and intention), does not take into account, seriously enough, an originary passivity or alterity.

The "promise of truth" and the slogan "*Die Sprache verspricht (sich),*" far from envisaging a present anchored more or less securely in the task that the self ought to be, affirm an aleatory structure indissociable from iterability and the possibility of mechanical repetition, from an absolute past that has never been and will never be present. It is only through this aporetic articulation of a certain anteriority and a certain futurity that a genuine commitment in the present, here and now, stands a chance. If there is something promissory about every mark or syntagm of marks, this promise has nothing to do with a pledge that may or may not be kept. What is at issue is not simply an act taking place in the present and able to prove its promisor reliable or otherwise in the future. Rather, this promise brings together in an undecidable fashion the apparently contradictory strands of perjury and sincerity, the necessary possibility of the former constituting the positive condition of (im)possibility for the latter. Thus construed, the promise designates not an empirical modality supervening upon language but the secret and excessive origin of a speech intimately articulated, albeit in a non-dialectical way, with secrecy and silence.

In light of such a reinscription of the promise, every discursive event implies an act of faith on the side of the addressee. Inasmuch as the promise constitutes a secret that is radically heterogeneous to interpretation, appropriation, or phenomenalization, it requires that the other take on trust my declaration or promise that what I say is the truth. Derrida reflects on this demand in a discussion of testimony toward the end of "Faith and Knowledge":

> The act of faith demanded in bearing witness exceeds, through its structure, all intuition and all proof, all knowledge ("I swear that I am telling the truth, not necessarily the 'objective truth,' but the truth of what I believe to be the truth, I am telling you this truth, believe me, believe what I believe, there, where you will never be able to see nor know the irreplaceable yet universalizable, exemplary place from which I speak to you; perhaps my testimony is false, but I am sincere and in good faith, it is not false <as> testimony").

What therefore does the promise of this axiomatic (quasi-transcendental) performative do that conditions and foreshadows "sincere" declarations no less than lies and perjuries, and thus all address of the other? It amounts to saying: "Believe what I say as one believes in a miracle." Even the slightest testimony concerning the most plausible, ordinary or everyday thing cannot do otherwise: it must still appeal to faith as would a miracle.[40]

This appeal to faith is interesting for me here because it underlines the aleatory and secret character of promissory speech. The motif of faith draws attention to the irreducibility of non-presence, to the impossibility of reaching a secure conclusion in relation to the content of speech, and, by extension, to the impossibility of a rigorous division between truthfulness and perjury. Far from being a contingent infelicity attributable to human finitude, perjury positively conditions truthful discourse while also disallowing the absolute heterogeneity between speech and silence, expression and secrecy. This differential movement gives rise to a necessary but impossible promise: necessary because I promise as soon as I open my mouth and impossible by virtue of the secrecy in which it is grounded. There is always something excessive about this promissory and secret speech. There is a nonsaturability that prevents the dichotomy between speech and silence, responsibility and irresponsibility, and, by the same token, the teleological subordination of the latter to the former. One point must be made in this context in relation to the "improbable encounters" between Derrida and Ricoeur.

On account of his insistence on the necessary possibilities of non-presence, secrecy, and even death, Derrida accords some primacy to discontinuity and interruption. For singular responsibility and truthful speech to be worthy of their name, and this is a demand taking place here and now, they have to presuppose a discontinuity with a preexisting order of ethical or linguistic rules. This temporal configuration interrupts the homogeneous horizon of univocity and ethical behavior opened up by the Idea. Strangely enough, precisely because this interruption disrupts horizontal continuity and progressiveness, it safeguards the status of the Idea as *infinitely* removed and unrealizable. The infinity of the Idea depends on the radical interruption of the forward movement of teleology, and the possibility of such an interruption is supplied by Derrida's thinking of the required possibility of non-presence rather than by Ricoeur's prioritization of unification. The only chance of the Kantian Idea is given by a discontinuity suppressed by Ricoeur's dialectics but reflected on by Derrida. This observation, far from seeking to assimilate Derridean *différance* to the Kantian Idea, gestures toward a non-teleological tension intrinsic to teleology, which, in Bennington's words, "arrives at its end only by cutting itself from the end to which it is, however, constitutively tending."[41]

In addition to his emphasis on discontinuity, which alone can account for the infinity of the Idea qua origin and end-point of every teleological movement, there is another strand in Derrida that complicates his relation to hermeneutics. By scrutinizing texts and by raising critical questions, Derrida's work is marked by a compulsion toward analysis, reflection, and interpretation. Bearing in mind that one must always respect the idiomaticity of Derrida's and Ricoeur's philosophical signatures, I believe one is justified in posing, with Rodolphe Gasché, the following rhetorical question: "Can one resist the temptation of figuring it [deconstruction] as a 'hermeneutics' of some sort?"[42]

Originary Mourning: In Memory of the Absolutely Other

I have argued thus far in favor of a quasi-transcendental secrecy whereby truthfulness is always articulated with perjury. If speech constitutes, for Ricoeur, a factor mediating but also providing access to a responsible and ethical self, Derrida shows that such a process is made (im)possible by an interruptive force according to which the possibility of the worst remains an absolutely irreducible and positive condition. It is on account of the latter that Derrida holds that any address to the other implies a moment of faith that no knowledge, intuition, or proof can hope to eliminate, a structure that appears to be applicable to the relation to the other in general. Why is a moment of faith always presupposed as the "ether" of a relation to the wholly other,[43] and why can this relation not be defined simply in terms of dialectics and a teleological continuity?

The link between secrecy and the chance of authentic responsibility is exemplified in Abraham's unique relation to God as the absolutely other. *The Gift of Death* makes much of the dissymmetry between Abraham and God because this absolute heterogeneity alone can give rise to an irreplaceable self and, by extension, to a singular responsibility. Also, in the first lecture of *Mémoires: For Paul de Man* entitled "Mnemosyne," Derrida, reflecting on his late friend's survival in him and the phrase "to be" or "to speak in his memory," grounds singularity in the experience of the other's death. When one is or speaks in bereaved memory of a friend, there is little doubt that that friend is no longer alive himself or herself. What survives in me or in us is only the memory of the deceased person. The other is forever gone, "irremediably absent, annulled to the point of knowing or receiving nothing himself of what takes place in his memory"; it would be not only nonsensical but also unfaithful "to delude oneself into believing that the other living *in us* is living *in himself*" (MPM, 21). On the occasion of a friend's death, one realizes that the other is nothing outside one, and comes face to face with an irrevocable absence, an infinite alterity one is unable to comprehend. The late friend remains hidden, heterogeneous, and secret. This radical absence makes the other appear as totally other than oneself.

Such infinite alterity, which is brought home to one most clearly, but neither necessarily nor exclusively, upon someone's death, constitutes, for Derrida, the a priori requirement ensuring that the other is not reduced to a modality of the self. According to a formula well known by now, the other, in order to be worthy of the name "other," has to retain the possibility of being irreparably absent or wholly different, whether he or she is actually absent, present, dead, or alive. The corollary of this argument is the irreducibility of alterity. If Derrida's writings may be said to have an "ethical import," although this is a phrase that has to be used with the greatest vigilance, this originates in his insistence on singularity and alterity, in his tendency to resist at all costs the other's appropriation by and subordination to the self.

In the "Perhaps or Maybe" interview with Alexander Garcia Düttmann from 1996, Derrida points out that "the other, even if he or she is a finite being, is infinitely other, and this infinity is precisely what resists any reappropriation; I cannot appropriate the alterity of the other."[44] If this infinite alterity is negated, reduced, sublated, or subordinated, one runs the risk of promoting a certain homogeneity, which has serious implications for the concept of responsibility and the ethical relation itself. If the latter is not to be reduced to a mutual affirmation of moral maxims happily shared by two homologous selves, it must be grounded in the necessary possibility that the other might always behave in a way that the self cannot predict or comprehend. Absolute alterity constitutes the positive condition of a genuine relation to the other, of an authentic responsibility for and to the other.

In this respect, Derrida's thinking appears to be very close indeed to that of Lévinas, the philosopher par excellence to have devoted his writings to doing justice to the absolutely other. It is on account of Lévinas's insistence on the other's radical exteriority that Ricoeur reproaches him for promoting a hyperbolic philosophical discourse affirming an absolute break. The Lévinasian other, argues Ricoeur, absolves itself from any relation "in the same movement by which the Infinite draws free from Totality" (OA, 336). Llewelyn also confirms Lévinas's determination to avoid the Cartesian assimilation of the other to an egological consciousness by construing alterity in terms of infinite and absolute exteriority: "The Other, *Autrui*, is not simply an alter ego, an appresented analogue of myself. He and I are not equals, citizens in an intelligible kingdom of ends. We are not relatives. We are not different as chalk and cheese. There is between us, in the Hegelian phrase that Lévinas adapts, an absolute difference."[45] Similarly, in "Violence and Metaphysics," Derrida points to Lévinas's wish to underline the other's infinitely excessive character in order to distance himself from Husserl's allegedly assimilative interpretation. Lévinas construes alterity as a radical exteriority irreducible to a spatial category and resistant to any inside-outside relation.[46]

Alterity appears to belong, for Derrida too, to an *absolutely* secret and invisible order, which should be approached not on the basis of actuality or presence but in terms of an a priori necessity. The other's unmasterability has to be presupposed in order for the other to be genuinely other. Throughout his writings, Derrida seeks to respect this absolute incomprehensibility and to conceptualize the other as what must fall outside any horizon of expectation, predictability, program, theory, thematization, calculation, causality, or presentation. The word *other* must designate someone or even something that always might blow my home away.

The Gift of Death approaches absolute alterity with the help of the distinction, discussed above, between limited and absolute invisibility marked by the difference between the Latin *absconditus* and the Greek *kryptos*. This analysis forms part of the commentary on the phrase from Matthew's gospel "your father who sees in secret (*qui videt in abscondito / ho blepōn en tō kruptō*)," and leads to the affirmation of an absolute dissymmetry between self and other: the other's or God's essential invisibility falls outside the register of sight altogether, for it refers to an order incongruous with the optical dimension.[47] Derrida insists on this dissymmetry, on the self's incapacity to experience or see the other who nonetheless looks at him or her: "There is no face-to-face exchange of looks between God and myself, between the other and myself" (GD, 91). Encountering such infinite alterity, the self enters into "an absolute relation with the absolute" (GD, 73), a secret nonrelation, let me provisionally say, comparable to the one Abraham bears witness to.[48]

Such a secret nonrelation amounts to an impossible experience to the extent that the self cannot experience absolute alterity *as such*. The phrase "absolute alterity" will always be marked by indeterminacy and the other will remain endlessly out of reach, unpresentable, totally heterogeneous, and dissymmetrical to the self. Derrida remarks that death is the most tempting figure for such absolute alterity because death constitutes an impossible experience of what will remain forever hidden for a mortal.[49] In this sense, both death and alterity are likened to an ultimate and unsurpassable limit that defies comprehension by absolving itself from any relation, by radically suspending all mediation.

This impossible situation can be portrayed more or less accurately by the term *aporia*, which designates the end of the road, an absolute limit that one cannot possibly cross. If there is something eminently aporetic about the other, it is because it resists presentation and defies any attempt at comprehension. It paralyzes thought and refers one to an impracticable limit. In *Aporias*, Derrida discusses such an uncrossable border and points out that what is at issue is "a certain *impossibility* as nonviability, as nontrack or barred path. It concerns the impossible or the impracticable" (AP, 13). The secrecy of the infinitely other implies an experience of the nonpassage where one does not know where one goes. Unable to anticipate or be prepared for the coming of the other, one succumbs to the experience of absolute inaccessibility and the impossible,

> the experience of what happens [*se passe*] and is fascinating [*passionne*] in this nonpassage, paralyzing us in this separation in a way that is not necessarily negative: before a door, a threshold, a border, a line, or simply the edge or the approach of the other as such. It should be a matter of [*devrait y aller du*] what, in sum, appears to block our way or to separate us in the very place where *it would no longer be possible to constitute a problem*, a project, or a projection, that is, at the point where the very project or the problematic task becomes impossible and where we are exposed, absolutely without protection, without problem, and without prosthesis, without possible substitution, singularly exposed in our absolute and absolutely naked uniqueness, that is to say, disarmed, delivered to the other. (AP, 12)

Although it is impossible for a finite being to experience the absolutely other, the requirement of absolute alterity constitutes the positive condition of a rigorous concept of not only "otherness" but also "singular selfhood." The unicity of the "I" and the irreplaceable self, the only one that deserves to be called "singular," become possible on the basis of a radical dissymmetry. In order for the self to gather itself around itself and to become conscious of its singularity, the terrible realization of an unbridgeable chasm between self and other has to be presupposed. The self is always already "in memory of the other," for it is predicated on a logically anterior alterity.

In turn, without this originary dissymmetry, there is no ethical relation and no responsibility *stricto sensu*. One has to appeal to a radical singularity lest the concept of responsibility be reduced to a mere affirmation of ethical rules and goals the self already shares with the other. The case of Abraham exemplifies the division between, on the one hand, an absolute responsibility where one's singularity binds one to the uniquely and absolutely other, and, on the other, a compromised responsibility where one's singularity is tempered by the generality of duty and language.[50] The responsibility that the singular self ought to assume before the other is terrifying, which is why Kierkegaard speaks about the temptation of the ethical.

The other's death constitutes an occasion upon which his or her radical absence and, by extension, my singularity are brought home to me. The experience of an "in me" or "in us," discussed in *Mémoires: For Paul de Man*, becomes possible thanks to the irrevocable absence of the other who has passed away. Faced with the event of the other's death, the self comes to realize not only the necessary possibility of his or her own death but also the fact that nobody else can die in his or her place, or relieve the self from the necessity that some day he or she will die. This is what provides access to the experience of a radical singularity. Heidegger was the philosopher who put forward most unequivocally the *Jemeinigkeit* of *Dasein* in the face of death.[51]

Drawing upon Heidegger's formulation, Derrida contends that one can certainly give his or her life for me, one can die for me in a specific situation and thereby give me a little longer to live but no one can offer me immortality. This irreplaceability with respect to death is the condition of sacrifice. No one can be delivered from one's singularity in the face of death, for no one can die in someone else's place: "To have the experience of one's absolute singularity and apprehend one's own death, amounts to the same thing. Death is very much that which nobody else can undergo or confront in my place. My irreplaceability is therefore conferred, delivered, 'given,' one can say, by death" (GD, 41). The process of interiorization depends on the apprehension of one's mortality, on an act of mourning in which the self is always already involved.

How does a finite being react before the impossible experience of infinite alterity and death, of infinite alterity as death? How does one respond to the frightening dissymmetry between oneself and the unassimilable other? According to Derrida, upon the encounter with a secrecy comparable to the *mysterium tremendum* of Christianity, one weeps and trembles.[52] Unable to comprehend the impossible possibility of the other's radical absence, my finite singularity is brought home to me, and I cannot help trembling at my incapacity to confront something that remains absolutely invisible. What makes me weep upon the death of a loved one is the realization of a terrible absence and of my unbearable solitude. Such a realization brings me face to face, so to speak, with the asymmetry between my finitude and the radical alterity of the other, whose memory I nonetheless keep in myself.

The self and mourning arise at the same time upon the encounter with a possibility the self cannot comprehend. If one weeps on the occasion of a friend's death, it is because one realizes not only one's radical solitude but also that one is nothing but memory. In Derrida's words, "the 'within me' and the 'within us' acquire their sense and their bearing only by carrying within themselves the death and the memory of the other; of an other who is greater than them, greater than what they or we can bear, carry, or comprehend, since we then lament being no more than 'memory,' 'in memory' " (MPM, 33–34).

What is one to make of this scene of mourning toward which the necessary possibility of otherness and death direct one? How can one cope with this frightful knowledge? What should one do in order to remain faithful to the other's alterity, to the memory of a close friend? If the self is always a mourning self in memory of the other who can die, in bereaved memory, is there such a thing as successful or true mourning? In a way, the answer has already been given. True mourning is not possible, if by this phrase one understands a process of bereavement whereby the person in mourning would be able fully to keep the other within himself or herself. An absolutely faithful interiorization is impossible not so much because the other's radical absence reveals to me my own finitude and, therefore, the limits of my ability to explain, comprehend, remember, and mourn. But most importantly, because infinite alterity imposes an *absolute* limit upon any aspiration to a true mourning. For the word *other* to have any meaning at all, what it designates must remain totally uninteriorizable. If there is a limit to our capacity to mourn and remember, this is

> because there is something of the other, and of memory as a memo-
> ry of the other, which comes from the other and comes back to the
> other. It defies any totalization, and directs us to a scene of allegory,
> to a fiction of prosopopeia, that is, to tropologies of mourning: to
> the memory of mourning and to the mourning for memory. This
> is why there can be no *true mourning*. (MPM, 29)

Reading de Man's comments on "true mourning," Derrida affirms that the phrase can signify nothing other than "the tendency to accept incomprehension, to leave a place for it" (MPM, 31).

What I have called "a priori requirement of absolute alterity" cannot be divorced from the idea of an other "worthy of its name" that Derrida often deploys in his later writings, an idea rooted in the philosophical demand for rational scrutiny and conceptual rigor. In "Afterword: Toward an Ethic of Discussion" (1988), he apparently subscribes to the "all or nothing" logic implicit in the phrase "worthy of its name" and demanded by philosophy as a rigorous science: "Every concept that lays claim to any rigor whatsoever implies the alternative of 'all or nothing.' . . . A concept determines itself only according to 'all or nothing.' . . . It is impossible or illegitimate to form a *philosophical concept* outside this logic."[53]

The argument I would like to put forward here is that this demand for philosophical exactitude, whose corollary is the affirmation of the absolutely other, is not absent from Ricoeur's discourse. One, however, cannot identify this demand within the course of his arguments and analyses, which always favor internal, dialectical relations between the terms under discussion. Rather, one can glimpse this demand precisely in the expression "worthy of the name" that has been interrupting his hermeneutic declarations since his early work.

In *The Symbolism of Evil* (1960), for example, how is one supposed to interpret the phrase "an ethical life worthy of that name"?[54] Does not Ricoeur's text make a demand upon the reader to think of an ethical life heterogeneous to a sphere of conventional ethics and generality? Even if Ricoeur does not say so in the expression's immediate context, it seems to me that "an ethical life worthy of that name" opens up the possibility of an appeal to the reader to distinguish a radical notion of "ethical life" from a readily available and ordinary meaning. Is it possible to divorce the phrase "worthy of the name" from an invitation to think hyperbolically?[55]

Already in *History and Truth* (1955), one comes across the following sentence highly reminiscent of a Derridean conceptuality: "Every event worthy of this name . . . has an infinite capacity for shocking."[56] By associating the event with shock and infinity, this sentence disrupts the belief in a unified horizon within which a finite subject might be said to experience or even appropriate an event. An "event worthy of this name" points to the exigency of conceiving of an absolute alterity that, even though it does not appear in reality and experience, is nonetheless demanded by a rigorous philosophical logos. Isn't the invocation of the event's *infinite* capacity for shocking comparable to Lévinas's hyperbolic argumentation that Ricoeur castigates in *Oneself as Another*? His very frequent recourse to the expression "worthy of the name" bespeaks a certain appeal for conceptual exactitude not dissimilar to that attested to by Lévinas's and Derrida's affirmation of "absolute alterity." Of course, due to his allegiance to dialectics and teleology, Ricoeur would subscribe neither to the paroxysm of hyperbole nor to the abyss separating the other from the self. Nevertheless, his texts call upon the reader to think such an abyss every time they differentiate the ordinary understanding of a word from a rigorous concept worthy of its name. In this respect, his relation to Derrida and Lévinas becomes significantly more nuanced than Ricoeur would probably like to admit.[57]

An Unexperienced Experience: The Absolute *Arrivant*

Despite the impossibility of encountering alterity as such, Derrida's phrase "the other's survival in me" entails iterability and a certain memory. In this light, absolute otherness is not equivalent to the irrelation that Ricoeur reproaches Lévinas for promoting. Derrida does not construe the other *simply* in terms of absoluteness. There is another strand to his approach, according to which the epithet *irreducible* might seem a more appropriate attribute of alterity. What is exactly the relation between the two philosophers with respect to otherness? Bennington, for instance, remarks that the other in Derrida, is not *absolutely* other, as this would deny the self any access to the other whatsoever, but *irreducibly* other.[58] If this is a legitimate description, how is it possible for Derrida's writings to radicalize the Lévinasian alterity, as Bennington claims? How can Lévinas's "absolutely other" be radicalized by a thinking that robs the other of its absoluteness?

If he asserts, with Lévinas, the force and necessity of absolute alterity, Derrida never loses sight of the impasses inherent in this assertion. With the aim of exploring these impasses, he has recourse, strangely enough, to Husserl. Here is a passage that signals the intricate relation between the three thinkers:

> What I have in common with Lévinas, as a common reference, is that I read Husserl intensely. In his *Cartesian Meditations* Husserl says that the *alter ego* can never become the object of a full intuition. I can have no direct access to what the other lives in him or herself, that is something which remains absolutely inaccessible for me, at least in the form of intuition. . . . What you live on your side I cannot share, [given] that here and now I occupy this absolute zero point, and that yours is infinitely different from mine. (PM, 13)

This passage alerts one to both an affinity and a difference between Derrida and Lévinas, which will reveal a further discrepancy between Derrida and Ricoeur. Firstly, although both Derrida and Lévinas read Husserl intensely, the former cautiously underlines that, for Husserl, the other's experience *in the form of intuition*, the other's experience *as such*, is "absolutely inaccessible" and "infinitely different" from mine. Secondly, Derrida's discovery of irreducible alterity in Husserl appears to be at odds with Ricoeur's view that Husserlian "appresentation" assimilates the other to the ego. Appresentation was claimed to valorize resemblance, and Ricoeur admitted that, at the gnoseological level, this is indeed a productive and justifiable operation. In addition, Ricoeur observed that Lévinas complains that Husserl's appresentation reduces the other to a phenomenon for the ego, thereby neutralizing its absolute alterity, a complaint that Derrida does not simply dismiss.

In contrast, however, to both Ricoeur and Lévinas, Derrida simultaneously argues not only that such a construal of appresentation does not do justice to the pains that Husserl took in order to respect otherness, but also that Lévinas's "absolutely other," far from operating at a totally different level from Husserl's, as Ricoeur would have it, presupposes the phenomenological analysis. Husserl's reflection on appresentation posits that the other as transcendental other, as another absolute origin and another zero point, cannot be given to the ego in an original and self-evident way. The introduction of "appresentation" marks a difference from originary intuition and highlights the alterity of the other's experience:

> The necessary reference to analogical appresentation, far from signifying an analogical and assimilatory reduction of the other to the same, confirms and respects separation, the unsurpassable necessity of (nonobjective) mediation. If I did not approach the other by way of analogical appresentation, if I attained to the other

immediately and originally, silently, in communion with the other's own experience, the other would cease to be the other. Contrary to appearances, the theme of appresentative transposition translates the recognition of the radical separation of the absolute origins, the relationship of absolved absolutes and nonviolent respect for the secret: the opposite of victorious assimilation. (VM, 124)

Derrida supports his claim by appealing to Husserl's distinction between humans and things as far as their alterity is concerned. Both natural things and human beings constitute transcendent bodies that present only one aspect of them at a time. My intuition of them cannot be complete and totalizing, for there is always something about them that remains hidden from my perception and that is indicated only by anticipation or analogy. There is, however, a crucial difference: on the one hand, the alterity of things is grounded in the fact that my perception remains infinitely incomplete at a time, but the possibility of an original presentation of their hidden aspects is always open; on the other hand, the other's alterity does not result from my incomplete perspectival intuition but from my inability to go around to see things from the other side, from the impossibility of experiencing what the other experiences himself or herself. A double alterity is at stake in the case of other humans: that of another body over there and the more radical alterity of an absolutely and irreducibly other zero point. In Derrida's words, "[T]he stranger is infinitely other because by his essence no enrichment of his profile can give me the subjective face of his experience *from his perspective*, such as he has lived it. Never will this experience be given to me originally, like everything which is *mir eigenes*, which is *proper* to me" (VM, 124).

Derrida underlines nonetheless that these two types of otherness must be thought together because the other's alterity would not even emerge without the alterity of bodies. By designating the other as an "alter ego," Husserl does not compromise his or her alterity. He thinks of the other in terms of an intentional modification of the ego, thereby taking into account the fact of a minimal phenomenalizability without which the other could not even appear before the ego as other. "Alter ego" and "appresentation" do not negate alterity, as attested to by the word "alter" and the prefix "ap-." "Alter ego" cannot be treated as if "alter" were just an epithet of a real subject, an accidental modification of a real identity: "The transcendental syntax of the expression *alter ego* tolerates no relationship of substantive to adjective, of absolute to epithet, in one sense or the other. This is its strangeness. A necessity due to the finitude of meaning: the other is absolutely other only if he is an ego, that is, in a certain way, if he is the same as I" (VM, 127).

On this reading, "alter ego" and "appresentation" gesture toward the impossibility of a complete mediation between self and other, while allowing for a minimal experience of the other. Ricoeur also affirms a similar impossibility, which he attributes to a factical necessity teleologically organized by an ideally infinite demand. Derrida, by contrast, by arguing that the other's infinite alterity must be given in a finite phenomenality, reverses the order of priority of the finite and the infinite, the empirical and the transcendental, and promotes an uncanny co-implication of possibility and impossibility.

It would be impossible to encounter the other, to respect it in experience and language if there were not some type of evidence of him or her. The other cannot be absolutely and infinitely other for fear of remaining completely hidden from the self. Such absolute alterity, however, is required a priori in order for the other to be worthy of its name. This double exigency motivates the phrase "irreducibly other," which designates that which the ego can never be but also that which appears before the ego, although never as such. Paradoxically, what becomes an intentional phenomenon for the ego is the impossibility of the other's transparent phenomenality. In this sense, alterity is essentially irreducible although it loses the absolute character of a positive plenitude attributed to it by Lévinas.

Does the affirmation of phenomenalizability commit a certain type of violence against the other? One could say that this is indeed the case on condition that one take into account that any discourse on alterity cannot help presupposing a minimal phenomenality without which one could not possibly think, speak, or write about the other. Whether one acknowledges the necessity of this originary violence or not, the other is never absolutely other but is always minimally phenomenalizable, capable of being exteriorized and transposed into the realm of space and light, which does not amount to saying that its alterity is negated or reduced. Its *irreducible* alterity can appear on the basis of this possibility alone, or, in other words, its radical dissymmetry from the self is possible on the basis of a minimal symmetry.[59]

To purport to leave the other unaffected by denying it the possibility of becoming a phenomenon for the ego, is this not the worst form of violence to the extent that it deprives the other of any relationality to the self? For Derrida, Lévinas's criticism of the Husserlian "alter ego" and refusal to attribute an egoity to the other constitute acts of a worse type of violence than the pre-ethical violence involved in the other's minimal phenomenality: "To refuse to see in it [the other] an ego in this sense is, within the ethical order, the very gesture of all violence. If the other was not recognized as ego, its entire alterity would collapse" (VM, 125). Why? Because, if the other were absolutely exterior to the ego, if it remained totally and safely unrelated to the self, then a stable identity could be ascribed to it, so it would end up being absolutely the same.

In order to be radically other, in order not to collapse to a modality of the same, the other would have to give up its positive self-identity, which is to say that it would have to be contaminated by the ego. Without such a parasitical commingling, the absolutely other and the absolutely same would be paradoxically one and the same thing. On this point Derrida concurs with Ricoeur who points out that, if Lévinas describes the other in terms of exteriority and irrelation, it is because he conceives of the ego already on the basis of sameness, identity, and, as a result, infinite separation from the other.[60] The only way of resisting endorsing self-identity is to affirm a co-implication of self and other, something that Husserl has successfully done by deploying the terms *ego* and *alter ego*. The infinitely other

> can be what it is only if it is other, that is, other *than*. Other than must be *other than* myself. Henceforth, it is no longer absolved of a relation to an ego. Therefore, it is no longer infinitely, absolutely other. It is no longer what it is. If it was absolved, it would not be the other either, but the Same. (2) The infinitely other cannot be what it is—infinitely other—except by being absolutely not the same. That is, in particular, by being other than itself (non ego). Being other than itself, it is not what it is. Therefore, it is not infinitely other, etc. (VM, 126)

Allowing for the possibility of gaining access to the egoity of the alter ego turns out to be the most peaceful gesture possible providing that one affirm, at the same time, the other's irreducible alterity. Derrida admits that it is always a matter of an economy of violence, as there is no pure peacefulness or nonviolence. Admitting to the possibility of the other's appearing on the basis of its "face" as a nonphenomenal phenomenon, and to the possibility of speaking of the other as radically other, is a relatively nonviolent gesture, even though it entails a certain "pre-ethical violence" (VM, 128–29).

By thus de-absolutizing alterity, Derrida refuses to subordinate it to the reign of the same. As a consequence, his thinking effects a radicalization of Lévinas's absolutizing reflection. The paradoxical character of this gesture is that the *irreducibly other* turns out to be, simultaneously, more and less other than the Lévinasian *absolutely other*: more other because, insofar as it is always already contaminated by the self, it cannot be subsumed under the category of the same; less other because it is not approached simply in terms of absolute alterity. This uncanny "less is more" logic, which cannot be divorced from *différance*, will help me below to flesh out the interrupting negotiation between self and other that Derrida puts forward.

"Violence and Metaphysics" argues that Lévinas, despite his declarations, presupposes the other's phenomenalizability by virtue of resorting to philosophical discourse and spatial conceptuality. Derrida recognizes that Lévinas, aware that the term *exteriority* neutralizes absolute alterity as it describes a spatial relation between an inside and an outside, was reluctant, over a certain period of time, to deploy this concept.[61] In *Totality and Infinity*, however, Lévinas makes abundant use of this term, whose signified content he strives to extricate from all spatial determination. If space is the site of the same, he tries to show that true exteriority is not spatial: while retaining the word *exteriority*, he endeavors to obliterate its ordinary meaning by contending that genuine exteriority is not spatial, that its truth is its nontruth, thereby acknowledging the necessity of having recourse to the language of totality in order to state infinite alterity as what exceeds totality. In spite of admitting to the impossibility of thinking alterity outside language, his discourse remains optimistic that a rigorous philosophical *logos* would be able to wrest the other from a conceptuality that correlates exteriority and spatiality.

What is one to make of Lévinas's deployment of an existing word in order to refer to what lies beyond the realm of the same and being, *epekeina tēs ousias*? Does his gesture not exemplify the trope of catachresis, which designates the abusive inscription of a sign, the imposition of a sign upon a meaning that does not have its own proper sign in language? Does such a catachrestic movement not entail an act of violence against the other at the very moment it purports to respect its alterity?

One of the paradoxical aspects of this catachresis is that, by using the *signifier* "exteriority" and by seeking to displace its usual spatial *meaning*, Lévinas inadvertently confirms the outside-inside spatial structure that exteriority as otherness was supposed to dislocate. To the extent that he has to use an already existing sensible form (the signifier "exteriority") in order to *exteriorize* an *interior* content (the signified "absolutely other"), no matter what he claims that content to be, Lévinas cannot help subscribing to the traditional, and to a certain extent inevitable, determination of language on the basis of the opposition between signifier and signified, the sensible and the intelligible, outside and inside. As a result, "absolute alterity," if it has any meaning at all, and given that meaning designates the interior sense of a sensible form, has to submit itself to a law of spatial relationality inseparable from language.

Commenting on such catachresis or forced metaphor, Derrida admits to the necessity of the other's expatriation into the realm of language, to the originary metaphoricity that precedes the distinction between the literal and the metaphorical:

> That it is necessary to state infinity's *excess* over totality *in* the language of totality; that it is necessary to state the other in the language of the Same; that it is necessary to think *true* exteriority as non-*exteriority*, that is, still by means of the Inside-Outside structure and by spatial metaphor; and that it is necessary still to inhabit the metaphor in ruins, to dress oneself in tradition's shreds and the devil's patches—all this means, perhaps, that there is no

philosophical logos which must not *first* let itself be expatriated into
the structure Inside-Outside. This deportation from its own site
toward the Site, toward spatial locality is the *metaphor* congenital to
the philosophical logos. Before being a rhetorical procedure within
language, metaphor would be the emergence of language itself. And
philosophy is only this language.[62] (VM, 112)

Lévinas is oblivious not to the necessity of transposing the other into the
determinate sphere of language but to the *implications* of this necessity, which
results in the following paradox. On the one hand, out of respect for alterity
and singularity, he conceives of the other as the absolute or positive infinite,
as what is beyond being. He dreams of a heterological thought delivered from
the constraints of discourse, of "a *pure* thought of *pure* difference" (VM, 151).
On the other hand, by speaking and writing about the other, Lévinas betrays
his heterological wish, for he introduces alterity into a discourse that is general-
izing, classifying, and reductive. Although he wishes to avoid encroaching on
the other's infinity, he commits an act of violence as soon as he articulates its
absolute alterity with finitude and determinateness.

If the infinitely other *as such* is simply impossible, unthinkable, and unut-
terable, naming it or attributing to it the epithets *infinite* or *absolute* translates it
into language, thereby robbing it of its freedom and positive infinity. The very
idea of a "positive infinity" is a contradiction in terms to the extent that there
is something essentially negative about "infinity," which, after all, designates
the *non*-finite. In order to be what it is, absolute and infinite, the other has
to submit itself to the law of language, and therefore to give up, to a certain
degree, both its absoluteness and its alleged positivity. In Derrida's words, "[T]he
other cannot be what it is, infinitely other, except in finitude and mortality
(mine *and* its). It is such as soon as it comes into language, of course, and only
then, and only if the word *other* has a meaning" (VM, 114–15). If *Totality and
Infinity* challenges the totalizing thought of Western ontology by focusing on
a positive infinite that exceeds this thought, Derrida, notes Bernasconi, draws
this challenge back within the sphere of philosophy and finitude.[63]

The other's absoluteness is betrayed as soon as alterity enters discourse,
and this betrayal cannot fail to remind one of Abraham's situation: he keeps
silent because language would betray his absolute singularity by transposing
him and his responsibility into the general and the universal. Here is Derrida
reflecting on such pre-ethical violence and the corollary de-absolutization
of alterity:

How to think the other, if the other can be spoken only as exteriority and through exteriority, that is, nonalterity? And if the
speech which must inaugurate and maintain absolute separation

is by its essence rooted in space, which cannot conceive separation and absolute alterity? . . . Does this not mean that discourse is
originally violent? And that the philosophical logos, the only one
in which peace may be declared, is inhabited by war? The distinction between discourse and violence always will be an inaccessible
horizon. Nonviolence would be the telos, and not the essence of
discourse. (VM, 116)

The diagnosis of this originary violence is not intended to make a case in
favor of silence. As already stressed, silence will never be justified, and Derrida
notes that "*finite* silence is also the medium of violence" (VM, 117). The point
is to show that it is always a matter of violence against violence, of an economy
of violence that is the only reasonable way of avoiding a good conscience. The
detection of violence at the source of discourse underscores the necessity not
only of resorting to language in order to think and speak about the other,
but also of compromising, however minimally, the other's absolute alterity on
account of its very transposition into discourse. Philosophical reflection on alterity cannot help the violence of linguistic expression and, as a result, can make
no pretence to a good conscience and a supposedly nonviolent irenics.

Nevertheless, this is not to suggest that "Violence and Metaphysics"
amounts to a critique of Lévinas, and I share Bernasconi's reservations about
commentators who insist that Derrida is arguing *against* Lévinas.[64] Firstly,
Derrida, as I showed in the last section, affirms the necessity of Lévinas's appeal
to an unthinkable, impossible, and unsayable alterity. Secondly, Lévinas was
himself aware of the difficulty of reconciling the demand of such infinite alterity with the fact that this demand has to be stated in the language of totality.
Accordingly, in "On the Trail of the Other" (1963), for instance, he poses the
following question: "Must it be that, up against the primarily unthinkable,
against transcendence and otherness, we give up philosophizing?"[65] Similarly,
in *Totality and Infinity*, one comes across the phrase "the infinite in the finite,"
which clearly recognizes a certain contact between self and other, and which,
moreover, is reminiscent of Derrida's declaration that "*the infinite* differance
[*sic*] *is finite*" (SP, 102).[66] It is in this light that Derrida underlines that his
commentary on the implications of Lévinas's discourse does not constitute a
critique: "We are not denouncing, here, an incoherence of language or a contradiction in the system. We are wondering about the meaning of a necessity:
the necessity of lodging oneself within traditional conceptuality in order to
destroy it" (VM, 111).[67]

Derrida's reflection accounts *simultaneously* for the necessity and the impossibility of thinking the infinitely other. The difficulty here is that the requirement
of absolute alterity is interlaced *with* the impossibility of having access to it, or,
in other words, the other's minimal phenomenalizability is always commingled

with the impossibility of the other appearing as such. This "with" does not point to two distinct modes of experiencing the other. Rather, it splits the instant into two and resists determining the other on the basis of identity, presentation, and experience. The other can be described as "the possibility of an impossibility" in more or less the same way in which Derrida delineates time and death by deploying this paradoxical phrase in "*Ousia* and *Grammē*" and *Aporias* respectively.[68] That the wholly other should remain unassimilable and unidentifiable is the positive condition of a genuine ethical relation, a structure that points toward an incalculable futurity. In order to allow for this imminence, for this coming of the other as an event for which I cannot possibly prepare myself and which has to take me completely by surprise, Derrida has recourse to various terms such as the perhaps, the event, the messianic, and the *arrivant*.

In *Aporias*, "the absolute *arrivant*" refers to what exceeds any horizon of expectation or identification, to an unpredictable event that one has to welcome without any assurance whatsoever. It implies a moment of absolute risk where even the possibility of the worst cannot be eliminated, although this possibility constitutes the positive condition of the better, the condition of ethics and politics. This is why the ethical relation implies a moment of faith where absolute nonrelation and interruption remain irreducible. The wholly other qua absolute *arrivant* is neither a friend nor an enemy. It is a figure without a face that defies any attempt at identification and undermines the conventional notion of the threshold or the border as a clear-cut demarcation line separating two distinct localities:

> [The absolute *arrivant*] surprises the host—who is not yet a host
> or an inviting power—enough to call into question, to the point
> of annihilating or rendering indeterminate, all the distinctive signs
> of a prior identity, beginning with the very border that delineated
> a legitimate home. . . . The absolute *arrivant* does not yet have a
> name or an identity. It is not an invader or an occupier, nor is it
> a colonizer, even if it can also become one. This is why I call it
> simply the *arrivant*, and not someone or something that arrives, a
> subject, a person, an individual, or a living thing. (AP, 34)

The wholly other constitutes a structure where the necessary possibility of inaccessibility is commingled with the chance of the coming of a friend, a chance nonetheless prevented from ever acquiring the status of an actual presence.

One's peculiar relation to the *arrivant* can be thought of in terms of "a relation without relation" or "an unexperienced experience," expressions intended to maintain the requirement that the other both remain absolutely beyond reach and be minimally accessible.[69] Such coupling of necessity and possibility implies an aleatory futurity, which the terms *relation* and *experience* fall short of accounting for as they cannot be disengaged from the values of presence and continuity. If experience, for example, always refers to the perception of an identical phenomenon,[70] "an unexperienced experience" designates a relation to something that remains phenomenalizable although it cannot be experienced as such. At issue here are not *two* distinct experiences. Rather, an unexperienced experience, which entails iterability, alterity, and the spacing movement of temporalization, constitutes the only chance of a self-evident experience, while disallowing the latter's construal in terms of actuality and plenitude. The experience of this aporia is the sine qua non of so-called experience and not the other way round, hence Derrida's rhetorical question: "Is an experience possible that would not be an experience of the aporia?" (AP, 15).

Taking into account the a priori requirement of absolute difference, Derrida allows for the possibility that the other may lack qualities such as subjectivity, humanity, and language. If these qualities are maintained, the other is reduced to a more or less determinable figure and, therefore, its alterity and the ethical relation itself are inevitably compromised. In "Perhaps or Maybe," he notes that, if I am sure

> that the other is a subject, then their surprise is under control: as a subject with a name or an identity the subject is identical with him or herself and, no matter how surprising they may be, if a human subject their surprise will be under control to some extent. Whereas the alterity I am referring to under the modality of maybe is perhaps radically inhuman, radically non-subjective, a non-subject. (PM, 4)

This corroborates the claim that the configuration of the wholly other radicalizes the thinking of alterity to such a degree that it complicates the ordinary understanding of the threshold or the border, and, as a result, the opposition between the human and the animal, or even the living and the nonliving, which has serious implications for one's responsibility toward the environment and animals.

Most discourses on ethics and responsibility, failing to take into consideration the irreducibly other, tend to embrace what Derrida terms a "sacrificial structure," which authorizes a noncriminal putting to death of animals while strictly prohibiting the murder of human beings.[71] Even Lévinas's philosophy, despite his laudable intention to respect alterity and to disrupt a traditional humanism, remains profoundly humanistic inasmuch as it does not sacrifice sacrifice and conceives the injunction "Thou shalt not kill" as prohibiting the murder of the other person and not of the living in general.[72] A similar argument holds for Ricoeur's reflection on selfhood, where the other is always the counterpart of a self construed on the basis of the question "Who?" And even when Ricoeur uses "otherness" to designate the passivity of the flesh and conscience, still, the latter constitute modalities of an alterity strictly applicable to human beings rather than animals. By contrast, an unconditional affirmation of the other would require that alterity remain irreducible to the otherness of another self, a subject, an ego, a human being, or someone capable of speech. The other calls me but the origin of this call must remain secret. If this is not the case, a homogeneity is established and the ethical relation is reduced to a programmatic and administrative enterprise.[73]

In *Counterpath: Traveling with Jacques Derrida*, Catherine Malabou has recourse to Derrida's term *non-arrival* (*le non arrivé*) in order to refer to this impossibility of identification and points to its curious indissociability from the absolute *arrivant*. To the extent that the "wholly other" is someone or something with no name, no identity, no proper place or country of origin, it designates what can never happen or arrive as such. In this paradoxical sense, the *arrivant* entails non-place and non-arrival, for it never properly arrives. At the same time, this very non-arrival constitutes the condition of possibility of the *arrivant*, thereby giving rise to the chance of the coming of the other, of ethics and politics. The chance of the event of the other originates in the impossibility of its full arrival, in a non-arrival that does not assume the status of a proper origin insofar as it is a non-place:

> Non-arrival can indeed be thought of as a point of departure, as departure from and resource for every event. But this chance is precisely not an origin from which what arrives derives. Non-arrival designates a non-place in the place and stead of the origin. In a sense this non-place is a *principle*. But it is a matter of a non-archeological *arkhē*, an an-archic archaism, in the double sense of a-principial and an-archivable. . . . An origin from which nothing can derive is obviously *atopian* and *anachronic*: it has neither place nor time. The origin of the event allows itself to be conceived of, therefore, as a non-place in space and as a non-time in time, as the very possibility, for the present of the now, of disjointing itself and detaching itself from itself.[74]

Thus construed, the sole chance of the wholly other is that it both arrive and not fully arrive, that it arrive without arriving, that it appear without presenting itself. The difficulty here is not only to think radical alterity by grasping together necessity and chance as a structure that lies beyond being, philosophical logos, and thought, but also to signal that this "beyond" does not submit itself to a logic of negativity or contradiction. Such a configuration of the other undermines the ordinary concept of the border or the limit and complicates as much the dialectical and continuist interpretation of the ethical relation as the watertight division between gnoseological necessity and ethical requirement.

Expropriation

Derrida's reflection on the absolute *arrivant* complicates a series of dialectical oppositions endorsed by Ricoeur's hermeneutics of the self such as singularity and generality, possibility and impossibility, finitude and infinity. The logic of the *arrivant* alone is able to make possible a singular self, while also respecting the other's singularity. The only chance of a rigorous concept of "singularity," of a singular decision and an uncompromised responsibility, depends on the necessary possibility of a radical interruption. In order to do justice to this essential moment of interruption and to the necessity of a minimal phenomenalizability, Derrida refers to the structure of an originary mourning whereby the self keeps within himself or herself an incomprehensible other. The latter's survival in me renders problematic the singular selfhood it makes possible, and bears witness to a *différance* of selfhood and alterity, singularity and generalizability. The relation without relation to the wholly other entails expropriation, as a result of which the other's survival in me cannot be regarded as the inclusion of a fantasy in a narcissistic subject closed upon itself.

This trace of the unassimilable other within me upsets the idea of a dialectical constitution of selfhood, for it implies a heterogeneity that forestalls a continuous and uninterrupted identity. Singularity is predicated upon discontinuity and iterability, which makes the singular self and the wholly other (im)possible. A specular relationship is revealed, one that displaces and precludes the self's totalizing gathering around itself. Here is Derrida on this specularity upon a friend's death:

> Upon the death of the other we are given to memory, and thus to interiorization, since the other, outside us, is now nothing. And with the dark light of this nothing, we learn that the other resists the closure of our interiorizing memory. With the nothing of this irrevocable absence, the other appears *as* other, and as other for us, upon his death or at least in the anticipated possibility of a death, since death constitutes and makes manifest the limits of a *me* or an *us* who are obliged to harbor something that is greater and other than them; something *outside of them within them*. (MPM, 34)

A large part of "Mnemosyne" is devoted to the commingling of the possibility of selfhood and the impossibility of "an anamnesic totalization of self," as well as to the ways in which de Man addressed this aporetic but inevitable process in some of his writings on autobiography.

The self's (de)constitution by the other's survival in it does not point to a peaceful coexistence of alterity and selfhood, nor is it a site of war and violence. Rather, it provides access to a singularized self as the effect of a differential trace. The alterity that *re-marks* one's identity right from the beginning renders concepts such as "subject," "ego," and "self" inadequate. If the singular self is grounded in a necessary possibility of non-presence it harbors within itself, it has to be less itself in order to stand a chance of becoming more singularly itself. This peculiar "less is more" logic infinitely complicates the hermeneutic belief in the self's dialectical augmentation, as it couples the possibility of the greatest profit to that of the greatest privation.[75]

This is what Derrida's untranslatable formula *"L'Un se garde de l'autre"* from *Archive Fever* encapsulates. One has to protect oneself from the wholly other, whose status as *arrivant* cannot eliminate the possibility that he or she might be a murderer. Simultaneously, one has to keep that other within oneself, being thereby expropriated by the very condition that can provide one's singularity. At issue is an aleatory movement that denies either the self or the other any definitive identity, and that replaces the idea of an absolute heterogeneity between them with that of an undecidable *différance*:

> As soon as there is the One, there is murder, wounding, traumatism. *L'Un se garde de l'autre.* The One guards against/keeps some of the other. It protects *itself* from the other, but, in the movement of this jealous violence, it comprises in itself, thus guarding it, the self-otherness or self-difference (the difference from within oneself) which makes it One. The "One differing, deferring from itself." The One as the Other. At once, at the same time, but in a same time that is out of joint, the One forgets to remember itself to itself, it keeps and erases the archive of this injustice that it is. (AF, 78)

"L'Un se garde de l'autre" captures the aporetic movement whereby one's singularity is anchored in something greater than oneself, in a greater other that expropriates one's unicity the very moment it makes its emergence possible. This chance of a singular self, argues Derrida, "cannot be absolutely stabilized in the form of the subject. The subject assumes presence, that is to say sub-stance, stasis, stance. Not to be able to stabilize itself *absolutely* would mean to be able *only* to be stabilizing itself. Ex-appropriation [*sic*] no longer closes itself; it never totalizes itself."[76] The trace of the other in me undercuts the notions of substratum, stability, or selfhood, for it takes seriously into consideration the wholly other qua originary passivity and possibility of the worst violence. Nevertheless, this possibility and the concomitant expropriation are not negative

limits. They constitute the conditions of a genuine relation to the other and of a responsibility irreducible to a calculative application of rules. The possibility of the worst, which turns out to be the positive condition for the better, cannot be teleologically organized in terms of a merely factical necessity looking forward to an infinite conceptual possibility, as is the case in Ricoeur.

The adverb *perhaps* is also used to portray this expropriating process that may give rise, here and now, to a singularly responsible self. The latter, however, cannot be construed as an autonomous subject, consciousness, will, action, decision, etc., as this would rob it of its structurally necessary "perhapsness." Derrida describes the disseminal identity the perhaps makes (im)possible as follows:

> The perhaps does not only condition the possibility of the coming of some*one*, but the coming of a plurality of some*ones*, and the possibility for me to be more or less than one. The polarity of subject and object reduces the perhaps, there is no perhaps in the subject-object correlation. The perhaps implies that others are plural singularities, and that on my side too there are pluralities of singularities—this isn't simply a formal way of putting it, I have the experience of "myself" as a multiplicity of places, images, imagos, there are others in me, I have experienced mourning where the other is in me, there is more than one other, we are numerous in ourselves, and there are a number of singularities over there, and that's why there is a perhaps, and why there are questions of ethics and politics. (PM, 13)

How is one to understand such a plural self including within itself a multiplicity of singular others that nonetheless must remain outside itself? Which is the best way to think about this specular *différance* between self and other? Since this specularity has been shown to defy the oppositional logic of speculative thought, and in light of the fact that philosophical logos is indissociable from such a logic, one has to resort to tropology and mythology in order to say the unsayable, in order to respect the impossible but necessary relation resulting from the perhaps.[77]

Accordingly, Derrida refers to the figure of prosopopeia that de Man discerns in William Wordsworth's "Essays upon Epitaphs," whose overarching metaphor is that of the journey of the contemplative soul compared to the sun in motion.[78] Reflecting on the relationship between the sun and the text of the epitaph, upon the *speaking* stone counterbalancing the *seeing* sun, de Man underlines that in this metaphorics, which "passes from sun to eye to language as name and as voice," the pivotal trope is that of prosopopeia. The latter designates "the fiction of an apostrophe to an absent, deceased, or voiceless entity, which posits the possibility of the latter's reply and confers upon it the power of speech."[79] If this tropological structure exemplifies the specularity (de)constitutive of selfhood, it is not simply because it points to the prosopopeia of the seeing sun looking down and conferring a face and a voice upon the epitaph. It is because it reveals what de Man elsewhere calls "a prosopopeia of prosopopeia": it is the naked name as the text on the stone that makes possible the face and eye of the sun. De Man's exegesis stresses the centrality of "the fiction of the voice-from-beyond-the-grave," and affirms that "an unlettered stone would leave the sun suspended in nothingness."[80]

There is no cause and effect relation here. The seeing sun is not the constituting provenance of the speaking stone. Nor is it the case that the text of the senseless epitaph enjoys a temporal anteriority with respect to the sun as a face that looks down on it. The "prosopopeia of prosopopeia" announces an abysmal co-implication originating in the impossible but necessary possibility of death and alterity, of death as alterity. It is in this sense that prosopopeia "deals with the giving and taking away of faces, with face and deface, *figure*, figuration and disfiguration."[81]

Ever since his first published texts, Derrida has been attentive to specularity or reflexivity as the quasi-transcendental condition of identity. In *Of Grammatology*, for instance, he maintains:

> There are things like reflecting pools, and images, an infinite reference from one to the other, but no longer a source, a spring. There is no longer a simple origin. For what is reflected is split *in itself* and not only as an addition to itself of its image. The reflection, the image, the double, splits what it doubles. The origin of the speculation becomes a difference. What can look at itself is not one; and the law of the addition of the origin to its representation, of the thing to its image, is that one plus one makes at least three. The historical usurpation and theoretical oddity that install the image within the rights of reality are determined as the *forgetting* of a simple origin.[82]

The wholly other does not amount to a simple origin but to an absolute secret giving rise to mourning, to the undecidable and specular (de)constitution of both self and other. The oppositional determination of source and reflection is, therefore, replaced by an aleatory reflexivity that divides what it constitutes the very moment of constituting it. Gasché remarks that reflexivity, thus interpreted, becomes the end of reflection and speculation in the ordinary sense of these words, for "it opens itself up to the thought of an alterity, a difference that remains unaccounted for by the polar opposition of source and reflection, principle and what is derived from it, the one and the Other."[83]

If Derrida's approach to the ethical relation stresses the necessity of interruption and articulates infinity with finitude, how exactly does it differ from Ricoeur's thinking, which would subscribe to both of these gestures? Ricoeur postulates a sphere of principle comprising the Kantian Idea of the good life as an infinite aim regulating a horizon within which the dialectic between selfhood and otherness takes place. Because complete mediation is out of the question, owing to the ineluctable fact of human finitude, the horizon is defined in terms of an infinite progress toward the Idea, which is to say that the finite domain is teleologically determined as always looking forward to an unrealizable *telos*. Such an account takes into consideration the need for the process toward infinity to be *empirically* discontinued. The very characterization of this progress in terms of infinity allows for interruptions here and there, for, if the infinite goal were ever to be actually reached, the idea of infinite progress would be automatically paralyzed.

For Derrida, however, it is not just a case of a progressive movement empirically interrupted every now and then but tending nonetheless asymptotically toward an infinitely distant ideal presence. Rather, *différance* points to a movement that allows for the other's infinite alterity, thereby giving rise to a genuine ethical responsibility, but that also prevents such responsibility, in principle and in fact, from acquiring the status of a full presence. The interruption here is not something contingent that happens *après coup* to an ideally infinite progress, but constitutes the necessary and positive condition of the very ideality and infinity of this progress. This interruptive structure results in a disjointed temporality that radically discontinues, *right from the beginning*, the process Ricoeur describes. By grounding infinite alterity and singular responsibility in the necessary possibility of difference, non-presence, death, and, in the final analysis, finitude, Derrida assigns to the latter not only a temporal but also a logical priority. As a consequence, he infiltrates infinity with finitude in such a way that the dichotomy between an infinite ideal and a field of factical experience becomes untenable. Derrida does not simply accentuate the role of an empirical finitude that Ricoeur's emphasis on the infinite task of reason possibly underplays. Although it is true that he strategically promotes finitude from its status as a negative fact to an indispensable condition, the necessary (im)possibility of difference radically blurs the borderline between the finite and the infinite, the empirical and the transcendental.

Ideal infinity is not conceived now in opposition to a finitude that is the necessary but negative pole of the binary. To the extent that infinite alterity has to appear before finite thought, it must be anchored in the order of finitude and phenomenality. Infinity as such cannot become the object of a finite consciousness, for it refers precisely to something that transcends the limits of empirical existence. In order to appear before consciousness, infinity has to give up its assuchness, its absolute character; it must subject itself to a finite form, which, paradoxically, becomes its quasi-transcendental provenance. Derrida's cryptic remark "*the infinite* differance [*sic*] *is finite*" signals his belief in an essential co-implication of the finite and the infinite that interrupts their teleological interpretation on the basis of an opposition between the potential and the actual, negativity and positivity, the contingent and the essential.

According to this gesture, absolute alterity and singular responsibility are inseparable from the requirement of infinite interruption; the latter, however, is grounded in facticity and finitude. The *thought* of infinity can only be promised in the finite, hence the exigency of some phenomenalizability and the configuration of this complex structure as an essential (im)possibility. If *différance* cannot be assimilated to the Idea in the Kantian sense, it is because it points to a necessary and a priori contamination, thereby radicalizing the relation between the two poles of any opposition and rendering their distinction impossible. This impossibility leads to a radical interruption of teleology, an interruption that does not befall a forward movement already on its way to a *telos*. *Différance* implies an absolutely irreducible interruption that, despite giving rise to effects of finitude and infinity, on which the thought of a continuous temporal process depends, disallows the pure and simple identity of these terms and infiltrates the very concept of continuity with a more originary discontinuity. The infinity of the progress toward the Idea is interrupted from the very beginning by virtue of its being rooted in a quasi-transcendental finitude. This thinking alone of the relation between the finite and the infinite can allow for a radical singularity worthy of its name and for the event of a singular decision, while simultaneously excluding the possibility of a conclusive de facto identification of a decision as ethical or otherwise.

Conclusion

Throughout this study, I have been concerned with exploring the difference between the thought of Ricoeur and Derrida, which, I have suggested, should be regarded through the prism of improbable encounters rather than a dialogue, a debate, or a confrontation. The first chapter demonstrated that, despite following Husserl in affirming the primacy of temporal continuity over against discontinuity, Ricoeur is dissatisfied with the phenomenological emphasis on a self-sufficient and self-constituting time-consciousness. He taps the resources of Freudian psychoanalysis precisely in order to question the sovereignty of the living present by admitting to the necessity and anteriority of unconscious activity with respect to conscious transparency. The perceptual present is now replaced by a reflective present posited as a task and pursued jointly by the analysand and the analyst. Reflective consciousness, then, arises as a philosophical configuration that admits to an ineluctable non-presence, which it nonetheless places under the service of an anticipated meaningfulness. The continuity between the *impossibility* of completely appropriating the meaning of unconscious impulses and the *possibility* of a progressive movement toward a limit-idea depends on the dialectical interpretation of a range of psychoanalytical terms such as perception and memory, consciousness and the unconscious, reality and pleasure, life and death.

A similar dialectical teleology was revealed by the exegesis of Ricoeur's hermeneutics of the self. In the first instance, Ricoeur affirms both the mediation of the speaking subject by language and the singularizing role of the instance of discourse. Subsequently, he discusses other types of mediation, whereby identity is destabilized by various factors such as time, textuality, finitude, and the alterity of other persons. These mediations result in a disappropriated self that has very little in common with the *solus ipse* of what Ricoeur calls "Husserlian egology." In the second instance of what turns out to be a twofold process, the reappropriated self, which becomes an ambition rather than a given, is posited as a *telos* never to be actually attained but regulating a horizon within which an infinite progress may be envisaged. Once again, Ricoeur affirms the possibility of such a progressive movement where one's thinking and actions ought to be guided by the Ideas of a unified history and of the good life with and for others in just institutions. Within this regulated horizon, a number of dialectical relations are said to take place such as that between *langue* and *parole*, generality and singularity, *idem* and *ipse*, text and reader, and, most importantly, selfhood and otherness. Complete mediation is not possible. Still, some directionality is ensured by the *telos* from which the whole process receives its meaning.

Chapters 2 and 4 indicated that Derrida's formulations cast doubt upon the hermeneutic belief in dialectics and teleology. As far as Ricoeur's construal of psychoanalysis is concerned, Derrida convincingly draws attention to specific Freudian motifs that undermine Freud's sustained commitment to interpretation. The oppositionality and directionality on which Ricoeur's argument depends are rendered problematic by certain psychoanalytical descriptions that complicate the boundary between the poles of Freud's distinctions. Both the early neurological account and later metapsychology contain moments that invite one to think these distinctions in terms of a peculiar commingling that robs their poles of a secure identity, thereby debilitating the process of dialecticization. Derrida shows that death and memory, far from functioning as negative and supplementary categories eclipsed by life and perception respectively, constitute positive conditions that remain *absolutely* irreducible. If he characterizes the role of these conditions as "quasi-transcendental," it is because the concomitant movement of *différance* prevents their conception on the basis of a transcendental origin or cause. According to a logic I have sought to explicate on many occasions, the necessary possibility of death and memory give rise to life and perception, whose corollary is that all these terms constitute, in the final analysis, *effects* structurally prevented from achieving plenitude or actual presence.

The same movement is responsible for transforming the relation between singularity and generality into a co-implication of generalizability and the chance of singularity. This co-implication, encapsulated in the word *iterability*, is an essential feature of *all* signification, and, by extension, of deixis. It both conditions the possibility of a singular referent and renders any pure singularity impossible. Derrida's thinking displaces the conventional link between speech, phenomenality, and singular responsibility by introducing an originary secrecy into the very heart of the signifying act. Secrecy, bound up with perjury or lying, is not construed as a factical eventuality befalling here and there an essentially truthful speech, but as the sine qua non that constitutes the only chance of truthfulness and a singularly assumed responsibility.

If the scene of communication between two interlocutors presupposes, by virtue of the irreducible possibility of perjury, a fiduciary act where the other has to believe what I am saying as if in a miracle, this logic of an a priori interruption is inherent in the ethical relation too. The possibility of ethics lies in the affirmation of an absolute disjunction between self and other, in a radical heterogeneity resistant to the values of reciprocity, friendship, and equality. The chance of the better here and now depends on the possibility of the worst. This means not simply that the infinite demand for the better is impossible because of one's finite limitations, but also, more radically, that the very infinity of this demand is anchored in a certain finitude in such a way that it becomes impossible to discriminate between the two in order then to organize them teleologically.

Following Derrida's proposition regarding his "tangential encounter" with Ricoeur, I have suggested that the relation between the two thinkers is not exhausted by a reflection on the so-called dialogue between deconstruction and hermeneutics. Although a "dialogue" or a "debate" is absolutely necessary, together with an array of concepts such as "difference," "position," "thesis," "opposition," "confrontation," etc., it is at the same time impossible. This is the case because, in the first place, Ricoeur's discourse cannot be homogenized into a seamless and unified corpus of hermeneutic assertions. Even in his reading of Freud, when Ricoeur is at his most dialectical, there are moments when the distribution of oppositional terms along the lines of a negative-positive relation is undermined. When, for instance, he points out that drives and their representatives cannot be portrayed in terms of the dichotomy between signifier and signified, for these representatives occupy the position of both signifier and signified, his text gestures toward a paradoxical commingling of the sensible and the intelligible highly reminiscent of Derridean iterability. The undecidability intrinsic to the latter takes radical alterity seriously into account but remains resistant to dialectics. A similar structure was revealed in Ricoeur's theory of discourse where a certain disjuncture between the more or less exemplary instance of discourse and the stigmatic instant in which this takes place calls upon the reader to think singularity as indissociable from a necessary possibility of repetition.

In the second place, to the extent that Derrida is attentive to the exigency of difference and discontinuity, deconstruction is able to account, more effectively than hermeneutics, for the self-interrupting movement ensuring the infinity of the Kantian Idea posited by hermeneutics. It is Derrida, rather than Ricoeur, who thinks through the conditions of possibility for the nonrealizability of the *telos*, and who, therefore, allows for the ideals of communication, the good life, a single humanity, and a single history, for the very infinity of these Kantian Ideas in the Ricoeurian sense. This is far from ascribing a teleological agenda to Derrida's construal, for the same interruptive movement undercuts the structuring of the infinite-finite relation in terms of identifiable positions and a progressive synthesis. Derrida both reflects on the necessity of interruption, which alone can guarantee the infinity of the prescribed task, and subjects all concepts in solidarity with such teleology to philosophical scrutiny. In doing so, is he not upholding, in a sense, one of the most fundamental traditions of philosophy, that of reflection, which constitutes Ricoeur's major intellectual concern?[1] I have already alluded to an analogous problem posed by Gasché, who suggests that deconstruction, in asking critical questions, can be figured as a "hermeneutics" of some sort.[2]

The point here is neither to assimilate Derrida's thinking to reflective philosophy and hermeneutics, nor to argue in favor of an unintentional strand of Ricoeur's discourse that would provide it with an aura of post-structuralism, postmetaphysics, or deconstruction. The expression "improbable encounters" points toward another logic and another thinking of difference and similarity, according to which the required possibility of absolutely differentiating between them is not simply coexistent with but the *same as* the impossibility of identifying, conclusively and definitely, an absolute difference. This complex logic divides the borderline between deconstruction and hermeneutics and also diagnoses a differential element and a porous frontier *within* the texts of each philosopher, thereby conceiving of their relation *simultaneously* in terms of negotiation and interruption. It is because of this internal limit that Ricoeur may always turn out to be closer to Derrida when one might think he is getting farther away from him, and vice versa.

I have argued that such a problematized frontier, such an uncanny encounter alone is able to account for each thinker's genuine irreplaceability, for a radical singularity that remains irreducible to the idea of an absolute heterogeneity in view of reconciliation but also to that of a leveling out of all difference. In order to do justice to Derrida's and Ricoeur's thinking, to the finesse of their philosophy and the unique fashion in which they have signed and countersigned the texts I have examined, one has to take into consideration the necessary possibility of interrupting a certain dialogue between them.

The intent of this study has been to introduce the idea of improbable encounters by focusing on specific thematic contexts whose incidence upon the thought of Derrida and Ricoeur has been significant. Although I have touched on other prominent concerns such as forgiveness, violence, testimony, faith, and the promise, it remains that the philosophical configurations and arguments advanced here should be further explored in relation to each of these thematic frameworks. I close this study with this incitement to further research into other improbable intersections between the two philosophers. The term *intersections*, which Ricoeur uses in his unpublished dedication of *The Rule of Metaphor* to Derrida,[3] is yet another complex way of portraying the relation between them to the extent that it points as much to the exigency of a conjoining as to that of following divergent routes. In this sense, the idea of "improbable encounters," for which I initially drew on Derrida, is something that Ricoeur would also endorse. After all, it was Ricoeur who already in 1965 wrote the following phrase: " 'Encounters' which are worthy of the name are very rare."[4] This sentence parallels the quotation from Derrida placed as an epigraph at the beginning of the book and bears witness to a conceptuality that the two thinkers more or less share but that has come to be associated primarily with Derrida. It invites one to think what an encounter worthy of the name might be. It appeals to the reader to conceive, perhaps in a hyperbolic fashion, of an encounter that should merit the attribute "genuine." It simultaneously announces that such encounters are very rare, perhaps improbable, or even impossible.

Appendix

"The Word: Giving, Naming, Calling"

Jacques Derrida

Without even admitting, sincerely, to a feeling of incompetence, I believe that
never will I have been so lacking the strength to approach, in a study or
philosophical discussion, the immense work of Paul Ricoeur. How can one
limit oneself only to one of the places, to one of the stations along such a
rich and long trajectory, spanning so many fields, themes, and problems: from
ethics to psychoanalysis, from phenomenology to hermeneutics and even theol-
ogy, through history and the responsibilities that it daily imposes on us, for
several decades, through the history of philosophy and the original interpretation of so many philosophers, from Aristotle and Augustine to Kant, from
Jaspers and Husserl to Heidegger and Lévinas, not to mention Freud and all
the Anglo-Saxon philosophers that Ricoeur has had the courage and lucidity,
so rare in France, to read, to make others read, and to take into consideration
in his most innovative work? This seems to me difficult and indeed impossible
if one does not want to betray, in a few pages, the unity of a style and of an
intention, of a *thought* but also of a passion and of a *faith, a thought faith and
a thinking faith*, of a commitment that, from the beginning, has never given
up a certain fidelity. To oneself as much as to others.

Re-reading what I have just written quite spontaneously ("difficult and
indeed impossible"), I smile. I belatedly point out that, during the last two
years, these two words were at the center of a debate between Paul Ricoeur
and me on evil and forgiveness (firstly, a private debate over lunch near the
Montsouris Park and, secondly, a public debate at the roundtables organized by
Antoine Garapon with the jurists and then by Laure Adler for France-Culture
at the Maison de l'Amérique latine). Against my apparently aporetic proposition
according to which forgiveness is, in a nonnegative sense, the *im-possible* itself

(one can forgive only the unforgivable; forgiving that which is already forgivable is not forgiving; and this does not amount to saying that *there is no* forgiveness but that forgiveness would have *to do the impossible*, as one says, in order to become *possible*: to forgive the unforgivable), Ricoeur put forward another formula more than once: "Forgiveness is not impossible, it is difficult."[1] What is the difference, and where does it come to pass, between the (nonnegative) "im-possible" and the "difficult," the very difficult, the most difficult possible, difficulty or the *unfeasible* itself? What is the difference between that which is radically difficult and that which appears to be im-possible? To put it telegraphically, the question could perhaps come down to that of the selfhood [*ipséité*] of the "I can."[2] Etymology confirms this pleonasm. The *ipse* is always the power or possibility of an "I" (I can, I want, I decide). The im-possible I am talking about perhaps signifies that *I cannot and must not* ever claim that it is within *my* power seriously and responsibly to say "I forgive" (or "I want" or "I decide"). It is only the other, myself as another, that within me wants, decides, or forgives, which does not absolve me of any responsibility; on the contrary.

This exchange without agreement or opposition has a strange "logic," whereby an encounter simultaneously tangential, tendentious, and intangible begins to emerge [*s'esquisse*] but also slips away [*s'esquive*] within the most amicable proximity ("we are alongside each other," he told me one day, recently, while we were trying once again to think *together* what had come to pass, what had not come to pass, between the two of us during a whole life). "To be alongside each other" (parallel ways that will meet perhaps in infinity, progressing or navigating side by side, edge to edge, an implicit alliance without conflict but respectful of an irreducible difference) could be one of the potentially richest "metaphors" that we could attempt to adjust, complicate, and indeed contest in order to express what is at issue in this "logic." If one were to deploy such a "logic" in many texts, while respecting not only silence and interruption, whether contingent or essential, but also what remains implicit or unsaid, one would be able to recognize in it the permanent law of a "singular" dialogue that has been enriching me for a long time. "Singular" is a citation whose context I will recall in a moment.

In order to bear witness to my constant admiration and to a friendship, I would go as far as to say to an affection that has not stopped growing, I have allowed myself to go back to what is dearest to my memory: to those moments, always memorable for me, when, over a period of about fifty years, I *saw, heard* or *met* Paul Ricoeur, when he gave me the chance to *speak* [*parler*] with him. And every single time this was for me an event. Since philosophy was never absent from these lively conversations [*paroles vives*], it will always, I hope, be discernible throughout the plain narrative of those blessed moments.

These were always occasions of speech [*moments de parole*], for Ricoeur is, in every sense of this term, a man of his *word* [*homme de parole*].[3] And he is a man of speech [*l'homme de la parole*] too. Immersing myself once again in his works, in a wandering fashion so as to find my way or, more precisely, the trajectory of a certain word [*parole*], I suddenly come across an article from 1967.[4] I discover that I had already marked, by means of a red line in the margin, a whole passage where, in agreement with Hjelmslev (in whom I was very interested at the time, myself also wondering, in a different way, about certain limitations of the structuralist "ideology" that dominated that era), Ricoeur wrote:

> In this respect, Hjelmslev is right. . . . Usage or use is at the inter-section of language and speech. We must conclude that the word *names* at the same time that the sentence says. It *names* in sentence position. In the dictionary, there is only the endless round of terms which are defined circularly, which revolve in the closure of the lexicon. But then someone speaks, someone says something. The word leaves the dictionary; it becomes word at the moment when man becomes *speech*, when *speech* becomes discourse and discourse a sentence. It is not by chance that, in German, *Wort*—"word"—is also *Wort*, "*speech*" (even if *Wort* and *Wort* do not have the same plural). Words are signs in *speech* position. Words are the point of articulation between semiology and semantics, in every *speech event*. . . . The sentence, we have seen, is an *event*; as such, its actual-ity is transitory, passing, ephemeral. But the word survives the sen-tence. As a displaceable entity, it survives the transitory instance of discourse and holds itself available for new uses. (emphasis JD)

In view of this last phrase, I had written in red: "in returning to the system." Ricoeur continued:

> Thus, heavy with a new use-value—as minute as this may be—it returns to the system. And, in returning to the system, it gives it a history.

In the margin, pleased with myself and with having anticipated the exact words of this conclusion, with a naïve self-satisfaction that is aggravated by the fact that I admit to it once again today, I wrote: "Here it is . . ."

I have said "half a century." Of this I will only recall here the encounters, the apparently transitory speech events [*événements de parole*] that my memory seeks to save as invaluable gifts. The first time that I saw and heard Paul Ricoeur, having only read very little of his work, was probably in 1953. I was then a student at the École Normale, and one of my best friends suggested that the two of us should attend a session of a discussion group that the journal *Esprit*,

I think, organized at Châtenay-Malabry. Marrou was there, whom I also heard then for the first time. I was impressed by Ricoeur's discourse: clarity, elegance, demonstrative force, and a thought-provoking authority without authority. The topic was history and truth as well as contemporary ethico-political problems. The next summer, having decided to devote my higher studies dissertation to the problem of genesis in Husserl, I spent many weeks at home in El Biar reading *Ideas I*. As is known, Ricoeur had translated, written an introduction for, commented on, and interpreted this book, so my reading was enlightened by his very rich scholarly notes. This is true even today, whenever I sometimes go back to this work. It was, then, this great reader of Husserl who first taught me, more rigorously than Sartre and even Merleau-Ponty, how to read phenomenology, and who, in a certain way, acted as my mentor from that moment onward. I also recall his articles on "Kant and Husserl," the *Crisis*, etc., which later became major references in my *Edmund Husserl's "Origin of Geometry": An Introduction*.[5]

After 1960, when I was a teaching assistant in general philosophy at the Sorbonne, I met Ricoeur for the first time when he was appointed (a little later, I think). At that time, teaching assistants had a strange role that one can hardly imagine nowadays. As the only assistant in general philosophy and logic, I was free to organize my teaching and seminars as I wished, without being controlled, except in a very abstract sense, by all the professors whose assistant, in principle, I was: Suzanne Bachelard, Canguilhem, Poirier, Polin, Ricoeur, and Wahl. I rarely met them outside of exams time, with the exception, perhaps, of Suzanne Bachelard and Canguilhem who, toward the end, was for me a fatherly friend whom I admired. One day, it must have been in 1962, I visited Ricoeur at his house at Châtenay-Malabry. During a stroll in his garden, he spoke to me enthusiastically about *Totality and Infinity*. This was the thesis that Lévinas was going to defend a few days later. The book had not been published yet. Ricoeur, who was a member of the examining committee, had just read it: a great book, he told me, an event. I was only familiar with Lévinas's texts on Husserl at the time. As a consequence, guided once again by Ricoeur's words, I read *Totality and Infinity* the next summer and wrote "Violence and Metaphysics,"[6] the first of a series of studies that I devoted to Lévinas in the course of the next thirty years. Therefore, I am also, in a way, indebted to Ricoeur for the friendship that, full of admiration, has since linked me to the person and work of Emmanuel Lévinas—and this too was the chance of a lifetime for me.

It was during those years at the Sorbonne but also during those following my departure for the École Normale Supérieure that we met at the seminar where Ricoeur, then director of the Husserl Archives (whose microfilms were in Paris), welcomed students, researchers, and colleagues so as to give them, more often than not, the opportunity of speaking [*leur donner la parole*] at the seminar. I recall giving a presentation there and meeting, in addition to Lévinas, several of those in Paris who were interested in Husserl in those years. Thanks to Ricoeur, the spirit that reigned at the seminars was exemplary: serenity, freedom, friendly discussion, rigor, and attempts at genuine research.

Several years later, in 1971, in Montreal, we had our first and longest oral discussion that has ever been published.[7] I have just re-read it for the first time after more than thirty years. Ricoeur had given the inaugural lecture of the conference entitled "Discours et communication." I spoke immediately after him ("Signature Event Context").[8] After the other presentations, the round-table lasted for two hours. It was largely dominated by what the chair of the discussion called a "singular amicable fight" between Ricoeur and me.[9] It takes up almost forty pages and I will not attempt to reconstitute it here, because of the lack of space and because there is no question of opening, within this testimonial, a fundamental philosophical debate. But as the conference proceedings are today hardly accessible, basically gone out of print, I will perhaps be allowed to obey the desire to cite only one extract from the transcript (undoubtedly inaccurate here and there), a brief and animated sequence. This sequence appears to me typical, which is why I dare to cite it, of a certain *chassé-croisé on the verge of and even above an abyss*, which perhaps represents a constant and quite faithful figure of our "singular" dialogue, whether spoken, written or silent. (This "*chassé-croisé*" is not equivalent to "being alongside each other"—and we are not finished yet with wearing out our metaphors). What is more, this sequence picks up the threads of an issue that I invoked above, that of semiotics and semantics, of the word, the sentence, nomination and speech [*la parole*], and the event.

Paul Ricoeur: . . . Then you are compelled to inflate the theory of writing, all of which has not been constructed in its proper place, within a theory of discourse. If you construct this theory of discourse, it can account for the characteristics of writing that you've demonstrated. It can do this because all the characteristics that you attributed to writing can be found within discursivity itself. This is a little of what I would like to discuss with you concerning the problem of discourse.

Jacques Derrida: Without a doubt, the lack, among others, of a theory of discourse is very noticeable, not only in the paper I delivered this morning but also in propositions I've risked elsewhere. In an entirely preliminary way, what's interested me in a theory of discourse, which in fact is necessary, is simply to record all of what is presupposed, in short, all the things left uncriticized, which, it seems to me, restrain right up to the present the attempts at a theory of discourse witnessed in linguistics as well as in philosophy. These presuppositions are the ones I very schematically outlined this morning, namely, that something like the event, for example, was obvious, that we would know what an event was. Now a theory of discourse presupposes a theory of the event, a theory of the act, a speech act theory, a theory of the act as singular event. I tried to mark in the theory of event, for example—but this concept is connected to a whole group of other concepts—I tried to mark what prevents every supposed event from being constituted as an event in this philosophic sense (singular, actual, present, irreplaceable, unrepeatable, etc.). The event's singularity is divided by the simple fact that the event was a genre of discourse, simply, a semiological event. And when you say that . . .

Paul Ricoeur: That's not the same thing.

Jacques Derrida: Yes, I'm going to try . . .

Paul Ricoeur: This distinction between semiology and semantics . . .

Jacques Derrida: Exactly . . . I'm coming to it . . .

Paul Ricoeur: appears to me absolutely fundamental . . .

Jacques Derrida: I'm coming to it.

Paul Ricoeur: and mixed together in a theory of writing. In lots of ways this theory is semiological, but it aims to resolve semantic problems with semiological resources.

Jacques Derrida: Yes, which brings me then to this point. In a certain way—I want to be precise—in a preliminary way, I have also attempted a critique of semiology. Therefore, it seems to me hard to enclose what I do in a semiology. . . . I have not at all tried to reduce discourse to a set of signs, but I have tried to keep us from forgetting that there are still signs in discourse, that discourse exists with the sign, with the differential chain, with spacing, etc. This is all of what we . . .

Paul Ricoeur: Yes, but I believe we really have to distinguish what we understand by spacing. The spacing found in discourse is not the same as what you find in the semiological order when a sign is distinct from another sign. This is the semiological spacing that may be phonic or graphic. Discursive spacing is something else entirely. . . . I agree when you say that discourse is always caught in signs, but discourse can also change this lattice. This is what translation does. Then the problem is to know what we translate; what we translate is the discourse's meaning. You make it pass from one semiological system to another. What's transferred? The characteristics of meaning. If you, however, lack a theory of meaning, you can't construct a theory of translation either.

Jacques Derrida: Was I mistaken about your restricting difference to the semiological as if semantic difference doesn't exist, as if difference doesn't also constitute the semantic?

Paul Ricoeur: Yes, but I don't capitalize the word *difference*. . . .

Jacques Derrida: You've often complained about my capitalizing *difference* . . . I've never done it . . .

Paul Ricoeur: but [you write it] with an "a" . . .

Jacques Derrida: But that gives the word another meaning . . .

Paul Ricoeur: That does give the word another meaning. There are differences between signs. Then there is the fact that the subject is not the predicate. Finally, there are differences everywhere. But what's important is that discourse produces, by its own differences which are not semiological differences, effects of discourse which are not effects of signs.

Jacques Derrida: I agree entirely. That's why I never said that difference might have to be restricted to the semiological element. . . .[10]

Another debate took place exclusively in writing and I think that we have never spoken about it in person. According to the rule that I have set myself, I will say nothing about it here. I will only give some minimal references to the interested reader. The same year, that is, in 1971, I published "White Mythology: Metaphor in the Text of Philosophy,"[11] of which Ricoeur put forward a sharply critical reading—though always generous and elegant—in his book *The Rule of Metaphor*.[12] Is it indiscreet to cite here the dedication of this work? I am doing this, nevertheless, as a privileged and unique witness because this unpublished dedication includes the word *intersections* (one of the several metaphors with which I have tried to describe the perpetual resumption of this "singular" dialogue: "to be alongside each other," he said recently, to which

I instantly responded "a *chassé-croisé*"): "For Jacques Derrida, this beginning of explanation in view of new *intersections*, this tribute of faithful thinking" (emphasis JD). Having attempted to respond to this sharp criticism in "The *Retrait* of Metaphor,"[13] and having decided not to reopen this discussion here (this, moreover, would be impossible given the current limitations), I will only recall one of Ricoeur's phrases. I recall this phrase not because I find it just or true (I have explained this elsewhere) but because it names life and death in a particularly striking way which touches me today more than ever for a thousand reasons and about which there would be so much to say. So here it is:

> Two assertions [*affirmations*] can be discerned in the tight fabric of Derrida's demonstration. The first has to do with the efficacy of worn-out metaphor in philosophical discourse, and the second with the deep-seated unity of metaphorical and analogical transfer of visible being to intelligible being.
>   The first assertion moves counter to our entire effort, which has been directed towards the discovery of living metaphor. The stroke of genius here is to enter the domain of metaphor not by way of its birth [*par la porte de la naissance*] but, if we may say so, by way of its death [*par la porte de la mort*].[14]

Even if I doubt that this is true of my text on metaphor, which is of little importance here today, I think that, well beyond this debate, Ricoeur has accurately and profoundly understood me and my philosophical gestures. I always go back to the invincible affirmation and reaffirmation of life, of the desire for life, alas, "through the door of death" [*par la porte de la mort*], on which my eyes are fixed at every instant. Of course, with as much fear and trembling for others, for those that I love, as for myself. Not so long ago Ricoeur told me: "Death does not make me fear, but solitude does." I think I had nothing to respond to this then, and I do not know any better today. Of course, I then hoped in myself, for myself, as I still do today, that he should be spared both for as long as possible. I hoped that his words [*sa parole*] no less than his writings should always watch over us.

One last "living" metaphor at the moment of signing off this testimonial of admiration and fidelity. It seems to me that we have always shared a belief, an act of faith, both of us, each in his own manner and from his proper place, his place of birth, his "perspective" (yes indeed) and the unique "door of death" [*porte de la mort*]. This belief binds us as a given word [*une parole donnée*] would. It gives to us and calls upon us to understand a simple but incredible thing that I would represent thus: over or across an impassable abyss that we do not know how to name, we can nonetheless speak to each other and understand each other. And we can even, this is the other gift that I receive from him, call each other.

We will be doing this again, as we just did a moment ago on the telephone, to exchange news and greetings.

31st December 2003

Translated by Eftichis Pirovolakis

Notes

Introduction

1. An English translation of this discussion by Leonard Lawlor appears as an appendix entitled "Philosophy and Communication: Round-table Discussion between Ricoeur and Derrida," in Leonard Lawlor, *Imagination and Chance: The Difference between the Thought of Ricoeur and Derrida* (Albany: State University of New York Press, 1992), 131–63.

2. Derrida's presentation "Signature événement contexte" and Ricoeur's "Discours et communication" were both published in *Actes du XVe Congrès de L'Association des Sociétés de Philosophie de Langue Française* (Montréal: Montmorency, 1973). Derrida's text, however, was first collected in *Marges de la philosophie* (Paris: Minuit, 1972), 365–93, a work translated into English by Alan Bass as *Margins of Philosophy* (Hemel Hempstead: Harvester Wheatsheaf, 1982). Derrida's essay has also been translated into English by Samuel Weber and Jeffrey Mehlman as "Signature Event Context," and reprinted in Jacques Derrida, *Limited Inc*, ed. Gerald Graff (Evanston: Northwestern University Press, 1988), 1–23. Although, as far as I know, no English translation of Ricoeur's presentation exists, the original French text has been reprinted in *Paul Ricoeur*, ed. Myriam Revault d'Allones and François Azouvi, L'Herne, no. 81 (Paris: Éditions de L'Herne, 2004), 51–67.

3. From *dis-* (expressing reversal) and *battere* or *batuere* ('to fight'), according to *The Oxford English Dictionary*, 2nd ed., prepared by J. A. Simpson and E. S. C. Weiner, 20 vols. (Oxford: Clarendon Press, 1989).

4. Jacques Derrida, "White Mythology: Metaphor in the Text of Philosophy," in *Margins of Philosophy*, 207–71; originally published as "La mythologie blanche: La métaphore dans le texte philosophique," *Poétique* 5 (1971): 1–52.

5. See Paul Ricoeur, *The Rule of Metaphor: The Creation of Meaning in Language*, trans. Robert Czerny with Kathleen McLaughlin and John Costello, SJ (London: Routledge, 2003), 336–48; originally published as *La métaphore vive* (Paris: Seuil, 1975).

6. Jacques Derrida, "The *Retrait* of Metaphor," trans. Frieda Gasdner, Biodun Iginla, Richard Madden, and William West, *Enclitic* 2, no. 2 (1978): 5–33. This essay, first published as "Le retrait de la métaphore" in *Poésie* 7 (1978): 103–26, was originally presented as a lecture to a colloquium on "Philosophy and Metaphor" at the University of Geneva in 1978, in which Ricoeur also participated.

7. Lawlor, who devotes the first part of his study to that aborted debate on metaphor, points out, in *Imagination and Chance*, 43, that Derrida "never addresses the foundation of Ricoeur's criticisms, his dialectical notion of distanciation. Similarly, Ricoeur's criticisms never address the foundation of the law of supplementarity, *différance*." See also Leonard Lawlor, "Dialectic and Iterability: The Confrontation between Paul Ricoeur and Jacques Derrida," *Philosophy Today* 32, no. 3 (1988): 181–94.

8. See Paul Ricoeur, *Memory, History, Forgetting*, trans. Kathleen Blamey and David Pellauer (Chicago: University of Chicago Press, 2004), 457 and 468–70; originally published as *La mémoire, l'histoire, l'oubli* (Paris: Seuil, 2000). See also Jacques Derrida, "On Forgiveness," trans. Michael Hughes, in *On Cosmopolitanism and Forgiveness*, trans. Mark Dooley and Michael Hughes (London: Routledge, 2001), 27–60; originally published as "Le Siècle et le pardon," *Le Monde des débats* (December 1999).

9. See Jacques Derrida, "The Word: Giving, Naming, Calling," trans. Eftichis Pirovolakis, appendix in this book, 167–75; originally published as "La parole: Donner, nommer, appeler," in Revault d'Allones and Azouvi, *Paul Ricoeur*, 19–25. Derrida also mentions here that this disagreement on evil and forgiveness gave rise to two further roundtable debates, in which both Derrida and Ricoeur participated; one was organized by Antoine Garapon, the other by Laure Adler.

10. Throughout the book, and in the interest of consistency with existing translations of Ricoeur's works, I will use the word *selfhood* to render the pivotal notion of "*ipséité*."

11. See Paul Ricoeur, "La promesse d'avant la promesse" (2004), in *La Philosophie au risque de la promesse*, ed. Marc Crépon and Marc de Launay (Paris: Bayard, 2004), 25–34.

12. See Jacques Derrida, "Questions à Jacques Derrida" (2004), in Crépon and de Launay, *La Philosophie au risque de la promesse*, 183–209, 195–200.

13. For some other references to each other's work, in addition to those already mentioned here, see Lawlor, *Imagination and Chance*, 4 nn. 2–3.

14. As far as Derrida is concerned, he displays the same reluctance in another of his encounters with hermeneutics, namely, his meeting with Hans-Georg Gadamer in April 1981 at a Paris symposium on "Text and Interpretation." Derrida's essay, "Interpreting Signatures (Nietzsche/Heidegger): Two Questions" (1986), focuses on Heidegger's construal of Nietzsche, and does not seem intended to develop a dialogue with Gadamer, whose name is mentioned at no point. Similarly, in his uncharacteristically short and inadequate response to Gadamer's presentation "Text and Interpretation," Derrida posed three brief and apparently misdirected questions to his interlocutor. One of my objectives here is to explore the reasons for Derrida's performative dramatization of such an interruptive logic. Derrida's response was entitled "Good Will to Power (A Response to Hans-Georg Gadamer)" (originally published as "Bonnes volontés de puissance [Une réponse à Hans-Georg Gadamer]," *Revue internationale de philosophie* 38, no. 151 (1984): 341–43), whereas the title of Gadamer's reply was "And Yet: The Power of Good Will" (my translation). These two texts have been given the simpler titles "Three Questions to Hans-Georg Gadamer" and "Reply to Jacques Derrida" respectively; and all four texts have been translated into English and collected, together with other essays relevant to this confrontation, in *Dialogue and Deconstruction: The Gadamer-Derrida*

Encounter, ed. Diane P. Michelfelder and Richard E. Palmer (Albany: State University of New York Press, 1989).

15. J. Hillis Miller, "But Are Things as We Think They Are?" review of *Time and Narrative*, by Paul Ricoeur, *The Times Literary Supplement* 9–15 October 1987, 1104–05. See Paul Ricoeur, *Time and Narrative*, trans. Kathleen McLaughlin and David Pellauer, 3 vols. (Chicago: University of Chicago Press, 1984–88); originally published as *Temps et récit*, 3 vols. (Paris: Seuil, 1983–85).

16. Stephen H. Clark, *Paul Ricoeur* (London: Routledge, 1990), 5–7. Clark's views regarding Ricoeur's post-structuralism are shared by G. B. Madison in "Ricoeur and the Hermeneutics of the Subject," in *The Philosophy of Paul Ricoeur*, ed. Lewis Edwin Hahn (Chicago: Open Court, 1995), 75–92, and also by Mario J. Valdés in "Introduction: Paul Ricoeur's Post-Structuralist Hermeneutics," in *A Ricoeur Reader: Reflection and Imagination*, ed. Mario J. Valdés (Hemel Hempstead: Harvester Wheatsheaf, 1991), 3–40.

17. See Lawlor, *Imagination and Chance*, 1–2.

18. Ibid., 123.

19. Ibid., 2–3.

20. Ibid., 123–29.

21. Similarly, in "Dialectic and Iterability," 182 and 193, Lawlor portrays the relation between the two thinkers in terms of a confrontation or an opposition that has to be resolved.

22. I fully share, in this sense, Lawlor's commitment to the values of lucidity and clarification. In *Imagination and Chance*, 7, Lawlor declares that his project amounts to a response to the demand "to clarify what takes place between Ricoeur and Derrida, to bring 'a minimum of lucidity' to hermeneutics and deconstruction."

23. Edmund Husserl, *Ideas: General Introduction to Pure Phenomenology* (1913), trans. W. R. Boyce Gibson (London: Allen and Unwin, 1931); translated by Ricoeur into French as *Idées directrices pour une phénoménologie: Introduction générale à la phénoménologie pure* (Paris: Gallimard, 1950).

24. For some of Ricoeur's later analyses of Husserl, see, for instance, MHF, 31–36 and 109–20, and *Oneself as Another*, trans. Kathleen Blamey (Chicago: University of Chicago Press, 1992), 322–26 and 331–35 (originally published as *Soi-même comme un autre* [Paris: Seuil, 1990]). Regarding the link between hermeneutics and phenomenology, see Paul Ricoeur, "Phenomenology and Hermeneutics," trans. John B. Thompson, in *From Text to Action: Essays in Hermeneutics II*, trans. Kathleen Blamey and John B. Thompson (Evanston: Northwestern University Press, 1991), 25–52; originally published as "Phénoménologie et herméneutique," *Man and World* 7, no. 3 (1974): 223–53. Also, John B. Thompson, in his *Critical Hermeneutics: A Study in the Thought of Paul Ricoeur and Jürgen Habermas* (Cambridge: Cambridge University Press, 1981), 36, describes Ricoeur's philosophy as an outstanding contribution to Heidegger's and Gadamer's hermeneutic phenomenology.

25. See W, 170.

26. Jacques Derrida, *Edmund Husserl's "Origin of Geometry": An Introduction*, trans. John P. Leavey Jr. (Lincoln: University of Nebraska Press, 1989); originally published as *Introduction à 'L'Origine de la géométrie' de Husserl* (Paris: Presses Universitaires

de France, 1962). Jacques Derrida, *The Problem of Genesis in Husserl's Philosophy*, trans. Marian Hobson (Chicago: University of Chicago Press, 2003); originally published as *Le problème de la genèse dans la philosophie de Husserl* (Paris: Presses Universitaires de France, 1990).

27. See Paul Ricoeur, *Freud and Philosophy: An Essay on Interpretation*, trans. Denis Savage (New Haven: Yale University Press, 1970); originally published as *De l'interprétation: Essai sur Freud* (Paris: Seuil, 1965). See also Jacques Derrida, "Freud and the Scene of Writing," in *Writing and Difference*, trans. Alan Bass (London: Routledge, 1978), 196–231; originally published as "Freud et la scène de l'écriture," *Tel Quel* 26 (Summer 1966): 10–41. ·

28. My thematic choices here are in agreement with Joanna Hodge's observation, in "Husserl, Freud, *A Suivre*: Derrida on Time," *The Journal of the British Society for Phenomenology* 36, no. 2 (May 2005): 188–207, 189, regarding the significance of "opening out a connection between Husserl's analyses of time and those of Freud." Lawlor pursues this connection neither in *Imagination and Chance*, nor, as Hodge politely points out, in his more recent *Derrida and Husserl: The Basic Problem of Phenomenology* (Bloomington: Indiana University Press, 2002). For Lawlor's discussion of Ricoeur's and Derrida's readings of Husserl's theory of temporalization, see *Imagination and Chance*, 83–87 and 107–09, and *Derrida and Husserl*, 70–72 and 183–88.

29. See Derrida, "Three Questions to Hans-Georg Gadamer," 53, and "Questions à Jacques Derrida," 196–200, where he differentiates psychoanalysis from hermeneutics, speech acts theory, and phenomenology.

30. In addition to *The Rule of Metaphor* and *Time and Narrative*, see Paul Ricoeur, *The Conflict of Interpretations: Essays in Hermeneutics*, ed. Don Ihde (Evanston: Northwestern University Press, 1974) (*Le conflit des interprétations: Essais d'herméneutique* [Paris: Seuil, 1969]); *Interpretation Theory: Discourse and the Surplus of Meaning* (Fort Worth: Texas Christian University Press, 1976); and *Hermeneutics and the Human Sciences: Essays on Language, Action, and Interpretation*, ed. and trans. John B. Thompson (Cambridge: Cambridge University Press, 1981).

31. Jacques Derrida, "The Time of a Thesis: Punctuations," trans. Kathleen McLaughlin, in *Philosophy in France Today*, ed. Alan Montefiore (Cambridge: Cambridge University Press, 1983), 34–50, 36–37.

32. Jacques Derrida, *Of Grammatology*, trans. Gayatri Chakravorty Spivak (Baltimore: Johns Hopkins University Press, 1976) (*De la grammatologie* [Paris: Minuit, 1967]); *Speech and Phenomena: And Other Essays on Husserl's Theory of Signs*, trans. David B. Allison (Evanston: Northwestern University Press, 1973) (the *Speech and Phenomena* text was originally published as *La voix et le phénomène: Introduction au problème du signe dans la phénoménologie de Husserl* [Paris: Presses Universitaires de France, 1967]); *Dissemination*, trans. Barbara Johnson (London: Athlone Press, 1981) (*La dissémination* [Paris: Seuil, 1972]); and *Positions*, trans. Alan Bass (London: Athlone Press, 1981) (*Positions: Entretiens avec Henri Ronse, Julia Kristeva, Jean-Louis Houdebine, Guy Scarpetta* [Paris: Minuit, 1972]).

33. In W, 170, Derrida remarks that it was Ricoeur who in 1962 drew his attention to Lévinas's unpublished at the time *Totality and Infinity*. As a result of his discussion with Ricoeur, Derrida read this work the next summer and published "Violence

and Metaphysics: An Essay on the Thought of Emmanuel Lévinas," *Writing and Difference*, 79–153; originally published as "Violence et métaphysique: Essai sur la pensée d'Emmanuel Lévinas," *Revue de métaphysique et de morale* 69, no. 3–4 (1964): 322–45, 425–73. See also Emmanuel Lévinas, *Totality and Infinity: An Essay on Exteriority* (1961), trans. Alphonso Lingis (Dordrecht: Kluwer Academic Publishers, 1991).

34. See TN, 3:215–16 and 258; "Freedom in the Light of Hope," trans. Robert Sweeney, *The Conflict of Interpretations*, 402–24, 412–20 ("Approche philosophique du concept de liberté religieuse," *Archivio di Filosofia* 38, no. 2–3 [1968]: 215–52); "Practical Reason," trans. Kathleen Blamey, TA, 188–207, 197–204 ("La raison pratique," *Rationality Today. La rationalité aujourd'hui*, ed. Th. F. Geraets [Ottawa: University of Ottawa Press, 1979], 225–48); and "Initiative," trans. Kathleen Blamey, TA, 208–22, 221 ("L'initiative," *Labyrinthe: parcours éthiques* [Bruxelles: Facultés universitaires Saint-Louis, 1986], 85–102). See also Pamela Sue Anderson's detailed discussion in *Ricoeur and Kant: Philosophy of the Will* (Atlanta: Scholars Press, 1993), 21–32; and David M. Kaplan, *Ricoeur's Critical Theory* (Albany: State University of New York Press, 2003), 12–13.

35. My approach, therefore, differs from any *regretful* and seriously reductive portrayal of the relation between deconstruction and hermeneutics as a non-dialogue or a "disjointed exchange"; see, for instance, Fred R. Dallmayr, "Prelude: Hermeneutics and Deconstruction: Gadamer and Derrida in Dialogue," in Michelfelder and Palmer, *Dialogue and Deconstruction*, 75–92, 77. For the phrase "worthy of its name" as used by Derrida and Ricoeur, see chapter 4, n. 1 and the section "Originary Mourning: In Memory of the Absolutely Other" respectively.

36. This expression has been motivated by Derrida's portrayal of his relation to Ricoeur in terms of a "tangential encounter" cited in the epigraph at the beginning of this Introduction. Derrida also referred to his exchange with John R. Searle as an " 'improbable' debate" (LI, 30–31). Moreover, Philippe Forget, the organizer of the Paris encounter between Derrida and Gadamer, described their meeting as an "improbable debate"; see Philippe Forget, "Argument(s)," trans. Diane Michelfelder, in Michelfelder and Palmer, *Dialogue and Deconstruction*, 129–49, 130.

37. In W, 168, Derrida uses this spatial imagery to respond to and qualify Ricoeur's depiction of their relation as "being alongside each other." Furthermore, Derrida delineates his relation to Gadamer's hermeneutics in a similar fashion in his "Rams: Uninterrupted Dialogue—Between Two Infinities, the Poem," trans. Thomas Dutoit and Philippe Romanski, in *Sovereignties in Question: The Poetics of Paul Celan*, ed. Thomas Dutoit and Outi Pasanen (New York: Fordham University Press, 2005), 135–63; originally published as *Béliers: Le dialogue ininterrompu: entre deux infinis, le poème* (Paris: Galilée, 2003). Finally, for a double and apparently contradictory use of the term *apposition*, see John Llewelyn, *Appositions of Jacques Derrida and Emmanuel Lévinas* (Bloomington: Indiana University Press, 2002), xiii.

38. In SP, 31, Derrida refers to this differentiation in terms of the distinction between commentary and interpretation. Such a deconstructive reading is exemplified by Derrida's analysis of Husserl discussed in chapter 2.

39. For the expression "philosophies of the subject," see Paul Ricoeur, "The Question of the Subject. The Challenge of Semiology" (1969), trans. Kathleen McLaughlin, *The*

Conflict of Interpretations, 236–66, 236–37; originally published as "La question du sujet: le défi de la sémiologie," *Le conflit des interprétations*, 233–62. See also OA, 4.

40. See Jacques Derrida, *Mémoires: For Paul de Man*, rev. ed., trans. Cecile Lindsay, Jonathan Culler, Eduardo Cadava, and Peggy Kamuf (New York: Columbia University Press, 1989), 21–39; originally published as *Mémoires pour Paul de Man* (Paris: Galilée, 1988).

41. See W, 168.

Chapter 1. Ricoeur on Husserl and Freud

1. Lawlor, *Imagination and Chance*, 83–84.

2. Ricoeur's discussion of the "archaeology of the subject" is found in FP, 419–58. In FP, 417–18 n. 99 and QS, 243, he points out that it was Maurice Merleau-Ponty who deployed this expression in order to designate the incarnation of instinctual drives; see Maurice Merleau-Ponty, "L'oeuvre et l'esprit de Freud," in *Parcours deux, 1951–1961* (Lagrasse: Verdier, 2000), 276–84.

3. See TN, 3:11–96.

4. In TN, 3:261–70 and especially 268–70, Ricoeur situates these theories of temporality on a scale ranging from archaism (Aristotle and Augustine) to hermeticism, and maintains that Kant and Husserl stand somewhere in the middle.

5. Edmund Husserl, *The Phenomenology of Internal Time-Consciousness* (1928), ed. Martin Heidegger, trans. James S. Churchill (The Hague: Martinus Nijhoff, 1964). The manuscripts that formed this text consisted of lecture notes from 1905 and supplementary material written between 1905 and 1911. This material, reworked by Husserl in collaboration with his assistant Edith Stein in 1917, appears as "Part A" of the critical scholarly edition *On the Phenomenology of the Consciousness of Internal Time (1893–1917)*, by Edmund Husserl, trans. John Barnett Brough (Dordrecht: Kluwer, 1991), vol. 4 of *Edmund Husserl: Collected Works*, 13 vols. (1980–2008). "Part B" of this work includes texts from 1893 to 1911 arranged chronologically and intended to shed light on Husserl's developing thought as well as on Stein's considerable interventions.

6. Ricoeur discusses Aristotle's definition of time in TN, 3:14–22. However, Aristotle's alleged cosmology cannot simply be opposed to a psychological account of time insofar as Aristotle first laid the foundations of such an account. After his declaration that we perceive movement and time together, Aristotle goes on to say that "even when it is dark and we are not being affected through the body, if any movement takes place in the mind we at once suppose that some time has indeed elapsed"; see Aristotle, *Physics*, trans. R. P. Hardie and R. K. Gaye, book IV: 219a4–6, vol. 1 of *The Complete Works of Aristotle*, ed. Jonathan Barnes, 2 vols. (Princeton: Princeton University Press, 1984). This suggests that Aristotle intended to correlate time and movement only inasmuch as they are both perceived by somebody, that is, only from the perspective of the soul. Although Ricoeur refers to this specific extract from Aristotle in TN, 3:277 n. 13, he insists that Aristotle did not stress perception or apprehension. Does Ricoeur not downplay this "psychological" aspect of Aristotle's text precisely in order to affirm a provisional chasm between a supposedly mathematizing definition and Husserl's phenomenological approach? By contrast, in "*Ousia* and *Grammē*: Note on a Note from

Being and Time," *Margins of Philosophy,* 29–67, 49 (originally published as "Ousia et grammè: note sur une note de *Sein und Zeit,*" in *L'endurance de la pensée: Pour saluer Jean Beaufret,* ed. Marcel Jouhandeau [Paris: Plon, 1968], 219–66), Jacques Derrida underlines that Aristotle unites time and movement in perception (*aisthēsis*), and designates this tripartite unity as a pure form of sensibility anticipating Kant's notion of "the nonsensuous sensuous": "Time is the form of that which can occur only *en tēi psukhēi.* The form of inner sense is also the form of all phenomena in general."

7. See also TN, 3:29, where Ricoeur points out that what gets emphasized by Husserl is "the continuity of the whole or the totality of the continuous, which the term duration (*Dauer*) itself designates. That something persists in change—this is what enduring means. The identity that results from this is no longer a logical identity but precisely that of a temporal totality."

8. See Paul Ricoeur, "Kant and Husserl," in *Husserl: An Analysis of His Phenomenology,* trans. Edward G. Ballard and Lester E. Embree (Evanston: Northwestern University Press, 1967), 175–201, 189–90; originally published as "Kant et Husserl," *Kant-Studien* 46, no. 1 (1954–55): 44–67. In this essay, Ricoeur appears curiously oblivious to a certain tension between the intuition of a determined content and an empty intention attendant upon Husserl's discussion of the Idea in the Kantian sense in, for instance, *Ideas I,* §§22, 74, 83, 143, and 149; see also chapter 2, n. 6. Finally, Derrida comments on Ricoeur's observation in *Edmund Husserl's "Origin of Geometry,"* 139–40.

9. See TN, 3:39.

10. In his transcendental exposition of the concept of time, Kant claims that analogy is indispensable in providing a representation of the inner intuition of time: "It [time] cannot be a determination of outer appearances; it has to do neither with shape nor position, but with the relation of representations in our inner state. And just because this inner intuition yields no shape, we endeavour to make up for this want by analogies"; see Immanuel Kant, *Critique of Pure Reason* (1781, 1787), trans. Norman Kemp Smith (London: Macmillan, 1929) A 33, B 50. I will discuss Freud's recourse to a scriptural and mechanical metaphorics in the second chapter.

11. The most important feature of the flux is its unity. Although there is a plurality of primal impressions and modifications leading to the constitution of immanent objects, Husserl indeed underlines that consciousness is characterized by a unitariness (*Einheitlichkeit*), which is the outcome of a connecting form applicable to the plurality of primary sensations: firstly, Husserl affirms the existence of the common form of the now, identical for a group of original sensations taking place "all-at-once" (*Zugleich*); secondly, he affirms the all-embracing and regular transformation of this all-at-once into a before, hence the principles of simultaneity and succession (PITC, §38, 102–105).

12. Husserl devotes §39 of PITC to the double intentionality of retention.

13. This is not to suggest that Ricoeur subscribes completely and unreservedly to the Kantian approach to time. Rather, he makes clear his wish dialectically to combine Kant's cosmological and Husserl's phenomenological interpretation, and emphasizes that neither account is sufficient unto itself. It seems, however, that Ricoeur's sympathies lie more with Kant than with Husserl.

14. See Augustine's reflection on time in his *Confessions,* trans. R. S. Pine-Coffin (Harmondsworth: Penguin, 1961) book XI: 253–80, 264. For Ricoeur's commentary on Augustine, see TN, 1:5–30 and 3:12–14.

15. See FP, 375–90, where Ricoeur goes as far as to suggest that Husserl's thinking can be said to be very close to Freudian psychoanalysis.

16. See Edmund Husserl, *Cartesian Meditations: An Introduction to Phenomenology* (1931), trans. Dorion Cairns (Dordrecht: Kluwer, 1993).

17. See SP, 84 n. 9.

18. Edmund Husserl, "Primal Consciousness and the Possibility of Reflection," Appendix IX, PITC, 161–63, 162–63. In view of similar denials of an unconscious non-presence, Freud complained that philosophy as philosophy of consciousness necessarily lacks an appropriate understanding of the unconscious, which often ends up being reduced to consciousness; see Rudolf Bernet, "Unconscious Consciousness in Husserl and Freud," trans. Christopher Jupp and Paul Crowe, in *The New Husserl: A Critical Reader*, ed. Donn Welton (Bloomington: Indiana University Press, 2003), 199–219, 199.

19. It has to be stressed here that Husserl himself was well aware of the incongruities and presuppositions discussed by Ricoeur, and accordingly confessed, very early on in his study, that his account of temporality is involved in "the most extraordinary difficulties, contradictions, and entanglements" (PITC, §1, 22).

20. This complaint about Husserl's theory of temporalization is reiterated in *Memory, History, Forgetting*, where Ricoeur stresses that "the transcendental consciousness of the flow designates itself there as the consciousness of a solitary I. . . . What seems to be lacking in the egological approach is the recognition of a primordial absence, the absence of a foreign I, of an other who is always already implied in the solitary consciousness of self" (MHF, 114–15); see also MHF, 31–36 and 109–20.

21. Lawlor, *Imagination and Chance*, 84.

22. See Thomas R. Koenig, "Psychoanalysis and Hermeneutics: A Psychoanalytico-Philosophical Reading of Freud," in *Tradition and Renewal: The Centennial of Louvain's Institute of Philosophy*, ed. D. A. Boileau and J. A. Dick, vol. 2 (Leuven: Leuven University Press, 1992), 93–115; and also John E. Smith, "Freud, Philosophy, and Interpretation," in Hahn, *The Philosophy of Paul Ricoeur*, 147–64.

23. Sigmund Freud, "Project for a Scientific Psychology" (1950 [1895]), in *The Standard Edition of the Complete Psychological Works of Sigmund Freud*, trans. James Strachey et al., 24 vols. (London: Hogarth Press and the Institute of Psycho-Analysis, 1953–74), 1:281–397. For Ricoeur's discussion of Freud's "energetics," see FP, 69–86.

24. The edition of the "Project" cited in *Freud and Philosophy* is from Sigmund Freud, *The Origins of Psycho-Analysis: Letters to Wilhelm Fliess, Drafts and Notes: 1887-1902*, ed. Marie Bonaparte, Anna Freud, and Ernst Kris, trans. Eric Mosbacher and James Strachey (London: Imago, 1954), 347–445.

25. See FP, 77. Freud claims that "*unpleasure* would have to be regarded as coinciding with a raising of the level of $Q\dot\eta$ or an increasing quantitative pressure: it would be the ω sensation when there is an increase of $Q\dot\eta$ in ψ. Pleasure would be the sensation of discharge" (SE, 1:312).

26. Sigmund Freud, *The Interpretation of Dreams* (1900), SE, vols. 4 and 5. For Ricoeur's commentary on this work, see FP, 87–114.

27. Ricoeur refers to Freud's anti-phenomenological reduction *of* consciousness in FP, 118, 121–22, and 391.

28. See Sigmund Freud, 'The Unconscious' (1915), SE, 14:159–215, 173.

29. See SE, 14:186–89, and FP, 119 and 393.

30. I will use "drive" to render Freud's "*Trieb*" with a view to indicating the irresistible nature of the pressure it exercises on the psychical apparatus. In the English translation of Freud's metapsychological papers and throughout Ricoeur's *Freud and Philosophy*, "*Trieb*" is usually translated by "instinct" in either its singular or plural form. For a detailed discussion of the translation of "*Trieb*" and its relation to Freud's "*Instinkt*," see Jean Laplanche and Jean-Bertrand Pontalis, *The Language of Psycho-Analysis*, trans. Donald Nicholson-Smith (London: Hogarth Press and the Institute of Psycho-Analysis, 1973), 214–17.

31. Sigmund Freud, "Instincts and Their Vicissitudes" (1915), SE, 14:109–40, 120.

32. Freud's descriptions are ambiguous insofar as he sometimes says that drives are themselves the psychical representatives of stimuli, while at other times drives are said to be represented in the psyche by the representatives; see Laplanche and Pontalis, *The Language of Psycho-Analysis*, 364–65.

33. In "Repression" (1915), SE, 14:141–58, 148, Freud points out that repression proper constitutes a second phase whereby mental derivatives of the already repressed representatives are repressed once again at the frontier of consciousness.

34. Whereas the ideational element of the psychical representative is defined in terms of an idea or a group of ideas cathected with a quota of physical energy (libido or interest) coming from a drive, the quota of affect corresponds to a drive detached from the idea and finding expression, proportionate to its quantity, in processes that are sensed as affects; see SE, 14:152–53.

35. Koenig, "Psychoanalysis and Hermeneutics," 94.

36. According to Freud's argument, qualities can originate neither in the external world, for what one encounters there is only masses in motion (quantities); nor in the φ neurones, for this would contradict the legitimate belief that the seat of consciousness is in the upper stories of the nervous system; nor in the ψ neurones, for the psychical process of remembering or reproducing performed by these neurones is definitely without quality.

37. The mutability of the content of these sensations, the transitoriness of consciousness and the easy linking of qualities simultaneously perceived attest to the permeability of the ω neurones.

38. See FP, 76 n. 17.

39. Ibid., 77–81.

40. Ricoeur notes here that the concept of the "libido" is the first one to receive by Freud such a double determination, both energetic and non-anatomical.

41. Sigmund Freud, "A Note upon the 'Mystic Writing-Pad' " (1925), SE, 19:225–32.

42. See also FP, 75 and 456–57.

43. Ibid., 104–105, 195, 203, 442, 444, and 452–53. See also MHF, 445–47.

44. Ricoeur discusses Hegel and his dialectical teleology, which is said to constitute the model for every teleology of consciousness, in FP, 462–68. See also G. W. F. Hegel, *Phenomenology of Spirit* (1807), trans. A. V. Miller (Oxford: Oxford University Press, 1977).

45. See Sigmund Freud, "New Introductory Lectures on Psycho-Analysis" (1933), SE, 22:1–182, 73. See also G. W. F. Hegel, *Phenomenology and Psychology*, §§453–54, 151–57, vol. 3 of *Hegel's Philosophy of Subjective Spirit*, ed. and trans. M. J. Petry, 3 vols. (Dordrecht: D. Reidel, 1978).

46. See FP, 456–58. Ricoeur's emphasis on the process of working-through and the value of "work" persists in MHF, 69–71, 77–80, and 445–46, and so does the belief that Freud's psychological categories are transposable to the plane of history and collective memory.

47. See Paul Ricoeur, "What is Dialectical?" in *Freedom and Morality*, ed. John Bricke (Lawrence: University of Kansas, 1976), 173–89, 186–87; originally published as "Le 'lieu' de la dialectique," in *Dialectics. Dialectiques*, ed. Ch. Perelman (The Hague: M. Nijhoff, 1975), 92–108.

48. See also Smith's discussion in "Freud, Philosophy, and Interpretation," 160–62.

49. See Jean-François Lyotard, *Discours, figure* (Paris: Klincksieck, 1971), 12–13, 48 n. 13 and 127 n. 20.

50. See FP, 399–403.

51. Ricoeur draws extensively here upon Jean Laplanche's and Serge Leclaire's "The Unconscious: A Psychoanalytic Study" (1966), trans. Patrick Coleman, "French Freud: Structural Studies in Psychoanalysis," special issue, *Yale French Studies* 48 (1972): 118–75.

52. Richard Kearney, ed., *Paul Ricoeur: The Hermeneutics of Action* (London: Sage Publications, 1996), 1, slightly modified.

Chapter 2. Derrida and Rhythmic Discontinuity

1. See, for instance, PG, 60, 63, 66–67, 69, 93–94, 96, and Derrida's brief comment on his use of the word *dialectic* in the "Preface to the 1990 Edition," in PG, xv–xvi.

2. What is at issue here is precisely an adjustment rather than a watertight division between *The Problem of Genesis* and *Speech and Phenomena*. Derrida's subtle discussions of "dialectics" and "contradiction" suffice to demonstrate that, already in the earlier work, he attempted to displace the ordinary understanding of these terms on the basis of a possible synthesis.

3. For a discussion of Husserl's so-called transcendental turn or change of direction after 1905, see Dermot Moran, *Edmund Husserl: Founder of Phenomenology* (Cambridge: Polity Press, 2005), 7–8 and 26–28.

4. See also Ricoeur's commentary on *Ideas I* in H, 13–34.

5. For the dichotomy between immanence and transcendence, see *Ideas I*, §42, 133–35.

6. On the indubitability of immanent perception, see *Ideas I*, §46, 143–46 and §49, 150–53. The ideal contents in question, grounded in acts of consciousness, are limited by the experience of a finite subject, so they cannot aspire to *absolute* ideality. This limitation led Husserl to distinguish between adequate and inadequate apodeictic

evidence. Immanent experience, despite its privileged status in comparison to sensible intuition, still remains yoked to finitude. Therefore, even the noematic correlate does not present itself with absolutely adequate evidence or exactitude. The latter, however, is posited as a Kantian Idea regulating the horizon within which the repetitious acts of consciousness take place: "As '*Idea*' (in the Kantian sense), *the complete givenness is nevertheless prescribed*—as a connexion of endless processes of continuous appearing. . . . This continuum is more closely defined as infinite in all directions, consisting in all its phases of appearances of the same determinable X" (*Ideas I*, §143, 397). For more references to the Kantian Idea in *Ideas I*, see chapter 1, n. 8, and for the distinction between adequate and inadequate evidence, see *Ideas I*, §§137–38, 382–87. Husserl's formulations appeal to the well-known Kantian distinction between, on the one hand, the infinite Ideas of reason whose "objects" can only be thought or intended, and, on the other, concepts whose objects can be circumscribed in intuition. Owing to its infinity and essential unrealizability, an Idea in the Kantian sense must take on a regulative role: the idea of a full presence is a priori prescribed as an ideal limit opening up a horizon of infinite approximation, where any finite intuition is doomed to remain, by definition, incomplete. In light of Husserl's admission to the impossibility of a fulfilled intuition and to the concomitant possibility of an intention of the infinite, Ricoeur's assertion that the distinction between intention and intuition is totally unknown in Husserl appears a little odd. The ideality of sense serves as a transition point from the finite to the infinite and the relationship between these two terms is viewed through the prism of a certain directionality or teleology. Derrida's following remark arises precisely from the inextricable link between ideality and the infinite Idea: "There is no *ideality* without there being an Idea in the Kantian sense at work, opening up the possibility of something indefinite, the infinity of a stipulated progression or the infinity of permissible repetitions" (SP, 9). Thanks to this transition to infinity, portrayed by Husserl in terms of a "passage to the limit" (see Derrida's *Edmund Husserl's "Origin of Geometry,"* 134), a horizon can be envisaged delimited and regulated by the Idea, which functions as a *telos* prescribing for reason and science infinite tasks while disallowing a complete mediation.

7. See Paola Marrati, *Genesis and Trace: Derrida Reading Husserl and Heidegger*, trans. Simon Sparks (Stanford: Stanford University Press, 2005), 9.

8. In his discussion of continuity and the temporal density of the living present in PG, 62–63, Derrida argues that what Husserl describes as a phenomenological necessity can be neither purely phenomenological nor constituting. By presenting the a priori synthesis of the original impression as phenomenological, Husserl wishes to limit his discussion of impression to the immanent consciousness of time, which he differentiates from sensation at an elementary physiological level. Derrida contests this differentiation and highlights that the a priori synthesis signals the articulation of the primary impression with a retentional modification described as intentional. The intentionality that this a priori synthesis entails "announces" a real object at which one may aim originarily. The impression of a sound, for instance, inasmuch as it is articulated with retention, is intentional; thus it presupposes the reception of a *real* sound on whose basis the constitutive activity of consciousness can subsequently take place. For Derrida, Husserl's a priori phenomenological synthesis is possible through another a priori synthesis that is ontological, fundamental, and more originary than the noematic lived experience. But

if this is the case, the supposedly purely phenomenological, constituting, and active character of transcendental experience is undermined. If the hyletic datum of the sound is initially passively received, the actuality of consciousness appears to depend on this originary passivity. The necessary articulation of impression and retention points toward an originary passive synthesis of time that renders problematic Husserl's transcendental project by reintegrating the worldly and the already constituted into the constituting. Although Derrida's point is highly reminiscent of the concerns that Ricoeur raises with respect to Husserl's reliance on a perceptual consciousness (see the first section of chapter 1), one has to be attentive to the different conclusions to which this observation leads the two thinkers; see, for example, PG, 63–64, where Derrida critically comments on Ricoeur's views on the role of activity and passivity in Husserl. See also Marrati's brilliant discussion of Derrida's point in *Genesis and Trace*, 12–15.

9. Derrida's argument in *Speech and Phenomena* is directed toward demonstrating that there can be no easy distinction between presentation and representation, insofar as the latter is always already at work, conditioning and making presentation possible. The irreducibility of representation from the sphere of perception is attested to by the prefix *vor-* of *Vorstellung*, which indicates a being-before consciousness, a certain availability to the gaze and, by implication, a certain outside.

10. See also Lawlor's comment on Ricoeur's note in *Imagination and Chance*, 85.

11. While discussing mental acts such as thinking of oneself as speaking or hearing oneself speak, Husserl affirms that no genuine communication or speech is involved as these acts "are themselves experienced by us at that very moment" (*im selben Augenblick*); see Edmund Husserl, "Investigation I," *Logical Investigations* (1900–01), trans. J. N. Findlay, 2 vols. (London: Routledge, 1970), 1: §8, 280. Moreover, Derrida cites the following passage from *Ideas I* confirming that lived experience given in the actual now is immediately and transparently present in the mode of certitude and absolute necessity: "*Every primordial dator Intuition is a source of authority (Rechtsquelle) for knowledge, . . . whatever presents itself in 'intuition' in primordial form* (as it were in its bodily reality), *is simply to be accepted as it gives itself out to be,* though *only within the limits in which it then presents itself* (*Ideas I*, §24, 92).

12. In *Ideas I*, §81, 237, Husserl maintains that "the actual *now* is necessarily something punctual and remains so, *a form that persists through continuous change of content.*"

13. I recall here a phrase already cited from section 17: "Only in *primary remembrance do we see what is past;* only in it is the past constituted" (PITC, §17, 64).

14. As I argued in chapter 1, despite being well aware that section 42 of *The Phenomenology of Internal Time-Consciousness* blurs the supposedly impermeable boundary between presentation and representation, Ricoeur does not follow through the significant implications of this thought.

15. Derrida introduces here for the first time his famous neologism *différance* in its noun form.

16. See Marrati, *Genesis and Trace*, 72.

17. Derrida deploys the idea of a "pure auto-affection, occurring in a self-proximity that would in fact be the absolute reduction of space in general" (SP, 79) in

order to describe the act of hearing oneself speak as well as the temporalizing process that gives rise to the transcendental subject. In SP, 83, he explains that he has drawn upon Heidegger for this concept (*Selbstaffektion*), and throughout the book he endeavors to show that auto-affection is never pure but always entails, even in Husserl, difference and repetition; see especially SP, 82–87. See also Marrati's illuminating discussion in *Genesis and Trace*, 75–76. This term inevitably bears witness to a complex link between Husserl and Kant. Ricoeur evaluates the latter's treatment of auto-affection in TN, 3:54–56.

18. See Geoffrey Bennington, " . . . You Meant," in *Other Analyses: Reading Philosophy* (2004), 83–94, 90, electronic book, http://www.bennington.zsoft.co.uk/. Derrida discusses the structure of necessary possibility in "Limited Inc a b c . . . ," trans. Samuel Weber, *Limited Inc.*, 29–110, 47–50 and 77; originally published as "Limited Inc a b c . . . ," *Glyph* 2 (1977): 1–81.

19. On minimal repeatability or iterability, see LI, 50–54 and 60–64. I discuss this motif in greater detail in the first two sections of chapter 4.

20. Derrida, "*Ousia* and *Grammē*," 55.

21. See Joanna Hodge's very helpful discussion of *différance* in *Derrida on Time* (London: Routledge, 2007), 83–87.

22. Jacques Derrida, "Differance," in SP, 129–60, 143; originally published as "La 'Différance,' " *Bulletin de la société française de philosophie* 62, no. 3 (1968): 73–101.

23. Although Husserl had already used the term *transcendental life* in the 1920s, he deploys it mainly in *The Crisis of European Sciences and Transcendental Phenomenology: An Introduction to Phenomenological Philosophy* (1936), trans. David Carr (Evanston: Northwestern University Press, 1970).

24. Commenting on the reading of Husserl offered in *Speech and Phenomena*, John D. Caputo argues that "Derrida does not quarrel about the reduction, does not question its possibility, does not want to short-circuit its critical operation. He only wants to see that it is carried out far enough, that the work of critique is not subverted in advance by a teleology of presence and fulfilment. . . . Phenomenological vigilance is not enough. It is satisfied with presence, intuition, self-showing—when that is precisely what needs to be questioned"; see John D. Caputo, "The Economy of Signs in Husserl and Derrida: From Uselessness to Full Economy," in *Deconstruction and Philosophy: The Texts of Jacques Derrida*, ed. John Sallis (Chicago: University of Chicago Press, 1987), 99–113, 100–101.

25. See Jacques Derrida, *Specters of Marx: The State of the Debt, the Work of Mourning, and the New International*, trans. Peggy Kamuf (London: Routledge, 1994), 18–20; originally published as *Spectres de Marx* (Paris: Galilée, 1993).

26. Ibid., 17–18.

27. In *Derrida on Time*, 35, Hodge affirms this radical strand in Husserl's analyses of time when she observes that "for Derrida, as indeed for Husserl, the characterisation of a 'natural' time of linearity and punctuality can emerge only on the basis of the workings of a temporality of delay, curvature, and an elliptical movement back and forth between intending act and intended content." Moreover, on page 25, Hodge differentiates between at least two groups of Husserlians: one of them emphasizes notions disruptive of the transcendental consciousness (passive synthesis, pre-predicative experience, intersubjectivity), whereas the other seeks to link Husserl to Hegel and an absolute

idealism. Although Ricoeur could arguably be subsumed under the first group, I think that neither group can easily accommodate Derrida's thinking.

28. Jacques Derrida, *Archive Fever: A Freudian Impression*, trans. Eric Prenowitz (Chicago: University of Chicago Press, 1996), 97; originally published as *Mal d'Archive: une impression freudienne* (Paris: Galilée, 1995).

29. See Jacques Derrida, "To Speculate—On 'Freud,'" *The Post Card: From Socrates to Freud and Beyond*, trans. Alan Bass (Chicago: University of Chicago Press, 1987), 257–409, 394–95; originally published as "Spéculer—Sur 'Freud,'" *La carte postale: De Socrate à Freud et au-delà* (Paris: Aubier-Flammarion, 1980), 275–437.

30. On the translation of the German *Bahnung* as "facilitation" or "breaching," see Alan Bass's comment in FSW, 200 n. 2.

31. Geoffrey Bennington, "Membranes," in *Other Analyses*, 97–123, 104. This section of the second chapter is greatly indebted to Bennington's essay.

32. See David Farrell Krell, *Of Memory, Reminiscence, and Writing: On the Verge* (Bloomington: Indiana University Press, 1990), 117. Freud admits that the duplex morphology of neurones, as it is not supported by contemporary histology, is a gratuitous hypothesis, a *constructio ad hoc* (SE, 1:302).

33. See Bennington, "Membranes," 107–108.

34. Rodolphe Gasché, *The Tain of the Mirror: Derrida and the Philosophy of Reflection* (Cambridge: Harvard University Press, 1986), 102.

35. Marian Hobson, *Jacques Derrida: Opening Lines* (London: Routledge, 1998), 154.

36. See Jacques Derrida, "From Restricted to General Economy: A Hegelianism without Reserve," in *Writing and Difference*, 251–77, 259–60; originally published as "De l'économie restreinte à l'économie générale: Un hégélianisme sans réserve," *L'arc: Georges Bataille* 32 (May 1967): 24–44. Also, "The inside of speculative philosophy sublates *its own* outside as a moment of its negativity," notes Derrida in "Outwork, Prefacing," in *Dissemination*, 1–59, 11; originally published as "Hors livre," in *La dissémination*, 7–67.

37. Hobson, *Jacques Derrida*, 159. See also Jacques Derrida, *Glas*, trans. John P. Leavey Jr. and Richard Rand (Lincoln: University of Nebraska Press, 1986), 244a; originally published as *Glas* (Paris: Galilée, 1974).

38. For some references to the term *quasi-transcendental*, see Derrida's SF, 403; LI, 152; "Ulysses Gramophone: Hear Say Yes in Joyce," trans. Tina Kendall and Shari Benstock, in *Acts of Literature*, ed. Derek Attridge (New York: Routledge, 1992), 253–309, 291 and 295 ("Ulysse gramophone: Ouï-dire de Joyce," in *Ulysse gramophone: Deux mots pour Joyce* [Paris: Galilée, 1987]); *On Touching—Jean-Luc Nancy*, trans. Christine Irizarry (Stanford: Stanford University Press, 2005), 67, 97, 119, 149, 287, 333 n. 32 (*Le Toucher, Jean-Luc Nancy* [Paris: Galilée, 2000]); *Paper Machine*, trans. Rachel Bowlby (Stanford: Stanford University Press, 2005), 52 and 83 (*Papier machine* [Paris: Galilée, 2001]); *Specters of Marx*, 168; Jacques Derrida and Elisabeth Roudinesco, *For What Tomorrow . . . : A Dialogue*, trans. Jeff Fort (Stanford: Stanford University Press, 2004), 145 (*De Quoi Demain . . .* [Paris: Librairie Arthème Fayard and Galilée, 2001]); *Glas*, 151–62a; "Faith and Knowledge: The Two Sources of 'Religion' at the Limits of Reason Alone," trans. Samuel Weber, in *Religion*, ed. Jacques Derrida and Gianni

Vattimo (Cambridge: Polity Press, 1998), 1–78, 36 and 63 ("Foi et savoir: Les deux sources de la 'religion' aux limites de la simple raison," in *La Religion: Séminaire de Capri*, ed. Jacques Derrida and Gianni Vattimo [Paris: Seuil, 1996], 9–86); "Des Tours de Babel," trans. Joseph F. Graham, in *Acts of Religion*, ed. Gil Anidjar (New York: Routledge, 2002), 103–34, 127 (originally published in bilingual form in *Difference in Translation*, ed. Joseph F. Graham [Ithaca: Cornell University Press, 1985], 165–248). For a discussion of this term and of Rodolphe Gasché's use of it, see Geoffrey Bennington, "Deconstruction and the Philosophers (The Very Idea)," in *Legislations: The Politics of Deconstruction* (London: Verso, 1994), 11–60, 29–30.

39. Sigmund Freud, "Beyond the Pleasure Principle" (1920), SE, 18:1–64.

40. For the essential indissociability of life and death instincts, see Nicholas Royle's illuminating discussion in *The Uncanny* (Manchester: Manchester University Press, 2003), 84–106, especially 91–94.

41. See SE, 1:352–57.

42. For a discussion of the main traits of *Nachträglichkeit* or deferred action, see Laplanche and Pontalis, *The Language of Psycho-Analysis*, 111–14.

43. See Sigmund Freud, "Repression" (1915), SE, 14:141–58, 153.

44. This lack of transparency attendant upon the movement of *Nachträglichkeit* is captured by its metaphorical portrayal by Derrida as "a mole-like progression" or "the subterranean toil of an impression" (FSW, 214). In *The Uncanny*, 241–44, Royle reflects on these tropological representations of *Nachträglichkeit*, which lead him to an insightful complication of the frontier between the human and the animal.

45. For some of Derrida's references to "a relation without relation," which he borrows from Maurice Blanchot, see *Altérités*, ed. Jacques Derrida and Pierre-Jean Labarrière (Paris: Osiris, 1986), 82, and SF, 260.

46. Derrida's discussion takes place in the context of a commentary on Paul de Man's reading of Hegel in "Sign and Symbol in Hegel's *Aesthetics*," *Critical Inquiry* 8 (Summer 1982): 761–75.

47. Derrida notes that the logic of *Nachträglichkeit* "turns out to disrupt, disturb, entangle forever the reassuring distinction . . . between the past and the future, that is to say, between the three actual presents" (AF, 80).

48. Derrida maintains that "the economic character of differance in no way implies that the deferred presence can always be recovered, that it simply amounts to an investment that only temporarily and without loss delays the presentation of presence, that is, the perception of gain or the gain of perception" (SP, 151).

49. See Geoffrey Bennington, "Circanalysis (The Thing Itself)," in *Interrupting Derrida* (London: Routledge, 2000), 93–109, 105–106.

50. See Krell, *Of Memory, Reminiscence, and Writing*, 183.

51. See also Freud, *The Origins of Psycho-Analysis*, 173–81 (letter 52 [6 Dec. 1896]).

52. Sigmund Freud, "The Claims of Psycho-Analysis to Scientific Interest" (1913), SE, 13:163–90, 177.

53. In Plato's *Theaetetus*, 191c-d, vol. 3 of *The Dialogues of Plato*, 4th ed., trans. Benjamin Jowett, 4 vols. (Oxford: Clarendon Press, 1953), Socrates invites Theaetetus to make the following assumption: "Imagine, then, that there exists in the mind of man

a block of wax. . . . Let us say that this tablet is a gift of Memory, the mother of the Muses; and that when we wish to remember anything which we have seen, or heard, or thought in our minds, we hold the wax to the perceptions and thoughts, and in that material receive the impression of them as from the seal of a ring."

54. See also chapter 1, n. 43.

55. In SE, 5:610–11, Freud accepts that the unconscious and consciousness should not be regarded as two localities in the mental apparatus and suggests replacing the topographical way of representation by a dynamic one. Hence Ricoeur's observation, in MHF, 445-46, that what differentiates the Freudian unconscious from the Bergsonian one is its greater dynamism. It is by virtue of the latter that Derrida notes that "the metaphorical concept of translation (*Übersetzung*) or transcription (*Umschrift*) is dangerous, not because it refers to writing, but because it presupposes a text which would be already there, immobile: the serene presence of a statue, of a written stone or archive whose signified content might be harmlessly transported into the milieu of a different language" (FSW, 211).

56. Similarly, in SE, 4:100, after giving two examples of the traditional decoding method, Freud concludes "that dreams really have a meaning and that a scientific procedure for interpreting them is possible"; hence his *relative* allegiance, in light of the complications mentioned above, to this method.

57. See FSW, 199.

58. Derrida, *Of Grammatology*, 73.

59. Krell, *Of Memory, Reminiscence, and Writing*, 186.

60. These tensions intrinsic to Freudian discourse are maintained in Jacques Derrida's "Resistances," in *Resistances of Psychoanalysis*, trans. Peggy Kamuf, Pascale-Anne Brault, and Michael Nass (Stanford: Stanford University Press, 1998), 1–38, where he identifies an aporia with respect to the two motifs of the concept of "analysis": the archaeological or anagogical one, and the lytological or philolytic one; originally published as "Résistances," in *Résistances de la psychanalyse* (Paris: Galilée, 1996).

61. Paul Ricoeur, "Reply to John E. Smith," in Hahn, *The Philosophy of Paul Ricoeur*, 165–68, 168.

62. See Introduction, n. 41.

Chapter 3. Ricoeur's Hermeneutics of the Self

1. See also Introduction, n. 34.

2. See Paul Ricoeur, "Structure, Word, Event," trans. Robert Sweeney, in *The Conflict of Interpretations*, 79–96, 86; originally published as "La structure, le mot, l'événement," *Esprit* 35, no. 5 (1967): 801–21. See also Émile Benveniste, *Problems in General Linguistics*, trans. Mary Elizabeth Meek (Coral Gables: University of Miami Press, 1971), 101–11. To these three levels Ricoeur adds the hermeneutic one, which is necessitated by the transition from speech to writing, and whose corresponding unit is the text.

3. For Ricoeur's discussion of this fundamental dichotomy, see RM, 76–87, and also IT, 8, where he maintains that "the distinction between semantics and semiotics is the key to the whole problem of language."

4. See Ferdinand de Saussure, *Course in General Linguistics*, ed. Charles Bally and Albert Sechehaye, trans. Roy Harris (London: Duckworth, 1983), 118.

5. See Benveniste, *Problems in General Linguistics*, 217.

6. See IT, 1–2. Also in RM, 81, Ricoeur points out that Plato conceptualized, in several of his dialogues, language as an interlacing (*sumplokē*) of a noun and a verb.

7. Ricoeur draws here upon Benveniste's *Problems in General Linguistics*, 227.

8. Quoted by Ricoeur in RM, 83.

9. See SWE, 86 and 92; see also IT, 9 and RM, 80.

10. As Derrida briefly remarks in W, 169, notwithstanding Ricoeur's prioritization of the instance of discourse and his emphasis on its actual and singular character, singularity is subsequently subordinated to the generality of meaningfulness thanks to the transitional function of words, which always survive the transitoriness of individual speech acts. In this light, the dialectic of code and message, of the virtuality of the system and the eventhood of the speech act, constitutes one phase of the signification process, which, for Ricoeur, always takes place within a horizon regulated by the Kantian Idea of univocity and successful communication. In the next phase of this process, the speech event must be eclipsed by an ideal meaning considered to be relatively permanent and eminently repeatable; see RM, 80 and IT, 10–12. See also Lawlor's very helpful and accurate discussion of the event-meaning dialectic in *Imagination and Chance*, 53–61.

11. Ricoeur maintains that the personal pronoun, for instance, possesses the "strange property of designating at once anyone who speaks and in speaking designates himself or herself, and the sole *I*, the one that I myself am, P. R."; quoted by Kathleen Blamey in "From the Ego to the Self: A Philosophical Itinerary," in Hahn, *The Philosophy of Paul Ricoeur*, 571–603, 597.

12. In *Problems in General Linguistics*, 224, Benveniste maintains that "it is in and through language that man constitutes himself as a *subject*, because language alone establishes the concept of 'ego' in reality, in *its* reality which is that of the being."

13. See Paul Ricoeur, "Structure and Hermeneutics," trans. Kathleen McLaughlin, in *The Conflict of Interpretations*, 27–61, 30; originally published as "Symbolique et temporalité," *Archivio di Filosofia* 33, no. 1–2 (1963): 5–41.

14. See Clark, *Paul Ricoeur*, 90.

15. See OA, 40–55. Moreover, in OA, 329–30, Ricoeur summarizes the ways in which the otherness of other people is implicit in his analyses of the speaking, narrating, reading, acting, and ethical self.

16. See TN, 3:246–49 and OA, 115–25.

17. In OA, 119–20, Ricoeur defines character as the distinctive traits or lasting dispositions that permit the re-identification of an individual as the same. He admits to the ineluctably temporal nature of character, thereby casting doubt onto his earlier conviction about its immutable status. This temporal dimension is then linked to the concept of "habit" and a set of acquired identifications with values, norms, ideals, etc. It is by virtue of the relative stability of these habits and identifications that character is said to assure "at once numerical identity, qualitative identity, uninterrupted continuity across change, and, finally, permanence in time which defines sameness" (OA, 122). The permanence in time involved here reveals a paradoxical overlapping of sameness (*idem*) and selfhood (*ipse*).

18. See Henry Isaac Venema, *Identifying Selfhood: Imagination, Narrative, and Hermeneutics in the Thought of Paul Ricoeur* (Albany: State University of New York Press, 2000), 139–43.

19. See OA, 140–48.

20. See ibid., 148–49, where Ricoeur also subsumes the so-called novel of apprenticeship and contemporary fiction in general under those "fictions of the loss of identity," a characteristic example of which is Robert Musil's *The Man without Qualities*, trans. Eithne Wilkins and Ernst Kaiser, 3 vols. (London: Secker and Warburg, 1960–61). Ricoeur maintains that the eighteenth-century English novel, Dostoevksy, and Tolstoy stand somewhere in the middle as far as the problematization of identity is concerned.

21. On the threat posed to selfhood by science fiction, see OA, 150–51.

22. For the expressions "Here I am!" and "Here I Stand!," see TN, 3:249 and OA, 165–68, where Ricoeur also explores the irresponsibility of the imaginary variations of literature as opposed to the true self-constancy and responsibility required of the ethical self. He borrows the biblical phrase "Here I am!" from Emmanuel Lévinas's *Otherwise than Being: Or, Beyond Essence* (1974), trans. Alphonso Lingis (Pittsburgh: Duquesne University Press, 1998), 114, 145–46, 149, and 185.

23. See TN, 1:70–71.

24. See Ricoeur's essay on "Appropriation" in *Hermeneutics and the Human Sciences*, 182–93; see also TA, 87–88.

25. In relation to literary texts where no narrative voice can be identified and the point of view constantly shifts, Ricoeur acknowledges Wayne Booth's preference for clarity and worthy universal values, although he also clearly distances himself from Booth's reactionary castigation of the unreliable narrator; see TN, 3:163 nn. 15 and 17. See also Wayne C. Booth, *The Rhetoric of Fiction*, 2nd ed. (Chicago: University of Chicago Press, 1983).

26. For a detailed discussion of the transition from the world of the text to that of the reader, and of refiguration or appropriation in terms of a textual "appeal to" or "call upon" the reader, see my " 'Donner À Lire': Unreadable Narratives," *Literature Interpretation Theory* 19, no. 2 (2008): 100–122.

27. Ricoeur compares here the positive contribution that narrativity makes to responsible selfhood to the process of psychoanalytical cure. The latter is also intended to cure by substituting for the bits and pieces of unintelligible stories a coherent narrative in which the analysand can recognize his or her self-constancy. This transformative operation, he adds, is applicable to individuals as much as to whole communities, as attested to by the history of biblical Israel.

28. Elsewhere, interpretation is portrayed as "the process by which disclosure of new modes of being . . . gives to the subject a new capacity for knowing himself. If the reference of the text is the project of a world, then it is not the reader who primarily projects himself. The reader rather is enlarged in his capacity of self-projection by receiving a new mode of being from the text itself" (IT, 94).

29. In TN, 3:226, 228, and 258–59, Ricoeur puts forward the Ideas of unfettered communication, of a single humanity, and of a single history, while in OA, 179, the Idea takes the form of the good life. In relation to his theory of discourse, the Idea

appears under the guise of univocity and successful communication. See also Lawlor, *Imagination and Chance*, 77 n. 53.

30. See Paul Ricoeur, "What Does Humanism Mean?," trans. David Stewart, in *Political and Social Essays*, ed. David Stewart and Joseph Bien (Athens: Ohio University Press, 1974), 68–87, 86; originally published as "Que signifie 'humanisme'?," *Comprendre* 15 (1956): 84–92. See also Paul Ricoeur, *Fallible Man*, trans. Charles A. Kelbley (New York: Fordham University Press, 1986), xliv, 66–71, 102–104, and 133–46; originally published as *L'homme faillible*, vol. 1 of *Finitude et culpabilité* (Paris: Aubier, 1960), 2 vols.

31. In OA, 169, almost twenty-five years after "The Question of the Subject," Ricoeur reaffirms the figure according to which the mediated and dispossessed self is always on a return path toward itself.

32. Aristotle, *Nicomachean Ethics*, trans. W. D. Ross (revised by J. O. Urmson), vol. 2 of *The Complete Works of Aristotle*.

33. See TN, 3:230–32. See also Ricoeur's essay on "Initiative" in TA 208–22.

34. See Paul Ricoeur, *Freedom and Nature: The Voluntary and the Involuntary*, trans. Erazim V. Kohák (Evanston: Northwestern University Press, 1966), 9–10; originally published as *Le Volontaire et l'involontaire* (Paris: Aubier, 1950). In *Identifying Selfhood*, 145, Venema refers to Ricoeur's description of voluntary and acting consciousness in *Freedom and Nature* and to a certain continuity in his thought, while at the same time warning against simply equating Ricoeur's subtle formulation of selfhood in *Oneself as Another* with his early voluntarism.

35. See the essays collected in Ricoeur's *From Text to Action* and in Kearney's *Paul Ricoeur: The Hermeneutics of Action*. See also the fourth section in this chapter and especially n. 59.

36. Venema, *Identifying Selfhood*, 144.

37. Ricoeur's formulation here clearly points towards a zigzag movement between the ideal limit and one's concrete choices. As Lawlor, in *Imagination and Chance*, 2, 5, 7, 25, 46, 92–93, 105, and 129, associates deconstruction with such a zigzag movement, I will try to show in the next chapter why this view does not do justice to Derrida's complex thinking.

38. Interestingly, although Ricoeur seeks to provide an account of friendship on the basis of benevolent mutuality, he acknowledges that friendship, for Aristotle, is an equivocal notion comprising three distinct modalities: for the sake of the good, of utility, and of pleasure (OA, 182). See also n. 50 below.

39. In OA, 187, Ricoeur wonders at what point in time Western thought started to form a more or less clear concept of otherness: was it with the Christian *agapē*, with the Hegelian struggle between two self-consciousnesses, or was it with the Lévinasian belief that there is no self without another who summons it to responsibility?

40. See n. 48 below.

41. One legitimate criticism leveled by Richard A. Cohen at Ricoeur is that he interprets the Lévinasian "injunction of the other" exclusively in terms of moral norms, obligation, and obedience to duty. To the contrary, argues Cohen, the authority of alterity in Lévinas operates at an originary level simply presupposed but not accounted for by Ricoeur's discourse; see Cohen, "Moral Selfhood: A Levinasian Response

to Ricoeur on Levinas," in *Ricoeur as Another: The Ethics of Subjectivity*, ed. Richard A. Cohen and James L. Marsh (Albany: State University of New York Press, 2002), 127–60, 133.

42. There appears to be a tension between Ricoeur's demand for benevolent spontaneity and his admission elsewhere that the self always perceives the other as a threat. In *Memory, History, Forgetting*, he accepts that "the other, because other, comes to be perceived as a danger for one's own identity" (MHF, 81). The other is first and foremost encountered as someone who threatens one's selfhood, hence one's tendency to reject and exclude it. See also Paul Ricoeur, "Memory and Forgetting," in *Questioning Ethics: Contemporary Debates in Philosophy*, ed. Richard Kearney and Mark Dooley (London: Routledge, 1999), 5–11, 8.

43. See respectively QS, 253 and TN, 3:226.

44. See OA, 297–356. The tenth study is divided into three sections: the first one is devoted to the motif of "attestation," the second one explores the ontological bearing of the distinction between sameness and selfhood, while the third section focuses on the dialectic between selfhood and otherness.

45. See CM, §§42–62, 89–151. See also Ricoeur's earlier discussion in "Husserl's Fifth Cartesian Meditation" (1967), in H, 115–42.

46. In light of the allusions, in OA, 320–27 and 332–34, to Maine de Biran's and Didier Franck's approaches to flesh and the lived body, it would be interesting to compare the views that Ricoeur advances here to Derrida's detailed reflection on these thinkers in *On Touching—Jean-Luc Nancy*, 140–58 and 226–43.

47. In OA, 331–32, Ricoeur compares Husserl's argument to Descartes' hyperbolic doubt.

48. Some of Lévinas's ideas on which Ricoeur's reading concentrates come from *Totality and Infinity*, 60–70.

49. For some of the passages that epitomize, for Ricoeur, this paroxysm, see Lévinas, *Otherwise than Being*, 99–129. For Lévinas's concept of "retraction" or "unsaying," see *Totality and Infinity*, 30, and *Otherwise than Being*, 7, 151 and 198 n. 7.

50. Ricoeur conveniently defines friendship in terms of symmetrical exchange alone and depreciates Aristotle's play on various boundary lines and admission to complications: "I shall leave aside the casuistry in the discussion of friendship that cuts through both of the treatises devoted to friendship in the *Nicomachean Ethics*. The philosopher continually plays on the boundaries, whether in the case of friendships among equals or unequals, or in that of borderline situations at the crossroads of disinterest, interest, and pleasure. My own interest lies solely in the dialectic of the self and the other in the treatment of *concepts* that structure friendship between people of goodwill" (OA, 184 n. 18).

51. Cohen, "Moral Selfhood," 130.

52. Ibid., 129.

53. Jacques Derrida, *The Gift of Death*, trans. David Wills (Chicago: University of Chicago Press, 1995), 24; originally published as "Donner la mort," in *L'Ethique du don: Jacques Derrida et la pensée du don*, ed. Jean-Michel Rabaté and Michael Wetzel (Paris: Transition, 1992).

54. Venema, *Identifying Selfhood*, 153.

55. Ibid., 153. Oddly, the terminology Venema endorses here ("enhance," "enlarge," "expand") is indebted to a transformative, dialectical conceptuality that Ricoeur has always embraced; see also the third section of this chapter.

56. Ibid., 156.

57. See OA, 189–91.

58. Venema, *Identifying Selfhood*, 155.

59. Ricoeur discusses action and agency in OA, 56–112, power in OA, 194–95 and 220, and the distinction between act and power in OA, 302–17.

60. See the eighth study, "The Self and the Moral Norm," in OA, 203–39.

61. Cohen, "Moral Selfhood," 134.

62. In the interest of accuracy, it has to be stressed that the category of the flesh is not for Ricoeur something simple but contains its own dialectic between passivity and activity, a dialectic anterior to the alterity or passivity of the other human being; see OA, 319–29, where he also discusses Heidegger's contribution to the "ontology of the flesh."

63. Blamey, "From the Ego to the Self," 594.

64. See Madison, "Ricoeur and the Hermeneutics of the Subject," 77 and 81–82.

65. See Paul Ricoeur, "Reply to G. B. Madison," in Hahn, *The Philosophy of Paul Ricoeur*, 93–95.

66. See Blamey, "From the Ego to the Self," 571.

67. See TN, 3:225–28, 235, and 257–59.

68. Ricoeur, "What Does Humanism Mean?," 86.

69. See also the first section of chapter 1.

70. Venema, *Identifying Selfhood*, 150.

71. Venema is right in noting that the other in Ricoeur is analogous to me. Yet he is once again a little unfair in construing this analogy, in *Identifying Selfhood*, 157, as affirming a simple identity: "The other must be like me, my duplicate needed to balance the dissymmetry of power of active selfhood and passive otherness. The other is just like me, the same as me, the other is me, or at least I must presume the other to be analogous to me."

72. See Cohen, "Moral Selfhood," 132.

Chapter 4. Secret Singularities

1. For some of the texts in which Derrida deploys the expression "worthy of its name," see MPM, 150; AF, 5; LI, 34; SEC, 13; GD, 7; "Resistances," 25; "On Forgiveness," 39; "Circumfession," in Geoffrey Bennington and Jacques Derrida, *Jacques Derrida*, trans. Geoffrey Bennington (Chicago: University of Chicago Press, 1993), 3–315, 47 (*Jacques Derrida* [Paris: Seuil, 1991]); *On Touching—Jean-Luc Nancy*, 298; *Paper Machine*, 161; Derrida and Roudinesco, *For What Tomorrow . . .* , 83; *Aporias: Dying—Awaiting (One Another at) the "Limits of Truth,"* trans. Thomas Dutoit (Stanford: Stanford University Press, 1993), 32 (published in French as *Apories: Mourir—s'attendre aux "limites de la vérité'"* [Paris: Galilée, 1996]); and Catherine Malabou and Jacques

Derrida, *Counterpath: Traveling with Jacques Derrida*, trans. David Wills (Stanford: Stanford University Press, 2004); 32 n. 9 and 56 (*La Contre-allée* [Paris: La Quinzaine Littéraire-Louis Vuitton, 1999]).

2. See Lyotard, *Discours, figure*, 115–16 n. 18. Although the fact that he draws heavily upon Benveniste may be taken to indicate his agreement with Ricoeur, Lyotard resists the dialectical articulation that Ricoeur favours. See also Bennington's discussion of Lyotard's objection to Derrida in "Index," in *Legislations: The Politics of Deconstruction*, 274–95, 284–93, and in *Lyotard: Writing the Event* (Manchester: Manchester University Press, 1988), 63–64.

3. Husserl, *Logical Investigations*, 1: §26, 313–19.

4. An important essay in the context of this discussion is Gottlob Frege's "On *Sinn* and *Bedeutung*" (1892), trans. Max Black, in *The Frege Reader*, ed. Michael Beaney (Oxford: Blackwell, 1997), 151–71.

5. See Jacques Derrida, "Structure, Sign, and Play in the Discourse of the Human Sciences," in *Writing and Difference*, 278–93, 281; originally published as "La structure, le signe et le jeu dans le discours des sciences humaines," in *L'écriture et la différence*, 409–28.

6. Geoffrey Bennington, "Derridabase," in Bennington and Derrida, *Jacques Derrida*, 3–316, 25.

7. See SEC, 10–11, SP, 91–93, and Husserl, *Logical Investigations*, 1: §9, 280–82 and §14, 290–91.

8. See SEC, 11–12.

9. See, for example, Derrida, *Of Grammatology*, 29 and 91.

10. See also LI, 44, 47–50, 53, and 61–62.

11. Gayatri Chakravorty Spivak, "Revolutions That as Yet Have No Model: Derrida's *Limited Inc*," *Diacritics* 10, no. 4 (1980): 29–49, 38.

12. Husserl, *Logical Investigations*, 1: §26, 316; see also SP, 95.

13. Derrida remarks that "death reveals that the proper name could always lend itself to repetition in the absence of its bearer, becoming thus a singular common noun, as common as the pronoun 'I,' which effaces its singularity even as it designates it, which lets fall into the most common and generally available exteriority what nevertheless *means* the relation to itself of an interiority" (MPM, 50).

14. Bennington, "Index," 293.

15. See J. L. Austin, *How to Do Things with Words*, 2nd ed., ed. J. O. Urmson and Marina Sbisà (Oxford: Oxford University Press, 1962), 60–62.

16. See SEC, 19–20.

17. See Bennington's brilliant analysis of the signature in "Derridabase," 148–66.

18. Bennington, "Index," 293.

19. See Paul de Man, "Sign and Symbol in Hegel's *Aesthetics*," 768, and Derrida's commentary on de Man in MPM, 55–56. See also G. W. F. Hegel, *The Encyclopaedia Logic*, trans. T. F. Geraets, W. A. Suchting, and H. S. Harris (Indianapolis: Hackett, 1991), §20, 50.

20. Derrida portrays the aporia of iterability in terms of a *différance* between "instant" and "instance" in Maurice Blanchot and Jacques Derrida, *The Instant of My*

Death / Demeure: Fiction and Testimony, trans. Elizabeth Rottenberg (Stanford: Stanford University Press, 2000), 39–43 and 46; Derrida's text was originally published as *Demeure: Maurice Blanchot* (Paris: Galilée, 1998). The uncanny relation between "instant" and "instance," which announces the double necessity of punctuality and universalizability, is encapsulated in the final phrase of Blanchot's short story in *The Instant of My Death / Demeure*, 10–11: "The instant of my death henceforth always in abeyance [*l'instant de ma mort désormais toujours en instance*]."

21. Furthermore, at a certain point in the animated exchange between the two thinkers at the Montreal conference on communication, Ricoeur concedes that iterability is indeed irreducible; see "Philosophy and Communication," 157.

22. See Jan Patočka, *Heretical Essays in the Philosophy of History* (1990), trans. Erazim Kohák, ed. James Dodd (Chicago: Open Court, 1996), 99–105.

23. On Plato's analogy of the cave, see Patočka, *Heretical Essays*, 104.

24. See GD, 1–34.

25. See Søren Kierkegaard, *Fear and Trembling* (1843), trans. Alastair Hannay (London: Penguin, 1985), 109.

26. Ibid., 135.

27. Ibid., 89.

28. Ibid., 137.

29. Ibid., 88 and 139.

30. See GD, 74.

31. See Jacques Derrida, "Passions: 'An Oblique Offering,' " trans. David Wood, in *Derrida: A Critical Reader*, ed. David Wood (Oxford: Blackwell, 1992), 5–35, 18–19.

32. Jacques Derrida, " 'Eating Well,' or the Calculation of the Subject: An Interview with Jacques Derrida," trans. Peter Connor and Avital Ronell, in *Who Comes after the Subject?*, ed. Eduardo Cadava, Peter Connor, and Jean-Luc Nancy (New York: Routledge, 1991), 96–119, 118; originally published as "Il faut bien manger, ou le calcul du sujet," *Cahiers Confrontation* 20 (Winter 1989): 91–114.

33. See also GD, 38–39, where Derrida contends that "dissimulation is never better dissimulated than by means of this particular kind of dissimulation that consists in making a show of exposing it, unveiling it, laying it bare."

34. Ricoeur quoted by Lawlor in *Imagination and Chance*, 59. The same idea is put forward in another context, where Ricoeur argues that "it is through a recognition of the failure of unity that the notion of a limiting idea will acquire all its meaning"; see Paul Ricoeur, "The Unity of the Voluntary and the Involuntary as a Limiting Idea," trans. Daniel O'Connor, in *The Philosophy of Paul Ricoeur: An Anthology of his Work*, ed. Charles E. Reagan and David Stewart (Boston: Beacon Press, 1978), 3–19, 17; originally published as "L'Unité du volontaire et de l'involontaire comme idée-limite," *Bulletin de la Société française de Philosophie* 45, no. 1, 1–2 (1951): 3–22, 22–29.

35. Derrida, *The Instant of My Death / Demeure*, 36.

36. Derrida, "Passions," 20.

37. On the derivation of "secret" from the Latin *secernere*, see GD, 13 and 20. In addition, Derrida points out that the choice of the term *secret* "is a strategy, in a definite philosophical scene, that wishes to insist on separation, isolation. Between *this*

secret and what is generally called secret, even if the two are heterogeneous, there is an analogy that makes me prefer the secret to the non-secret, the secret to the public expression, exhibition, phenomenality. I have a taste for the secret, it clearly has to do with non-belonging"; see "I Have a Taste for the Secret," in Jacques Derrida and Maurizio Ferraris, *A Taste for the Secret* (1997), trans. Giacomo Donis, ed. Giacomo Donis and David Webb (Cambridge: Polity Press, 2001), 3–92, 58–59.

38. Ricoeur reiterates this belief in "La promesse d'avant la promesse."

39. De Man's phrase is from his *Allegories of Reading: Figural Language in Rousseau, Nietzsche, Rilke, and Proust* (New Haven: Yale University Press, 1979), 277.

40. Derrida, "Faith and Knowledge," 63–64.

41. Geoffrey Bennington, "Almost the End," in *Interrupting Derrida*, 141–52, 151.

42. Rodolphe Gasché, "Deconstruction and Hermeneutics," in *Deconstructions: A User's Guide*, ed. Nicholas Royle (Basingstoke: Palgrave, 2000), 137–50, 150.

43. See Derrida, "Faith and Knowledge," 64.

44. Jacques Derrida, "Perhaps or Maybe," *PLI Warwick Journal of Philosophy* 6 (Summer 1997): 1–18, 13.

45. Llewelyn, *Appositions of Jacques Derrida and Emmanuel Lévinas*, 4.

46. See VM, 112. This essay first appeared in 1964 in *Revue de métaphysique et de morale* and was subsequently revised and included in *L'écriture et la différence*, 117–228. See Introduction, n. 33, and, for a discussion of the significant revision that the essay underwent in 1967, see Robert Bernasconi, "The Trace of Lévinas in Derrida," in *Derrida and Différance*, ed. David Wood and Robert Bernasconi (Evanston: Northwestern University Press, 1988), 13–29.

47. See GD, 88–92. The other's essential invisibility is applicable to one's relation to oneself too, insofar as the very possibility of a present self, of an "I am," is predicated upon a temporalizing movement indissociable from otherness and non-presence, as I argued in chapter 2. I will discuss the ensuing expropriated self in the final section of this chapter.

48. Derrida confirms the absolute character of alterity in "I Have a Taste for the Secret," 57, where he yokes together the absolute secret and the wholly other. The etymology of "absolute" (*ab-solutum*) points to a radical interruption, where the other remains cut off from any bond, out of reach and detached from the experience of a finite being.

49. See Derrida, "I Have a Taste for the Secret," 57–58.

50. This necessary distance between self and other should be applied to the self's reliance on ethico-theoretical maxims too. I am truly responsible only to the extent that I refuse to compromise my identity, decision, and action by inscribing them within the horizon of a calculative general ethics. Derrida often refers to Kant's cautious distinction between "acting *from duty*" and "acting *in accordance with duty*" as a criterion of differentiating authentic responsible behavior from simply aping what one takes to be responsible behavior. Derrida, however, goes a step farther to say that, in order to assume a genuine responsibility and to refuse to compromise one's singularity, one should act *out of duty*, one should resist a course of action administratively prescribed by ethics. For some of Derrida's comments on the Kantian distinction, see Derrida, "Passions," 8–9

and 33 n. 12; GD, 63; and AP, 16–17; see also Immanuel Kant, *Critique of Practical Reason* (1788), trans. and ed. Mary Gregor (Cambridge: Cambridge University Press, 1997), 69. Regarding the translation of Kant's "*aus Pflicht*" and "*pflichtmässig*," I have followed Bennington's suggestion in *Interrupting Derrida*, 37. See also Immanuel Kant, *The Metaphysics of Morals* (1797), trans. and ed. Mary Gregor (Cambridge: Cambridge University Press, 1996), for the relevant distinction between morality and ethics, right and virtue. Ricoeur apparently endorses this division in light of his insistence, in *Oneself as Another*, on the difference between deontology and teleology.

51. See Martin Heidegger, *Being and Time* (1927), trans. John Macquarrie and Edward Robinson (Oxford: Blackwell, 1962), §47, 284.

52. See GD, 53–57, and AF, 77, for a brief comment on trembling and singularity. See also Patočka, *Heretical Essays*, 106.

53. Jacques Derrida, "Afterword: Toward an Ethic of Discussion" (1988), trans. Samuel Weber, in *Limited Inc*, 111–60, 116–17.

54. Paul Ricoeur, *The Symbolism of Evil*, trans. Emerson Buchanan (Boston: Beacon Press, 1967), 136; originally published as *La Symbolique du mal*, vol. 2 of *Finitude et culpabilité* (Paris: Aubier, 1960), 2 vols.

55. Here are just some of the texts in which Ricoeur deploys the idea or the phrase "worthy of the name" while discussing a range of concepts such as narrative plot, laws, literary hermeneutics, practices, practical wisdom, life, art, criticism and critique, a philosophy of history, philosophers, a theory of recognition, the event, juridical theory, etc.: TN, 1:56 and 178; TN, 2:8; TN, 3:174; OA, 57, 241, and 316; MHF, 61, 171, and 293; H, 168; RM, 368; *The Course of Recognition*, 18; QS, 250; FM, 68, 106, and 136; and *The Just*, trans. David Pellauer (Chicago: University of Chicago Press, 2000), xxii (*Le Juste* [Paris: Esprit, 1995]).

56. Paul Ricoeur, *History and Truth*, trans. Charles A. Kelbley (Evanston: Northwestern University Press, 1965), 247; originally published as *Histoire et vérité* (Paris: Seuil, 1955).

57. For another improbable encounter between Derrida and Ricoeur, see my " 'Donner À Lire': Unreadable Narratives," 113–19, where I provide a deconstructive reading of Ricoeur's narrative function of "refiguration" in *Time and Narrative*.

58. See Bennington, "Deconstruction and Ethics," *Interrupting Derrida*, 34–46, 37.

59. See VM, 126.

60. However, although Ricoeur is keen to dialecticize the supposed irrelation between self and other, Derrida suggests, against Lévinas's will, that such a dialectic is already implicit in Lévinas's discourse.

61. See VM, 112.

62. For a detailed discussion of originary metaphoricity as the condition of language, see Derrida's "White Mythology: Metaphor in the Text of Philosophy."

63. See Bernasconi, "The Trace of Lévinas in Derrida," 15.

64. Ibid., 18.

65. Emmanuel Lévinas, "On the Trail of the Other" (1963), trans. Daniel Hoy, *Philosophy Today* 10 (1966): 34–46, 37.

66. See Lévinas, *Totality and Infinity*, 50.

67. Lévinas's acknowledgment, in the final analysis, of the other's minimal phenomenalizability leads to the admission of an originary violence, something that is in agreement with Howard Caygill's observation, in *Lévinas and the Political* (London: Routledge, 2002), 3, that, for Lévinas, it is irresponsible to speak of peace without war, and that violence is inextricable from ethics.

68. See Derrida "*Ousia* and *Grammē*," 55, and AP, 68–72.

69. For the "relation without relation," see chapter 2, n. 45. The expression "unexperienced experience" is also Blanchot's, and Derrida has recourse to it in *The Instant of My Death / Demeure*, 47 and 65; see also Maurice Blanchot, *The Writing of the Disaster*, new ed., trans. Ann Smock (Lincoln: University of Nebraska Press, 1995), 67.

70. See VM, 152.

71. See Derrida, " 'Eating Well,' " 112.

72. Ibid., 112–13.

73. In " 'Eating Well,' " 110–11, Derrida argues that "something of this call of the other must remain nonreappropriable, nonsubjectivable, and in a certain way nonidentifiable, a sheer supposition, so as to remain *other*, a *singular* call to response or to responsibility. This is why the determination of the singular 'Who?'—or at least its determination as subject—still remains problematic. And it *should* remain so. This obligation to protect the other's otherness is not merely a theoretical imperative."

74. Malabou and Derrida, *Counterpath: Traveling with Jacques Derrida*, 142.

75. See Derrida, "Passions," 12.

76. Derrida, " 'Eating Well,' " 106.

77. As far as mythology is concerned, Derrida provides an approximation of the specular (de)constitution of the self by alluding to Psyche, who was prohibited, by Aphrodite's irrational decree, from coming into full contact with Eros. The myth reveals an unovercomeable distance, which does not amount to an absolute separation; see Jacques Derrida, "Psyche: Inventions of the Other," trans. Catherine Porter, in *Reading de Man Reading*, ed. Lindsay Waters and Wlad Godzich (Minneapolis: University of Minnesota Press, 1989), 25–65, 38–39 (collected in French as "Psyché: Invention de l'autre," in *Psyché: Inventions de l'autre* [Paris: Galilée, 1987], 11–61).

78. See Paul de Man, "Autobiography as De-Facement," in *The Rhetoric of Romanticism* (New York: Columbia University Press, 1984), 67–81, 74–75. See also William Wordsworth, "Essays upon Epitaphs," in *The Prose Works of William Wordsworth*, ed. W. J. B. Owen and Jane Worthington Smyser, 3 vols. (Oxford: Clarendon Press, 1974), 2:43–119, 52–53. De Man focuses on the deconstructive effects of Wordsworth's use of metaphor and prosopopeia. The functioning of these tropes in Wordsworth's essay complicates the hierarchical structure of dichotomies that the poet wishes nonetheless to endorse, such as life and text, the literal and the figural, life and death, soul and body, conceptuality and materiality, truth and fiction.

79. De Man, "Autobiography as De-Facement," 75–76; see also MPM, 27.

80. De Man, "Autobiography as De-Facement," 77. For the "prosopopeia of prosopopeia," see Paul de Man, "Hypogram and Inscription: Michael Riffaterre's Poetics of Reading," *Diacritics* 11, no. 4 (Winter 1981): 17–35, 34.

81. De Man, "Autobiography as De-Facement," 76.

82. Derrida, *Of Grammatology*, 36–37.

83. Gasché, *The Tain of the Mirror*, 102.

Conclusion

1. See David Wood, "Vigilance and Interruption: Derrida, Gadamer, and the Limits of Dialogue," in *Philosophy at the Limit* (London: Unwin Hyman, 1990), 118–31, 129.

2. See Gasché, "Deconstruction and Hermeneutics," 150.

3. "For Jacques Derrida, this beginning of explanation in view of new *intersections*, this tribute of faithful thinking" (W, 174).

4. Ricoeur, *History and Truth*, 52.

Appendix. "The Word: Giving, Naming, Calling"

[The French text of this essay, entitled "La parole: Donner, nommer, appeler," was published in *Paul Ricoeur*, ed. Myriam Revault d'Allones and François Azouvi, L'Herne, no. 81 (Paris: Éditions de L'Herne, 2004), 19–25. I have a great debt of gratitude to Geoffrey Bennington and Céline Surprenant for their invaluable help. Without their knowledgeable suggestions and generous advice, the English translation would have been much less accurate. I would also like to thank Sean Gaston for his kindness and insightful comments. I have indicated the recurrence of the term *la parole* in Derrida's text by inserting it in square brackets. The English translation "the word" in the title does not do justice to all senses of *la parole* to which Derrida alludes, more or less obliquely, in the essay and which can be legitimately associated with Ricoeur's philosophy. Some of these senses are the following: "speech act" or "speech event" to be opposed to the Saussurean *langue* but also to writing, "word" qua linguistic unit on the borderline between the lexical and the syntactic levels of language, "word" in the sense of a commitment or a promise to the other and, finally, "the Word" in the religious sense of the term. See also Derrida's comments in Note 3 below.—Trans.]

1. "Difficult Forgiveness" is the very title of the epilogue to Paul Ricoeur's *Memory, History, Forgetting*, trans. Kathleen Blamey and David Pellauer (Chicago: University of Chicago Press, 2004), in which he discusses, in a friendly way, some of my views on the history, and more particularly the contemporary history, of forgiveness (468 and 490).

2. [I have used the word *selfhood* to render "*ipséité*" in the interest of consistency with existing translations of Ricoeur's works.—Trans.]

3. If I had the strength, time and space, I would like to follow the trajectory of the word *parole* in Ricoeur's work, its role in confession, testimony, and forgiveness, at least since *The Symbolism of Evil*, trans. Emerson Buchanan (Boston: Beacon Press, 1967) (on the first page of the introduction entitled "Phenomenology of 'Confession,'" Ricoeur announces: "[Confession] is an *utterance* [*parole*], an utterance of man about himself; and every utterance can and must be taken up into the element of philosophic discourse" [emphasis PR, translation slightly modified]), and up to what he says about testimony in *Memory, History, Forgetting*, 165 ("What makes it an institution is, first of all, the stability of testimony ready to be reiterated, and next the contribution of the trustworthiness of each testimony to the security of the social bond inasmuch as this rests on confidence in the *word* [*la parole*] of other people" [emphasis JD, translation slightly

modified]), by way of "L'herméneutique du témoignage," in *Lectures 3, Aux frontières de la philosophie* (Paris: Seuil, 1992), an admirable and very rich essay that proved indeed valuable to me during a seminar on testimony that lasted three years (on page 117, for instance, Ricoeur writes: "The meaning of testimony, then, appears to be inverted; the word does not designate any more an act of *speech* [*parole*]; an eye-witness's oral account of an event that he has witnessed; testimony is the act itself in that it attests, by exteriorization, to one's inner self, one's conviction and faith. And yet, there is no interruption of meaning.... From testimony in the sense of a report of the facts, one passes, by way of a gradated transition, to attestation by action and death; the witness's involvement in the testimony is the fixed point around which a whole range of meanings revolves. It is this involvement that marks the difference between a false witness and a truthful and trustworthy one" (emphasis JD, my translation). And always at the limit of philosophy: "The concept of testimony that extricates itself from biblical exegesis is hermeneutic in a double sense. Firstly, in the sense that it *gives* [*donne*] to interpretation a content to interpret. Secondly, in the sense that it *calls for* [*appelle*] an interpretation" (my translation).

In the association of the two verbs *to give* [*donner*] and *to call for* [*appeler*], I discern the signature and idiomatic gesture of Paul Ricoeur. A little farther on, on page 130, he adds: "Testimony is the ἀνάγκη στῆναι of an interpretation. A hermeneutics without testimony is condemned to an infinite regress, in a perspectivism with neither beginning nor end. This is a hard word [*parole*] for the philosopher to hear" (my translation).

4. Paul Ricoeur, "Structure, Word, Event," trans. Robert Sweeney, in *The Conflict of Interpretations: Essays in Hermeneutics*, ed. Don Ihde (Evanston: Northwestern University Press, 1974), 79–96, 92. I underline the words *speech* [*parole*], *names, event,* and *history.*

5. [Jacques Derrida, *Edmund Husserl's "Origin of Geometry": An Introduction,* trans. John P. Leavey Jr. (Lincoln: University of Nebraska Press, 1989).—Trans.]

6. [Jacques Derrida, "Violence and Metaphysics: An Essay on the Thought of Emmanuel Lévinas," in *Writing and Difference,* trans. Alan Bass (London: Routledge, 1978), 79–153.—Trans.]

7. *Actes du XVe Congrès de l'Association des Sociétés de Philosophie de Langue Française,* Proc. of Conference on "Communication," 1971, University of Montréal (Montréal: Montmorency, 1973).

8. [Ricoeur's presentation, "Discours et communication," which has not been translated into English, has been reprinted in Revault d'Allones and Azouvi, *Paul Ricoeur,* 51–67. For an English translation of Derrida's presentation, see Jacques Derrida, "Signature Event Context," trans. Samuel Weber and Jeffrey Mehlman, in *Limited Inc,* ed. Gerald Graff (Evanston: Northwestern University Press, 1988), 1–23.—Trans.]

9. *Actes du XVe Congrès de l'Association des Sociétés de Philosophie de Langue Française,* 404.

10. [See "Philosophy and Communication: Round-table Discussion between Ricoeur and Derrida," trans. Leonard Lawlor, appendix, in Leonard Lawlor, *Imagination and Chance: The Difference between the Thought of Ricoeur and Derrida* (Albany: State University of New York Press, 1992), 131–63, 136–38, slightly modified.—Trans.]

11. Jacques Derrida, "White Mythology: Metaphor in the Text of Philosophy," in *Margins of Philosophy*, trans. Alan Bass (Hemel Hempstead: Harvester Wheatsheaf, 1982), 207–71.

12. Paul Ricoeur, *The Rule of Metaphor: The Creation of Meaning in Language*, trans. Robert Czerny with Kathleen McLaughlin and John Costello, SJ (London: Routledge, 2003), 336–48.

13. Jacques Derrida, "The *Retrait* of Metaphor," trans. Frieda Gasdner, Biodun Iginla, Richard Madden, and William West, *Enclitic* 2, no. 2 (1978): 5–33. This essay, translated by Peggy Kamuf, also appears in Jacques Derrida's *Psyche: Inventions of the Other*, vol. 1 (Stanford: Stanford University Press, 2007), 48–80.

14. Ricoeur, *The Rule of Metaphor*, 336.

Bibliography

Primary Texts by Jacques Derrida

Derrida, Jacques. *Edmund Husserl's "Origin of Geometry": An Introduction.* Trans. John P. Leavey Jr. Lincoln: University of Nebraska Press, 1989 (*Introduction à 'L'Origine de la géométrie' de Husserl.* Paris: Presses Universitaires de France, 1962).

———. "Violence and Metaphysics: An Essay on the Thought of Emmanuel Lévinas." In *Writing and Difference*, 79–153 ("Violence et métaphysique: Essai sur la pensée d'Emmanuel Lévinas." *Revue de métaphysique et de morale* 69, no. 3–4 [1964]: 322–45, 425–73).

———. "Freud and the Scene of Writing." In *Writing and Difference*, 196–231 ("Freud et la scène de l'écriture." *Tel Quel* 26 [Summer 1966]: 10–41).

———. *Writing and Difference.* Trans. Alan Bass. London: Routledge, 1978 (*L'écriture et la différence.* Paris: Seuil, 1967).

———. "Structure, Sign, and Play in the Discourse of the Human Sciences." 1967. In *Writing and Difference*, 278–93 ("La structure, le signe et le jeu dans le discours des sciences humaines." In *L'écriture et la différence*, 409–28).

———. "From Restricted to General Economy: A Hegelianism without Reserve." In *Writing and Difference*, 251–77 ("De l'économie restreinte à l'économie générale: Un hégélianisme sans réserve." *L'arc: Georges Bataille* 32 [May 1967]: 24–44).

———. *Of Grammatology.* Trans. Gayatri Chakravorty Spivak. Baltimore: Johns Hopkins University Press, 1976 (*De la grammatologie.* Paris: Minuit, 1967).

———. *Speech and Phenomena: And Other Essays on Husserl's Theory of Signs.* Trans. David B. Allison. Evanston: Northwestern University Press, 1973 (*La voix et le phénomène: Introduction au problème du signe dans la phénoménologie de Husserl.* Paris: Presses Universitaires de France, 1967).

———. "Form and Meaning: A Note on the Phenomenology of Language." In *Speech and Phenomena*, 107–28 ("La forme et le vouloir-dire: note sur la phénoménologie du langage." *Revue internationale de philosophie* 21, no. 81 [1967]: 277–99).

———. "Differance." In *Speech and Phenomena*, 129–60 ("La 'Différance.' " *Bulletin de la société française de philosophie* 62, no. 3 [1968]: 73–101).

———. "*Ousia* and *Grammē*: Note on a Note from *Being and Time*." In *Margins of Philosophy*, 29–67 ("Ousia et grammè: note sur une note de *Sein und Zeit*." In *L'endurance de la pensée. Pour saluer Jean Beaufret*, ed. Marcel Jouhandeau, 219–66. Paris: Plon, 1968).

——. "The Pit and the Pyramid: Introduction to Hegel's Semiology." In *Margins of Philosophy*, 69–108 ("Le puits et la pyramide: introduction à la sémiologie de Hegel." In *Hegel et la pensée moderne*, ed. Jacques d'Hondt, 27–83. Paris: Presses Universitaires de France, 1970).

——. "White Mythology: Metaphor in the Text of Philosophy." In *Margins of Philosophy*, 207–71 ("La mythologie blanche: La métaphore dans le texte philosophique." *Poétique* 5 [1971]: 1–52).

——. *Margins of Philosophy*. Trans. Alan Bass. Hemel Hempstead: Harvester Wheatsheaf, 1982 (*Marges de la philosophie*. Paris: Minuit, 1972).

——. *Dissemination*. Trans. Barbara Johnson. London: Athlone Press, 1981 (*La dissémination*. Paris: Seuil, 1972).

——. "Outwork, Prefacing." 1972. In *Dissemination*, 1–59 ("Hors livre." In *La dissémination*, 7–67).

——. "Signature Event Context." 1972. Trans. Samuel Weber and Jeffrey Mehlman. In *Limited Inc*, 1–23 ('Signature événement contexte." In *Marges de la philosophie*, 365–93).

——. *Positions*. Trans. Alan Bass. London: Athlone Press, 1981 (*Positions: Entretiens avec Henri Ronse, Julia Kristeva, Jean-Louis Houdebine, Guy Scarpetta*. Paris: Minuit, 1972).

——. *Glas*. Trans. John P. Leavey Jr. and Richard Rand. Lincoln: University of Nebraska Press, 1986 (*Glas*. Paris: Galilée, 1974).

——. "Limited Inc a b c. . . ." Trans. Samuel Weber. In *Limited Inc*, 29–110 ("Limited Inc a b c. . . ." *Glyph* 2 [1977]: 1–81).

——. "The *Retrait* of Metaphor." Trans. Frieda Gasdner, Biodun Iginla, Richard Madden, and William West. *Enclitic* 2, no. 2 (1978): 5–33 ("Le retrait de la métaphore." *Poésie* 7 [1978]: 103–26).

——. "To Speculate—On 'Freud.'" In *The Post Card: From Socrates to Freud and Beyond*, trans. Alan Bass, 257–409. Chicago: University of Chicago Press, 1987. ("Spéculer—Sur 'Freud.'" In *La carte postale: De Socrate à Freud et au-delà*, 275–437. Paris: Aubier-Flammarion, 1980).

——. "The Time of a Thesis: Punctuations." 1983. Trans. Kathleen McLaughlin. In Montefiore, *Philosophy in France Today*, 34–50.

——. "Three Questions to Hans-Georg Gadamer." Trans. Diane Michelfelder and Richard Palmer. In Michelfelder and Palmer, *Dialogue and Deconstruction*, 52–54 ("Bonnes volontés de puissance [Une réponse à Hans-Georg Gadamer]." *Revue internationale de philosophie* 38, no. 151 [1984]: 341–43).

——. "Des Tours de Babel." Trans. Joseph F. Graham. In *Acts of Religion*, ed. Gil Anidjar, 103–34. New York: Routledge, 2002 ("Des Tours de Babel." In *Difference in Translation*, ed. Joseph F. Graham, 165–248. Ithaca: Cornell University Press, 1985).

——. "Interpreting Signatures (Nietzsche/Heidegger): Two Questions." 1986. Trans. Diane Michelfelder and Richard Palmer. In Michelfelder and Palmer, *Dialogue and Deconstruction*, 58–71.

——. "Psyche: Inventions of the Other." Trans. Catherine Porter. In *Reading de Man Reading*, ed. Lindsay Waters and Wlad Godzich, 25–65. Minneapolis: University of Minnesota Press, 1989 ("Psyché: Invention de l'autre." In *Psyché: Inventions de l'autre*, 11–61. Paris: Galilée, 1987).

———. "Ulysses Gramophone: Hear Say Yes in Joyce." Trans. Tina Kendall and Shari Benstock. In *Acts of Literature*, ed. Derek Attridge, 253–309. New York: Routledge, 1992 ("Ulysse gramophone: Ouï-dire de Joyce." In *Ulysse gramophone: Deux mots pour Joyce*. Paris: Galilée, 1987).

———. *Limited Inc.* Ed. Gerald Graff. Evanston: Northwestern University Press, 1988.

———. "Afterword: Toward an Ethic of Discussion." 1988. Trans. Samuel Weber. In *Limited Inc*, 111–60.

———. *Mémoires: For Paul de Man.* Rev. ed. Trans. Cecile Lindsay, Jonathan Culler, Eduardo Cadava, and Peggy Kamuf. New York: Columbia University Press, 1989 (*Mémoires pour Paul de Man*. Paris: Galilée, 1988).

———. " 'Eating Well,' or the Calculation of the Subject: An Interview with Jacques Derrida." Trans. Peter Connor and Avital Ronell. In *Who Comes after the Subject?*, ed. Eduardo Cadava, Peter Connor, and Jean-Luc Nancy, 96–119. New York: Routledge, 1991 ("Il faut bien manger, ou le calcul du sujet." *Cahiers Confrontation* 20 [Winter 1989]: 91–114).

———. *The Problem of Genesis in Husserl's Philosophy.* Trans. Marian Hobson. Chicago: University of Chicago Press, 2003 (*Le problème de la genèse dans la philosophie de Husserl*. Paris: Presses Universitaires de France, 1990).

———. "Circumfession." 1991. In Bennington and Derrida, *Jacques Derrida*, 3–315.

———. "Passions: 'An Oblique Offering.' " Trans. David Wood. In *Derrida: A Critical Reader*, ed. David Wood, 5–35. Oxford: Blackwell, 1992.

———. *The Gift of Death.* Trans. David Wills. Chicago: University of Chicago Press, 1995 ("Donner la mort." In *L'Ethique du don: Jacques Derrida et la pensée du don*, ed. Jean-Michel Rabaté and Michael Wetzel. Paris: Transition, 1992).

———. *Specters of Marx: The State of the Debt, the Work of Mourning, and the New International.* Trans. Peggy Kamuf. London: Routledge, 1994 (*Spectres de Marx*. Paris: Galilée, 1993).

———. *Aporias: Dying—Awaiting (One Another at) the "Limits of Truth."* Trans. Thomas Dutoit. Stanford: Stanford University Press, 1993 (*Apories: Mourir—s'attendre aux "limites de la vérité."* Paris: Galilée, 1996).

———. *Archive Fever: A Freudian Impression.* Trans. Eric Prenowitz. Chicago: University of Chicago Press, 1996 (*Mal d'Archive: une impression freudienne*. Paris: Galilée, 1995).

———. "Faith and Knowledge: The Two Sources of 'Religion' at the Limits of Reason Alone." Trans. Samuel Weber. In *Religion*, ed. Jacques Derrida and Gianni Vattimo, 1–78. Cambridge: Polity Press, 1998 ("Foi et savoir: Les deux sources de la 'religion' aux limites de la simple raison." In *La Religion: Séminaire de Capri*, ed. Jacques Derrida and Gianni Vattimo, 9–86. Paris: Seuil, 1996).

———. "Resistances." In *Resistances of Psychoanalysis*, trans. Peggy Kamuf, Pascale-Anne Brault, and Michael Nass, 1–38. Stanford: Stanford University Press, 1998 ("Résistances." In *Résistances de la psychanalyse*. Paris: Galilée, 1996).

———. "Perhaps or Maybe." *PLI Warwick Journal of Philosophy* 6 (Summer 1997): 1–18.

————. "I Have a Taste for the Secret." 1997. In Jacques Derrida and Maurizio Ferraris, *A Taste for the Secret*. Trans. Giacomo Donis. Ed. Giacomo Donis and David Webb, 3–92. Cambridge: Polity Press, 2001.

————. *Demeure: Maurice Blanchot*. Paris: Galilée, 1998.

————. "On Forgiveness." Trans. Michael Hughes. In *On Cosmopolitanism and Forgiveness*, trans. Mark Dooley and Michael Hughes, 27–60. London: Routledge, 2001 ("Le Siècle et le pardon." *Le Monde des débats* [December 1999]).

————. *On Touching—Jean-Luc Nancy*. Trans. Christine Irizarry. Stanford: Stanford University Press, 2005 (*Le Toucher, Jean-Luc Nancy*. Paris: Galilée, 2000).

————. *Paper Machine*. Trans. Rachel Bowlby. Stanford: Stanford University Press, 2005. (*Papier machine*. Paris: Galilée, 2001).

————. "Rams: Uninterrupted Dialogue—Between Two Infinities, the Poem." Trans. Thomas Dutoit and Philippe Romanski. In *Sovereignties in Question: The Poetics of Paul Celan*, ed. Thomas Dutoit and Outi Pasanen, 135–63. New York: Fordham University Press, 2005 (*Béliers: Le dialogue ininterrompu: entre deux infinis, le poème*. Paris: Galilée, 2003).

————. "The Word: Giving, Naming, Calling." 2004. Trans. Eftichis Pirovolakis ("La parole: Donner, nommer, appeler." In Revault d'Allones and Azouvi, *Paul Ricoeur*, 19–25).

————. "Questions à Jacques Derrida." 2004. In Crépon and Launay, *La Philosophie au risque de la promesse*, 183–209.

————. *Psyche: Inventions of the Other*. Vol. 1. Stanford: Stanford University Press, 2007.

Primary Texts by Paul Ricoeur

Ricoeur, Paul. *Freedom and Nature: The Voluntary and the Involuntary*. Trans. Erazim V. Kohák. Evanston: Northwestern University Press, 1966 (*Le Volontaire et l'involontaire*. Paris: Aubier, 1950).

————. "The Unity of the Voluntary and the Involuntary as a Limiting Idea." Trans. Daniel O'Connor. In *The Philosophy of Paul Ricoeur: An Anthology of his Work*, ed. Charles E. Reagan and David Stewart, 3-19. Boston: Beacon Press, 1978 ("L'Unité du volontaire et de l'involontaire comme idée-limite." *Bulletin de la Société française de Philosophie* 45, no. 1, 1–2 [1951]: 3–22, 22–29).

————. "Kant and Husserl." In *Husserl*, 175–201 ("Kant et Husserl." *Kant-Studien* 46, no. 1 [1954–55]: 44–67).

————. *History and Truth*. Trans. Charles A. Kelbley. Evanston: Northwestern University Press, 1965 (*Histoire et vérité*. Paris: Seuil, 1955).

————. "What Does Humanism Mean?" Trans. David Stewart. In *Political and Social Essays*, 68-87 ("Que signifie 'humanisme'?" *Comprendre* 15 [1956]: 84–92).

————. *Finitude et culpabilité*. 2 vols. Paris: Aubier, 1960.

————. *Fallible Man*. Trans. Charles A. Kelbley. New York: Fordham University Press, 1986 (*L'homme faillible*. Vol. 1 of *Finitude et culpabilité*).

————. *The Symbolism of Evil*. Trans. Emerson Buchanan. Boston: Beacon Press, 1967

(*La Symbolique du mal*. Vol. 2 of *Finitude et culpabilité*)..

———. "Structure and Hermeneutics." Trans. Kathleen McLaughlin. In *The Conflict of Interpretations*, 27–61 ("Symbolique et temporalité." *Archivio di Filosofia* 33, no. 1–2 [1963]: 5–41).

———. *Freud and Philosophy: An Essay on Interpretation*. Trans. Denis Savage. New Haven: Yale University Press, 1970 (*De l'interprétation: Essai sur Freud*. Paris: Seuil, 1965).

———. *Husserl: An Analysis of His Phenomenology*. Trans. Edward G. Ballard and Lester E. Embree. Evanston: Northwestern University Press, 1967.

———. "Husserl's Fifth Cartesian Meditation." 1967. In *Husserl*, 115–42.

———. "Structure, Word, Event." Trans. Robert Sweeney. In *The Conflict of Interpretations*, 79–96 ("La structure, le mot, l'événement." *Esprit* 35, no. 5 [1967]: 801–21).

———. "Freedom in the Light of Hope." Trans. Robert Sweeney. In *The Conflict of Interpretations*, 402–24 ("Approche philosophique du concept de liberté religieuse." *Archivio di Filosofia* 38, no. 2–3 [1968]: 215–52).

———. *The Conflict of Interpretations: Essays in Hermeneutics*. Ed. Don Ihde. Evanston: Northwestern University Press, 1974 (*Le conflit des interprétations: Essais d'herméneutique*. Paris: Seuil, 1969).

———. "The Question of the Subject: The Challenge of Semiology." 1969. Trans. Kathleen McLaughlin. In *The Conflict of Interpretations*, 236–66 ("La question du sujet: le défi de la sémiologie." In *Le conflit des interprétations*, 233–62).

———. "The Model of the Text: Meaningful Action Considered as a Text." *Social Research* 38 (1971): 529–62.

———. "Discours et communication." 1973. In Revault d'Allones and Azouvi, *Paul Ricoeur*, 51–67 (*Actes du XVe Congrès de L'Association des Sociétés de Philosophie de Langue Française*, 23–48).

———. *Political and Social Essays*. Ed. David Stewart and Joseph Bien. Athens: Ohio University Press, 1974.

———. "Phenomenology and Hermeneutics." Trans. John B. Thompson. In *From Text to Action*, 25–52 ("Phénoménologie et herméneutique." *Man and World* 7, no. 3 [1974]: 223–53).

———. "What is Dialectical?" In *Freedom and Morality*, ed. John Bricke, 173–89. Lawrence: University of Kansas, 1976 ("Le 'lieu' de la dialectique." In *Dialectics. Dialectiques*, ed. Ch. Perelman, 92–108. The Hague: M. Nijhoff, 1975).

———. *The Rule of Metaphor: The Creation of Meaning in Language*. Trans. Robert Czerny with Kathleen McLaughlin and John Costello, SJ. London: Routledge, 2003 (*La métaphore vive*. Paris: Seuil, 1975).

———. "The Hermeneutical Function of Distanciation." Trans. John B. Thompson. In *From Text to Action*, 75–88 ("La fonction herméneutique de la distanciation." In *Exegesis: Problèmes de méthode et exercises de lecture*, ed. Fr. Bovon and Gr. Rouiller, 201–15. Paris: Delachaux et Niestlé, 1975).

———. *Interpretation Theory: Discourse and the Surplus of Meaning*. Fort Worth: Texas Christian University Press, 1976.

———. "Practical Reason." Trans. Kathleen Blamey. In *From Text to Action*, 188–207 ("La raison pratique." In *Rationality Today. La rationalité aujourd'hui*, ed. Th. F.

Geraets, 225–48. Ottawa: University of Ottawa Press, 1979).

———. "Narrative Time." *Critical Inquiry* 7 (Autumn 1980): 169–90 ("La fonction narrative et l'expérience humaine du temps." *Archivio di Filosofia* 80, no. 1 [1980]: 343–67).

———. *Hermeneutics and the Human Sciences: Essays on Language, Action, and Interpretation.* Ed. and trans. John B. Thompson. Cambridge: Cambridge University Press, 1981.

———. "Appropriation." 1981. In *Hermeneutics and the Human Sciences*, 182–93.

———. *Time and Narrative.* Trans. Kathleen McLaughlin and David Pellauer. 3 vols. Chicago: University of Chicago Press, 1984–88 (*Temps et récit.* 3 vols. Paris: Seuil, 1983–85).

———. "The Text as Dynamic Identity." In *Identity of the Literary Text*, ed. Mario J. Valdés and Owen Miller, 175–86. Toronto: Toronto University Press, 1985.

———. *From Text to Action: Essays in Hermeneutics II.* Trans. Kathleen Blamey and John B. Thompson. Evanston: Northwestern University Press, 1991 (*Du texte à l'action: Essais d'herméneutique II.* Paris: Seuil, 1986).

———. "Initiative." Trans. Kathleen Blamey. In *From Text to Action*, 208–22 ("L'initiative." In *Labyrinthe: parcours éthiques*, 85–102. Bruxelles: Facultés universitaires Saint-Louis, 1986).

———. *Le mal: Un défi à la philosophie et à la théologie.* Genève: Labor et Fides, 1986.

———. *Oneself as Another.* Trans. Kathleen Blamey. Chicago: University of Chicago Press, 1992 (*Soi-même comme un autre.* Paris: Seuil, 1990).

———. "Narrative Identity." Trans. David Wood. In *On Paul Ricoeur: Narrative and Interpretation*, ed. David Wood, 188–99. London: Routledge, 1991.

———. *Lectures 3, Aux frontières de la philosophie.* Paris: Seuil, 1992.

———. *The Just.* Trans. David Pellauer. Chicago: University of Chicago Press, 2000 (*Le Juste.* Paris: Esprit, 1995).

———. "Reply to John E. Smith." 1995. In Hahn, *The Philosophy of Paul Ricoeur*, 165–68.

———. "Reply to G. B. Madison." 1995. In Hahn, *The Philosophy of Paul Ricoeur*, 93–95.

———. "Reply to Patrick L. Bourgeois." 1995. In Hahn, *The Philosophy of Paul Ricoeur*, 567–70.

———. "Imagination, Testimony, and Trust: A Dialogue with Paul Ricoeur." 1999. In Kearney and Dooley, *Questioning Ethics*, 12–17.

———. "Memory and Forgetting." 1999. In Kearney and Dooley, *Questioning Ethics*, 5–11.

———. *Memory, History, Forgetting.* Trans. Kathleen Blamey and David Pellauer. Chicago: University of Chicago Press, 2004 (*La mémoire, l'histoire, l'oubli.* Paris: Seuil, 2000).

———. *The Course of Recognition.* Trans. David Pellauer. Cambridge: Harvard University Press, 2005 (*Parcours de la reconnaissance.* Paris: Stock, 2004).

———. "La promesse d'avant la promesse." 2004. In Crépon and Launay, *La Philosophie au risque de la promesse*, 25–34.

Secondary Texts

Actes du XVe Congrès de L'Association des Sociétés de Philosophie de Langue Française. Proc. of Conference on "Communication," 1971, University of Montréal. Montréal: Montmorency, 1973.

Anderson, Pamela Sue. *Ricoeur and Kant: Philosophy of the Will.* Atlanta: Scholars Press, 1993.

Aristotle. *The Complete Works of Aristotle.* Ed. Jonathan Barnes. 2 vols. Princeton: Princeton University Press, 1984.

————. *Nicomachean Ethics.* Trans. W. D. Ross (revised by J. O. Urmson). Vol. 2 of *The Complete Works of Aristotle.*

————. *Physics.* Trans. R. P. Hardie and R. K. Gaye. Vol. 1 of *The Complete Works of Aristotle.*

Augustine. *Confessions.* Trans. R. S. Pine-Coffin. Harmondsworth: Penguin, 1961.

Austin, J. L. *How to Do Things with Words.* 2nd ed. Ed. J. O. Urmson and Marina Sbisà. Oxford: Oxford University Press, 1962.

Bennington, Geoffrey, and Jacques Derrida. *Jacques Derrida.* Trans. Geoffrey Bennington. Chicago: University of Chicago Press, 1993 (*Jacques Derrida.* Paris: Seuil, 1991).

Bennington, Geoffrey. *Lyotard: Writing the Event.* Manchester: Manchester University Press, 1988.

————. "Derridabase." 1991. In Bennington and Derrida, *Jacques Derrida,* 3–316.

————. *Legislations: The Politics of Deconstruction.* London: Verso, 1994.

————. "Deconstruction and the Philosophers (The Very Idea)." 1994. In *Legislations,* 11–60.

————. "Index." 1994. In *Legislations,* 274–95.

————. "Membranes." 1994–95. In *Other Analyses,* 97–123.

————. *Interrupting Derrida.* London: Routledge, 2000.

————. "Deconstruction and Ethics." 2000. In *Interrupting Derrida,* 34–46.

————. "Circanalysis (The Thing Itself)." 2000. In *Interrupting Derrida,* 93–109.

————. "Almost the End." 2000. In *Interrupting Derrida,* 141–52.

————. ". . . You Meant." 2000. In *Other Analyses,* 83–94.

————. "Time After Time." *Journal of the British Society for Phenomenology* 32, no. 3 (2001): 300–311.

————. *Other Analyses: Reading Philosophy.* 2004. Electronic book. http://www.bennington.zsoft.co.uk/.

Benveniste, Émile. *Problems in General Linguistics.* Trans. Mary Elizabeth Meek. Coral Gables: University of Miami Press, 1971.

————. *Indo-European Language and Society.* Trans. Elizabeth Palmer. London: Faber and Faber, 1973.

Bernasconi, Robert. "The Trace of Lévinas in Derrida." In *Derrida and Différance,* ed. David Wood and Robert Bernasconi, 13–29. Evanston: Northwestern University Press, 1988.

Bernet, Rudolf. "Unconscious Consciousness in Husserl and Freud." Trans. Christopher Jupp and Paul Crowe. In *The New Husserl: A Critical Reader,* ed. Donn Welton, 199–219. Bloomington: Indiana University Press, 2003.

Blamey, Kathleen. "From the Ego to the Self: A Philosophical Itinerary." In Hahn, *The Philosophy of Paul Ricoeur*, 571–603.

Blanchot, Maurice. *The Writing of the Disaster*. New ed. Trans. Ann Smock. Lincoln: University of Nebraska Press, 1995.

Blanchot, Maurice, and Jacques Derrida. *The Instant of My Death / Demeure: Fiction and Testimony*. Trans. Elizabeth Rottenberg. Stanford: Stanford University Press, 2000.

Booth, Wayne C. *The Rhetoric of Fiction*. 2nd ed. Chicago: University of Chicago Press, 1983.

Caputo, John D. "The Economy of Signs in Husserl and Derrida: From Uselessness to Full Economy." In *Deconstruction and Philosophy: The Texts of Jacques Derrida*, ed. John Sallis, 99–113. Chicago: University of Chicago Press, 1987.

Caygill, Howard. *Lévinas and the Political*. London: Routledge, 2002.

Clark, Stephen H. *Paul Ricoeur*. London: Routledge, 1990.

Cohen, Richard A., and James L. Marsh, eds. *Ricoeur as Another: The Ethics of Subjectivity*. Albany: State University of New York Press, 2002.

Cohen, Richard A. "Moral Selfhood: A Levinasian Response to Ricoeur on Levinas." In Cohen and Marsh, *Ricoeur as Another*, 127–60.

Crépon, Marc, and Marc de Launay, eds. *La Philosophie au risque de la promesse*. Paris: Bayard, 2004.

Dallmayr, Fred R. "Prelude: Hermeneutics and Deconstruction: Gadamer and Derrida in Dialogue." In Michelfelder and Palmer, *Dialogue and Deconstruction*, 75–92.

De Man, Paul. *Allegories of Reading: Figural Language in Rousseau, Nietzsche, Rilke, and Proust*. New Haven: Yale University Press, 1979.

———. "Hypogram and Inscription: Michael Riffaterre's Poetics of Reading." *Diacritics* 11, no. 4 (Winter 1981): 17–35.

———. "Sign and Symbol in Hegel's *Aesthetics*." *Critical Inquiry* 8 (Summer 1982): 761–75.

———. "Autobiography as De-Facement." In *The Rhetoric of Romanticism*, 67–81. New York: Columbia University Press, 1984.

Derrida, Jacques, and Pierre-Jean Labarrière, eds. *Altérités*. Paris: Osiris, 1986.

Derrida, Jacques, and Elisabeth Roudinesco. *For What Tomorrow . . . : A Dialogue*. Trans. Jeff Fort. Stanford: Stanford University Press, 2004 (*De Quoi Demain. . . .* Paris: Librairie Arthème Fayard and Galilée, 2001).

De Saussure, Ferdinand. *Course in General Linguistics*. Ed. Charles Bally and Albert Sechehaye. Trans. Roy Harris. London: Duckworth, 1983.

Forget, Philippe. "Argument(s)." Trans. Diane Michelfelder. In Michelfelder and Palmer, *Dialogue and Deconstruction*, 129–49.

Frege, Gottlob. "On *Sinn* and *Bedeutung*." 1892. Trans. Max Black. In *The Frege Reader*, ed. Michael Beaney, 151–71. Oxford: Blackwell, 1997.

Freud, Sigmund. *The Standard Edition of the Complete Psychological Works of Sigmund Freud*. Trans. James Strachey et al. 24 vols. London: Hogarth Press and the Institute of Psycho-Analysis, 1953-74.

———. *The Interpretation of Dreams*. 1900. Vols. 4 and 5 of *The Standard Edition*. 1953.

———. "The Claims of Psycho-Analysis to Scientific Interest." 1913. In Vol. 13 of *The Standard Edition*, 163–90. 1955.

———. "Remembering, Repeating, and Working-Through." 1914. In Vol. 12 of *The Standard Edition*, 145–56. 1958.

———. "Instincts and Their Vicissitudes." 1915. In Vol. 14 of *The Standard Edition*, 109–40. 1957.

———. "Repression." 1915. In Vol. 14 of *The Standard Edition*, 141–58. 1957.

———. "The Unconscious." 1915. In Vol. 14 of *The Standard Edition*, 159–215. 1957.

———. "Beyond the Pleasure Principle." 1920. In Vol. 18 of *The Standard Edition*, 1–64. 1955.

———. "The Ego and the Id." 1923. In Vol. 19 of *The Standard Edition*, 1–66. 1961.

———. "A Note upon the 'Mystic Writing-Pad.'" 1925. In Vol. 19 of *The Standard Edition*, 225–32. 1961.

———. "New Introductory Lectures on Psycho-Analysis." 1933. In Vol. 22 of *The Standard Edition*, 1–182. 1964.

———. "Project for a Scientific Psychology." 1950 (1895). In Vol. 1 of *The Standard Edition*, 281–397. 1966.

———. *The Origins of Psycho-Analysis, Letters to Wilhelm Fliess, Drafts and Notes: 1887–1902*. Ed. Marie Bonaparte, Anna Freud, and Ernst Kris. Trans. Eric Mosbacher and James Strachey. London: Imago, 1954.

Fynsk, Christopher. *Heidegger: Thought and Historicity*. Ithaca: Cornell University Press, 1986.

Gadamer, Hans-Georg. "Text and Interpretation." Trans. Dennis J. Schmidt and Richard Palmer. In Michelfelder and Palmer, *Dialogue and Deconstruction*, 21–51.

———. "Reply to Jacques Derrida." Trans. Diane Michelfelder and Richard Palmer. In Michelfelder and Palmer, *Dialogue and Deconstruction*, 55–57.

Gasché, Rodolphe. *The Tain of the Mirror: Derrida and the Philosophy of Reflection*. Cambridge: Harvard University Press, 1986.

———. "Deconstruction and Hermeneutics." In Royle, *Deconstructions: A User's Guide*, 137–50.

Gaston, Sean. *Derrida and Disinterest*. London: Continuum, 2005

———. *Starting with Derrida: Plato, Aristotle, and Hegel*. London: Continuum, 2007.

Hahn, Lewis Edwin, ed. *The Philosophy of Paul Ricoeur*. Chicago: Open Court, 1995.

Hegel, G. W. F. *The Encyclopaedia Logic*. Trans. T. F. Geraets, W. A. Suchting, and H. S. Harris. Indianapolis: Hackett, 1991.

———. *Philosophy of Mind*. Trans. William Wallace. Oxford: Clarendon Press, 1991.

———. *Phenomenology of Spirit*. 1807. Trans. A. V. Miller. Oxford: Oxford University Press, 1977.

———. *Phenomenology and Psychology*. Vol. 3 of *Hegel's Philosophy of Subjective Spirit*, ed. and trans. M. J. Petry. 3 vols. Dordrecht: D. Reidel, 1978.

Heidegger, Martin. *Being and Time*. 1927. Trans. John Macquarrie and Edward Robinson. Oxford: Blackwell, 1962.

Hobson, Marian. *Jacques Derrida: Opening Lines*. London: Routledge, 1998.

Hodge, Joanna. "Husserl, Freud, *A Suivre*: Derrida on Time." *The Journal of the British Society for Phenomenology* 36, no. 2 (May 2005): 188–207.

———. *Derrida on Time*. London: Routledge, 2007.

Husserl, Edmund. *Logical Investigations*. 1900–1901. Trans. J. N. Findlay. 2 vols. London: Routledge, 1970.

———. *Ideas: General Introduction to Pure Phenomenology*. 1913. Trans. W. R. Boyce Gibson. London: George Allen and Unwin, 1931.

———. *Idées directrices pour une phénoménologie: Introduction générale à la phénoménologie pure*. Trans. Paul Ricoeur. Paris: Gallimard, 1950.

———. *The Phenomenology of Internal Time-Consciousness*. 1928. Ed. Martin Heidegger. Trans. James S. Churchill. The Hague: Martinus Nijhoff, 1964.

———. "Primal Impression and its Continuum of Modifications." Appendix I. In *The Phenomenology of Internal Time-Consciousness*, 129–32.

———. "Primal Consciousness and the Possibility of Reflection." Appendix IX. In *The Phenomenology of Internal Time-Consciousness*, 161–63.

———. *On the Phenomenology of the Consciousness of Internal Time (1893–1917)*. Trans. John Barnett Brough. Dordrecht: Kluwer Academic Publishers, 1991. Vol. 4 of *Edmund Husserl: Collected Works*. 13 vols. 1980–2008.

———. *Cartesian Meditations: An Introduction to Phenomenology*. 1931. Trans. Dorion Cairns. Dordrecht: Kluwer Academic Publishers, 1993.

———. *The Crisis of European Sciences and Transcendental Phenomenology: An Introduction to Phenomenological Philosophy*. 1936. Trans. David Carr. Evanston: Northwestern University Press, 1970.

Jones, Ernest. *Sigmund Freud: Life and Work*. 3 vols. London: Hogarth Press, 1954–57.

Kant, Immanuel. *Critique of Pure Reason*. 1781, 1787. Trans. Norman Kemp Smith. London: Macmillan, 1929.

———. *Critique of Practical Reason*. 1788. Trans. and ed. Mary Gregor. Cambridge: Cambridge University Press, 1997.

———. *The Metaphysics of Morals*. 1797. Trans. and ed. Mary Gregor. Cambridge: Cambridge University Press, 1996.

Kaplan, David M. *Ricoeur's Critical Theory*. Albany: State University of New York Press, 2003.

Kearney, Richard, and Mark Dooley, eds. *Questioning Ethics: Contemporary Debates in Philosophy*. London: Routledge, 1999.

Kearney, Richard, ed. *Paul Ricoeur: The Hermeneutics of Action*. London: Sage Publications, 1996.

Kierkegaard, Søren. *Fear and Trembling*. 1843. Trans. Alastair Hannay. London: Penguin, 1985.

Koenig, Thomas R. "Psychoanalysis and Hermeneutics: A Psychoanalytico-Philosophical Reading of Freud." In *Tradition and Renewal: The Centennial of Louvain's Institute of Philosophy*, ed. D. A. Boileau and J. A. Dick, 93–115. Vol. 2. Leuven: Leuven University Press, 1992.

Krell, David Farrell. *Of Memory, Reminiscence, and Writing: On the Verge*. Bloomington: Indiana University Press, 1990.

Laplanche, Jean, and Jean-Bertrand Pontalis. *The Language of Psycho-Analysis.* Trans. Donald Nicholson-Smith. London: Hogarth Press and the Institute of Psycho-Analysis, 1973.

Laplanche, Jean, and Serge Leclaire. "The Unconscious: A Psychoanalytic Study." 1966. Trans. Patrick Coleman. "French Freud: Structural Studies in Psychoanalysis," special issue, *Yale French Studies* 48 (1972): 118–75.

Lawlor, Leonard. "Dialectic and Iterability: The Confrontation between Paul Ricoeur and Jacques Derrida." *Philosophy Today* 32, no. 3 (1988): 181–94.

———. *Imagination and Chance: The Difference between the Thought of Ricoeur and Derrida.* Albany: State University of New York Press, 1992.

———. *Derrida and Husserl: The Basic Problem of Phenomenology.* Bloomington: Indiana University Press, 2002.

Lévinas, Emmanuel. *Totality and Infinity: An Essay on Exteriority.* 1961. Trans. Alphonso Lingis. Dordrecht: Kluwer Academic Publishers, 1991.

———. "On the Trail of the Other." 1963. Trans. Daniel Hoy. *Philosophy Today* 10 (1966): 34–46.

———. *Otherwise than Being: Or, Beyond Essence.* 1974. Trans. Alphonso Lingis. Pittsburgh: Duquesne University Press, 1998.

Llewelyn, John. *Appositions of Jacques Derrida and Emmanuel Lévinas.* Bloomington: Indiana University Press, 2002.

Lyotard, Jean-François. *Discours, figure.* Paris: Klincksieck, 1971.

———. *The Differend: Phrases in Dispute.* 1983. Trans. Georges Van Den Abbeele. Manchester: Manchester University Press, 1988.

Madison, G. B. "Ricoeur and the Hermeneutics of the Subject." In Hahn, *The Philosophy of Paul Ricoeur,* 75–92.

Malabou, Catherine. *The Future of Hegel: Plasticity, Temporality, and Dialectic.* Trans. Lisabeth During. London: Routledge, 2005.

Malabou, Catherine, and Jacques Derrida. *Counterpath: Traveling with Jacques Derrida.* Trans. David Wills. Stanford: Stanford University Press, 2004 (*La Contre-allée.* Paris: La Quinzaine Littéraire-Louis Vuitton, 1999).

Merleau-Ponty, Maurice. "L'oeuvre et l'esprit de Freud." In *Parcours deux, 1951–1961,* 276–84. Lagrasse: Verdier, 2000.

Marrati, Paola. *Genesis and Trace: Derrida Reading Husserl and Heidegger.* Trans. Simon Sparks. Stanford: Stanford University Press, 2005.

Michelfelder, Diane P., and Richard E. Palmer, eds. *Dialogue and Deconstruction: The Gadamer-Derrida Encounter.* Albany: State University of New York Press, 1989.

———. "Introduction." In *Dialogue and Deconstruction,* 1–18.

Miller, J. Hillis. "But Are Things as We Think They Are?" Review of *Time and Narrative,* by Paul Ricoeur. *The Times Literary Supplement,* 9–15 October 1987, 1104–1105.

Montefiore, Alan, ed. *Philosophy in France Today.* Cambridge: Cambridge University Press, 1983.

Moran, Dermot. *Edmund Husserl: Founder of Phenomenology.* Cambridge: Polity Press, 2005.

Musil, Robert. *The Man without Qualities*. Trans. Eithne Wilkins and Ernst Kaiser. 3 vols. London: Secker and Warburg, 1960–61.

Nancy, Jean-Luc. "The Unsacrificeable." Trans. Richard Livingston. *Yale French Studies* 79 (1991): 20–38.

Nietzsche, Friedrich. "On the Uses and Disadvantages of History for Life." In *Untimely Meditations,* trans. R. J. Hollingdale, 58–123. Cambridge: Cambridge University Press, 1983.

The Oxford English Dictionary. 2nd ed. Prepared by J. A. Simpson and E. S. C. Weiner. 20 vols. Oxford: Clarendon Press, 1989.

Patočka, Jan. *Heretical Essays in the Philosophy of History.* 1990. Trans. Erazim Kohák. Ed. James Dodd. Chicago: Open Court, 1996.

"Philosophy and Communication: Round-table Discussion between Ricoeur and Derrida." Trans. Leonard Lawlor. Appendix. In Lawlor, *Imagination and Chance*, 131–63.

Pirovolakis, Eftichis. " 'Donner À Lire': Unreadable Narratives." *Literature Interpretation Theory* 19, no. 2 (2008): 100–122.

Plato. *The Dialogues of Plato.* 4th ed. Trans. Benjamin Jowett. 4 vols. Oxford: Clarendon Press, 1953.

———. *Theaetetus.* Vol. 3 of *The Dialogues of Plato.*

———. *Phaedrus.* Vol. 3 of *The Dialogues of Plato.*

Revault d'Allonnes, Myriam, and François Azouvi, eds. *Paul Ricoeur.* L'Herne, no. 81. Paris: Éditions de L'Herne, 2004.

Royle, Nicholas. *The Uncanny.* Manchester: Manchester University Press, 2003.

———. *Jacques Derrida.* London: Routledge, 2003.

Royle, Nicholas, ed. *Deconstructions: A User's Guide.* Basingstoke: Palgrave, 2000.

Sallis, John, ed. *Deconstruction and Philosophy: The Texts of Jacques Derrida.* Chicago: University of Chicago Press, 1987.

Searle, John R. *Speech Acts: An Essay in the Philosophy of Language.* Cambridge: Cambridge University Press, 1969.

Smith, John E. "Freud, Philosophy, and Interpretation." In Hahn, *The Philosophy of Paul Ricoeur,* 147–64.

Spivak, Gayatri Chakravorty. "Revolutions That as Yet Have No Model: Derrida's *Limited Inc.*" *Diacritics* 10, no. 4 (1980): 29–49.

Thompson, John B. *Critical Hermeneutics: A Study in the Thought of Paul Ricoeur and Jürgen Habermas.* Cambridge: Cambridge University Press, 1981.

Valdés, Mario J., ed. "Introduction: Paul Ricoeur's Post-Structuralist Hermeneutics." In *A Ricoeur Reader: Reflection and Imagination,* 3–40. Hemel Hempstead: Harvester Wheatsheaf, 1991.

Venema, Henry Isaac. *Identifying Selfhood: Imagination, Narrative, and Hermeneutics in the Thought of Paul Ricoeur.* Albany: State University of New York Press, 2000.

Wood, David. *The Deconstruction of Time.* Atlantic Highlands: Humanities Press International, 1989.

———. "Vigilance and Interruption: Derrida, Gadamer, and the Limits of Dialogue." In *Philosophy at the Limit,* 118–31. London: Unwin Hyman, 1990.

Wordsworth, William. "Essays upon Epitaphs." In *The Prose Works of William Wordsworth,* ed. W. J. B. Owen and Jane Worthington Smyser, 2:43–119. 3 vols. Oxford: Clarendon Press, 1974.

Index